WALKING
ON THE MOON

WALKING
ON THE MOON

**The Untold Story of the Police and
the Rise of New Wave Rock**

Chris Campion

First published in Great Britain
2010 by Aurum Press Ltd
7 Greenland Street
London NW1 0ND
www.aurumpress.co.uk

First published in the United States and Canada
2010 by John Wiley & Sons, Inc.,
Hoboken, New Jersey

A catalogue record for this book is available from the British Library.

ISBN 978 1 84513 575 1

10 9 8 7 6 5 4 3 2 1
2015 2014 2013 2012 2011 2010

Text design by Forty-Five Degrees Design LLC

Typeset in Mimion by SX Composing DTP, Rayleigh, Essex

Printed in the UK by the MPG Books Group

For Julia

CONTENTS

1	Orphans	1
2	Carpetbaggers	16
3	Queens of New York	31
4	Vive le Punk	41
5	Paging Doctor Rock	53
6	Welcome to America	68
7	Ladies and Gentlemen, the Sensational New Blow Waves	84
8	The Organization	101
9	Police the World	112
10	Gimme Shelter	129
11	The New Wave Crusade	145
12	Dystopia in Utopia	165
13	Destabilize, Desynchronize	180
14	Rock of Charity	202
15	Classical Gas	229
16	Recede, Retire, Retread	254
Acknowledgments		272
Photographer Biographies		274
Notes		276
Sources		293
Index		305

1

ORPHANS

"I remember a very damp, cold, mildewed basement in the depths of winter". This is how Andy Summers recalled the inauspicious circumstances in which the Police started out. In November 1977, towards the end of the first year of their existence, the band were using a half-constructed basement, in a flat on the Finchley Road in North London, as a rehearsal space. It was owned by a gay hairdresser who, Summers remembers, had his eye on Stewart Copeland.

Amid the wreckage of that basement, while attempting to keep their heads above the cloud of dust and fumes and dodge the amorous attentions of Stewart Copeland's male admirer, they began to formulate a sound around a song that Sting had brought to the group: a ballad set to a bossa nova rhythm about a man's infatuation with a prostitute named Roxanne.

"We started to fool around with 'Roxanne,'" said Summers. "He had, as I remember, just the verse, and we kept playing with it. Sting always denies this, but I remember Stewart kind of teaching him where to put the bass line, because Stewart was more into the reggae thing than Sting was at that point."

Stewart Copeland agreed with Summers. "One time we had a party at Sting's, and I, kinda working on a hunch that he'd relate immediately to the music, brought along a bunch of Wailers' albums, some Burning Spear, some dub records, et cetera. And sure enough, Sting just latched on immediately to the rhythmic slant of the music, all the possibilities."

Sting's take is markedly different. He asserted that 'Roxanne' was fully-formed when he first brought it to the group and that Copeland's intervention resulted in just a slight geographical realignment of his original rhythm—a tango, rather than a "jazz-tinged bossa nova"—giving it a "lopsided Argentinean gait."

The feint of memory, slanted by the temptation to self-aggrandize, produces a Rashomon effect: this is the story of the Police. An inevitability in a group made up of such dominant personalities. But the seeds of dysfunction were also built into the group dynamic. An intense sibling rivalry simmered below the surface at all times. One oldest child (Sting). One youngest (Copeland). The third (Summers), a generation older, acting as a counterpoint and a pivot between the other two, but also seeking their approval and validation.

With just six months between them in age, Sting and Stewart Copeland bickered like brothers and were constantly at loggerheads. Sting had been born at the beginning of October 1951; Copeland in the middle of July the following year. Summers had arrived ten years earlier, in December 1942. He relished his position as the experienced elder in the group, even though his emotional maturity was stunted somewhere around the other two.

They behaved like rowdy teenagers: carping, sniping, play-fighting, cracking one-liners as a form of one-upmanship, and batting insults back and forth. One candid and extremely rare roundtable interview with all three for a July 2000 magazine profile, conducted many years after the band had broken up, illustrated how easily hostilities could break out.

While discussing their music, Sting and Summers made the mistake of couching their conversation in musical terms. This infuriated Copeland, the only member of the band unable to read music, who complained that they were purposely trying to exclude him by talking in a language he didn't understand. His protests fell on hostile ears.

"Stewart, those are called 'notes,'" Sting quipped.

"You want to hear an oxymoron?" Summers chimed in. "Musical drummer!"

"Hey, Andy," Copeland retorted. "What do you throw a drowning guitarist? His amp!"

But it was Sting who got the last word in. "What has three legs and a cunt?" he fired back at Copeland. "A drum stool!"

This exchange couldn't be written off as just light-hearted banter. It was more sardonic and bitter than that. Despite their ages—Sting and Copeland were just shy of fifty when this exchange occurred, Summers was approaching sixty—their relationship was still clearly underpinned by a simmering adolescent rivalry.

The same love-hate dynamic that had driven them all the way to the top.

Up there, where the atmosphere was thin, they lived in a bubble, protected from the rigours of the world but also trapped inside a pressurized container that amplified every thought, every action, every sound. The odds of ever reaching that rarefied position had been stacked heavily against them. But somehow they made it, catapulted to the stars in a junk bucket powered by hubris and jury-rigged for success. The junk bucket transformed into a juggernaut that hurtled around the globe two, three, four times over. Inside, an umbilical cord connected all three occupants, sustaining them while constraining all movement.

As time went on, they yearned for individual freedom. They struggled, pushed and pulled against one another until, eventually, the cord snapped. The juggernaut ran out of fuel and ground to a halt. And there it remained for twenty-five years, like a rusted satellite floating in space; always visible but in perpetual stasis, evidence of a distant memory. A monument to the time when the Police were the biggest band in the world.

Pop music is a dream. The promise of a perfect moment deferred. The music business is a machine in perpetual motion, passion conscripted into the service of industry. Music culture is born of tempestuous change and an incestuous genealogy, each iteration of genre birthed by, but also forged in reaction to, the one before. Each owing a debt for its existence to the last.

And then there was the Police. They seemed to come from nowhere. A group with no discernible parentage, no distinct musical lineage or acknowledged antecedents. Orphans. Three individuals whose only commonality was the colour of their hair, dyed peroxide blond. Hair had long been a signifier for youth movements. Superficially, these three looked like punk rockers, but they didn't really dress like them, and they certainly didn't sound like them. They had picked out a musical style for themselves seemingly at random, an amalgam of Western pop and Jamaican rhythms but blanched of roots and ethnicity: white reggae. It was a sound that would become their own and remain their own.

The Police piggy-backed the punk scene and rode it to new wave success. They expressed no allegiance to any particular subculture or movement, musical or otherwise, but played by their own rules and single-mindedly pursued an internationalist agenda. Along the way, they changed the expectations of what a band that struck out on its own could realistically hope to achieve. Their success was an anomaly, a phenomenon.

This was not a group formed out of the camaraderie of youth or the shared discovery and learning of music. It was a common alliance forged through shared ambition and the determination to succeed. Even so, there could scarcely be a less-likely bunch of musical bedfellows. The trio came from disparate backgrounds and their personalities were at odds with each other.

Born in the United States but raised in Beirut, drummer and group founder Stewart Copeland was the scion of two spies. A perpetual adolescent who was garrulous, nervy, and arrogant. Bassist and front man Sting (born Gordon Matthew Thomas Sumner) was the son of a milkman from Tyneside. Raised as a Catholic, he flirted with Marxism in his youth and trained as an primary school teacher. Introverted and intensely self-assured, he cultivated a dark charm as a performer. Guitarist Andy Summers was born in a caravan in Somerset and grew up in Bournemouth; he was devoted to his guitar and possessed of a particularly dry humour but could also be moody and resentful.

Their personae were tailor-made for profiles in teen magazines, and it was the teenyboppers who picked up on them first, embracing them as a pop band. Music aficionados were not quite so easily won over. The Police moved as a unit, were clearly outsiders, and therefore viewed with suspicion. Not only their credibility but their provenance was called into question by music critics, who found it difficult to work out whether the Police were a pop act masquerading as a rock band, or vice versa.

The band responded by putting on a ruthless charm offensive and actively courting the media. The Police were as much a media event as a musical phenomenon. As such, they changed the parameters of rock success, not only how to achieve it but how to maintain it. They thrived on manipulation and constructed a myth around themselves as outsider heroes who had conquered the world on their own terms. The myth was so pervasive that they acquired "classic rock" status the moment they first left the world stage in 1984. Yet their reign at the top was remarkably brief: just a five-year span between their first hit single, "Roxanne" to the last date on the world tour for their final album, *Synchronicity*.

During that same period, the record industry underwent enormous changes, moving from bust to boom. The artist-friendly labels that had started in the sixties became profit-driven corporate entities in the eighties. Compact discs were introduced. MTV was launched. Image superseded virtuosity as the quality deemed most valuable by the music business. Rock music would never be the same again.

After a twenty-three-year hiatus, when all but the hardiest of fans had given up on ever seeing the Police perform again, the band took the music world by surprise and burst back into public life. For the whole of 2007 and most of 2008, the Police dominated headlines, resuming their position at the top of the pop heap as if they had never been away. Only the lines and creases in their faces were proof that the trio had been off the scene for close to a quarter of a century.

In the intervening period, only Sting had remained in the public eye, seemingly compelled to maintain his status in the higher echelon of performing artists. In 2007, he was reputed to be worth £250 million and lived in lordly splendour. His main residence was a grand seventeenth-century Jacobean manor, set within an eight-hundred acre estate in the Wiltshire countryside. He spent his summers at another palatial residence, a sixteenth-century Tuscan estate called Tenuta del Palagio. Both homes were equipped with state-of-the-art recording studios. His portfolio of property also included a beach-side house in the exclusive Malibu Colony and an eighteen-room apartment in Manhattan overlooking Central Park. But his phenomenal wealth couldn't protect him from criticism. By 1990, Sting's credibility took a knock with his admission that he enjoyed marathon tantric sex sessions with his wife, Trudie Styler. From that point on, he became a figure of fun and his sexual prowess became more of a talking point than his music. But when the Police returned, all of that seemed to have been forgotten.

The fans came flocking back too. But now they weren't simply those who had been there the first time around, in the seventies and eighties. They brought their children as well, a generation who had grown up thinking of the Police as a classic rock band, like the Beatles and the Stones.

The music world the Police re-entered had also undergone dramatic changes. Again, it was sinking into a recession. Record sales were dropping but tours brought in ever higher revenues. As they whirled around the globe on what would be billed as the third highest-grossing concert tour of all time, the Police seemed more than equipped to ride those changes. The outing was also billed as the group's swansong, an absolutely final world tour to provide their fans with a definitive end to the Police story.

*

Each musician had his own reason for the dogged pursuit of success. The most tenacious was clearly Andy Summers. A decade older than the other two, he was of the same generation as the Beatles and had already been playing as a professional musician for sixteen years before he joined the Police.

Summers was a war baby, a child born of the bomb—literally, according to family lore. While his mother, Jean, was employed at a munitions factory in Lancashire during World War II, she was overcome by fumes that induced contractions. Andrew James Somers (he later changed the spelling) was born on New Year's Eve in 1942. He would be the second of four children, with one older brother. A younger brother and a sister came later.

He was born in the small country town of Poulton-le-Fylde, near where his father, Maurice, was stationed as a serviceman with the Royal Air Force. Summers recalled that due to the shortage of housing during wartime, his parents lived in a gypsy caravan for the first two years of his life. This detail, revealed on the first page of his autobiography, served to generate an image of Summers as a free-spirited romantic, rather than serious and tightly wound.

At war's end, the family moved to the seaside resort of Bournemouth, all the way down on the south coast of England, where Maurice resumed civilian life as a restaurateur.

Summers's own account of his Police prehistory reads like a storeyed career through the annals of rock greatness. The guitarist pops up Zelig-like in the lineup of several seminal groups: he was a member of the Animals and Soft Machine, played shows alongside Pink Floyd, jammed with Jimi Hendrix, and did stints as a sideman to Kevin Coyne and Kevin Ayers.

His first gig as a professional musician was playing in the house band at the Majestic, a kosher hotel that was a popular destination for Jewish holidaymakers in Bournemouth. From 1961 to 1969, Summers clung to the coattails of George "Zoot" Money, a gregarious, flame-haired Hammond organ player of Italian stock. Money, who also grew up in Bournemouth, rescued Summers from his hotel lounge gig and asked him to join his newly formed Big Roll Band.

Money moved to London in 1961 after being spotted by the manager of British bluesman Alexis Korner, whose group Blues Incorporated would serve as the launch pad for many future music stars, including members of the Rolling Stones, the Animals, and Cream. Summers and the other two members of the Big Roll Band followed him there. In London, they expanded to a six-piece (adding a sax player and a vocalist) and enthralled audiences at the Flamingo Club in Soho, knocking out energetic covers of American R&B tunes. The Big Roll Band soon became a well-regarded staple of the London scene playing on the same bill as the Animals and Georgie Fame and the Blue Flames. Despite releasing two albums on Columbia Records and scoring a minor hit with a track called "Big Time Operator," the Big Roll Band never quite managed to capitalise on the local fame.

By 1966, sharp suits and neat hair were on the way out. Paisley shirts and acid rock were on the way in. Summers convinced Money that the Big Roll Band had to roll with the changes, too. They downsized to a four-piece again and changed their name to the mythical-sounding Dantalian's Chariot. Their music took on a psychedelic hue, and they acquired an oil wheel to project on top of them at live performances in London's Middle Earth club. The group didn't last more than a year.

Summers was then asked to join Canterbury psych band the Soft Machine—which had just come off an extensive US tour with the Jimi Hendrix Experience and was due to start another within weeks—but was dismissed a few weeks into their tour. Founding member Kevin Ayers told Summers there wasn't room for two guitarists in the group. "My playing was pushing the band in a direction that didn't suit Kevin," Summers contended, "and in my view he simply could not keep up with it." Summers had been in the band a total of two months.

Stranded in New York, he managed to contact Money, then playing in Eric Burdon's New Animals. A space had just opened up for a guitarist, and Summers jumped at the chance. He makes great truck of his tenure with the Animals, which included an appearance on one album (*Love Is*) and playing on a poorly organized Japanese tour toward the end of 1968 that ended with a nasty run-in with the Yakuza. In actuality, he was a member of the group for just six months. Burdon disbanded the New Animals shortly after returning from Japan and got back together with the old Animals, reforming the original lineup of the group in December 1968 to play a one-off benefit gig in their hometown of Newcastle.

Summers had floated through the sixties, indulging, by his own account, in his fair share of free love and pharmaceutical experimentation. Now his free ride had come to an end. He was only twenty-six years old, and his career had reached an impasse. Stranded again, this time in Los Angeles, he bided his time for four years, studying classical guitar while earning a meagre crust by teaching it as well. He fell in love, got married, and prepared to settle down. But there was a need gnawing inside him to pick up where he had left off with his music career. In 1973, Summers returned to England with his new wife, Kate.

By contrast, Sting's early life in the industrial north of England was devoid of sunshine and bereft of glamour and opportunity. He was born and raised in the Tyneside town of Wallsend, so named because it marked the eastern extent of Hadrian's Wall, a second-century relic of the Roman occupation that once provided fortification against incursions by Celtic hordes from the north. In the nineteenth century, the area became associated with another kind of fortification, the construction of vast sea vessels made of steel: warships, container ships, and passenger liners such as the SS *Mauritania*.

Still, to the teenage Gordon Sumner, Wallsend must have felt like the world's end: old-fashioned, parochial, limiting. He would come to feel trapped there. To the west of the Sumners' family home was the Wallsend Golf Course, which had covered over a former coal pit. To the south was a railway line. And just below that were the docks of the venerable Swan Hunter shipyard; the skyline at the end of Sting's street was dominated by the vast ships that were constructed there. His father and his grandfather had both worked in the shipyards (as fitter's engineer and shipwright, respectively). As the oldest son, this would probably have been Sting's calling, too, had his father, Ernie, not changed careers and become a milkman. His mother, Audrey, was a hairdresser by trade and an enthusiastic piano player at home, something for which she apparently displayed considerable talent. Her playing and the rock 'n' roll 78s she brought home to play on the family's turntable provided her son with an early introduction to music.

When Sting was five, the family moved into a two-storey apartment above the dairy that Ernie had taken over as manager. There, as a child, Sting became an inadvertent witness to an event that seemed strange and awkward at the time, even inconsequential, but later took on immense significance in his life. Early one morning, before going to school, Sting stumbled upon his mother engaged in a tryst with the young man who had been hired to help out in the dairy. Hearing his mother's urgent moans behind a closed door at the end of the house, he feared that something frightful was happening and instinctively attempted to enter in order to comfort and help her. But his way was blocked, his mother offering hurried reassurances for her indiscretion.

This event set off a long estrangement from his mother, whom he began to regard as a flighty, emotional creature. The realization that her infidelity had continued throughout his parents' marriage harboured in Sting a deep hostility and mistrust. His father, typical of men of the time, kept a tight lid on his emotions. The young child sought affection and approval that were not forthcoming. As a result, Sting became introverted and aloof. He inherited a guitar from an uncle, later bought another with pocket money saved from his job on the milk round, and was swept away by the sounds he plucked out of them in his bedroom. Music became a means to spirit himself away from the humdrum world of the everyday and into an eternal "now" built on fantasy. It also provided a buffer against the humiliation he had experienced during a strict Catholic school upbringing at the hands of nuns. Music was a source of comfort throughout the loneliness of childhood and adolescence, something onto which he could latch his hopes and dreams while embarking on his first steps in the adult world.

Sting abhorred the lot of the working stiff; he found desk jobs stultifying and was generally unwilling to conform. At the age of eighteen, he made a point of turning up late every day at his first office job—as a clerk at the local tax office—until, after six months, there was no option for the office but to fire him.

He enrolled instead in a local teacher-training college, where he met lifelong friend Gerry Richardson. The two bonded over music and began to play in a college band called Earthrise. Sting swapped his guitar for a bass. Richardson and Sting both subsequently became members of two different bands simultaneously: the Phoenix Jazzmen and the Newcastle Big Band. Sting once described the latter as "twenty-five pissheads on a Sunday lunchtime trying to get through to the end of an arrangement." He cut his teeth playing traditional jazz in residencies at local hotels, working men's clubs, and bingo halls, and performing party standards like the "Hokey Cokey" at dinner dances. He also played backup music for strippers in seedy northern clubs. It was during his time with the Phoenix Jazzmen that he received a nickname (from the trombonist in the band) that would stick with him for life: "Sting," after his favourite item of clothing—a yellow and black striped football jersey.

In 1974, Sting graduated from college and found a position at a Catholic primary school in a small mining village near Newcastle, teaching five- to seven-year-olds. He formed a new band, Last Exit, with Richardson (with whom he also shared a house) and two other local musicians. The name was taken from *Last Exit to Brooklyn*, Hubert Selby's abrasive novel about fifties New York street life. But the music they played was so anodyne as to render any association meaningless—one profile described their repertoire as consisting of "Stevie Wonder soul, Fleetwood Mac blues, Chick Corea hyperfunk." Last Exit's stock in trade was ersatz jazz-funk allied to achingly conventional love songs. Here, too, were born the roots of rivalry that Sting would carry over into the Police, as he and Richardson competed to come up with original songs for the band to play during a residency established at the Gosforth Hotel.

Sting had become extremely conscious of the importance of presentation from a very early age after attending a private school on a scholarship and mixing with children from a different class. From then on, upward mobility was the goal, whether it was achieved through sex or music. During Sting's teenage years, he learned to mesmerize girls like a snake charmer and reinvented himself as the "Don Juan of North Shields" (just up the road from Wallsend). "I used to get girls pregnant all the time," he boasted. When his first serious girlfriend became pregnant, he left her in the lurch for another partner, who offered the promise of greater intellectual stimulation. He, in turn, was dumped by her. The vicious cycle of love and the active part he played in it would increasingly find voice in his songs. His first girl-friend would in years to come commit suicide. The event inspired a song, "The Bed's Too Big without You," that seemed to be less a tribute to her memory than an attempt to work through his own sorrowful guilt over abandoning her.

At the same time that Sting reinvented himself as a lothario, he primed himself for success, mimicking the announcers on the BBC to soften his speaking voice and remove the most obvious traces of his vowelled Newcastle accent. He met and wooed his first wife, actress Frances Tomelty, while performing in the band that accompanied a Christian rock musical, *Rock Nativity*. Tomelty was a headstrong woman from Northern Ireland. The affair with her was so all-consuming that the pair commuted between London and Newcastle to see each other for two years, until she became pregnant with their first child at the beginning of 1976. Tomelty became Last Exit's manager and shopped their demo tapes around to record companies in London. She also tutored Sting in the art of stagecraft.

For two years, Last Exit played residencies at the Lion's Inn pub at Blakey Ridge, an isolated sixteenth-century inn located on the highest point on the Yorkshire Moors, and at the Gosforth Hotel in Newcastle, where the band built up a reputation as local heroes. But the shows began to feel as stultifying as the desk jobs Sting had left behind. The band members were treading water, rather than moving up, and Sting was beginning to get restless.

Stewart Copeland had less of a burning desire to succeed than the other two did, but he had been reared to believe that his primacy was an inalienable right. Copeland's father, Miles Copeland II, was one of the founding members of the Central Intelligence Agency. Stewart's mother worked for the British secret service. Although Stewart was born in Alexandria, Virginia (in what he once described as "a suburb of the CIA," close to the organization's headquarters in Langley), he was raised in Beirut, Lebanon—then considered the model of a westernized Arab city—where he led a privileged and cosseted life. His family lived in a grand apartment in the city, and Stewart was looked after by a nanny. The first band he joined as a drummer made its debut in the protected environs of the American Embassy Beach Club in Beirut.

Copeland's passion for bashing the drums far outweighed any natural musical ability he had. He couldn't read a note of music and had flunked the entrance exam for the music programme at the University of California at Berkeley. He majored in communications and public policy instead, later describing it as "a greater engine for my career than a musical education would have been." But he did have one distinct advantage: both of his older brothers had entered the music business before him.

By the early seventies, oldest brother Miles had already built up a successful management business representing British progressive rock groups like Wishbone Ash and Renaissance. He had started his own management agency, British Talent Managers (BTM), which, by the mid-seventies, would also incorporate a boutique record label (BTM Records) distributed through RCA. Ian, the middle of the three brothers, was employed by a venerable old booking agency in London named John Sherry Enterprises and was also working on building up his own roster of acts. He booked a Scottish funk act called the Average White Band as support on tour with Eric Clapton, inadvertently launching their career. The two brothers swapped acts back and forth like trading cards.

Nepotism came as second nature to the Copeland clan. Miles aided his brother's drumming ambitions by parachuting him into the lineup of two of the bands that he managed. The first, a group called Stonefeather, mutinied and split in reaction to the enforced placement of their new eighteen-year-old drummer—especially given that their manager had fired the previous drummer. The second was Curved Air, a moderately successful British progressive rock band that had gone through numerous lineup changes since forming in 1969. Stewart Copeland was the drummer for the band's last two years and final two albums.

To draw attention to the start of his tenure with Curved Air, Copeland wrote a letter under an assumed name to the *Melody Maker* music weekly, praising his own talents as a drummer. He was rewarded with a half-page article in an April 1975 issue, accompanied by a large photograph of himself behind the kit. The headline to the piece, "Seeing through Curved Air's Copeland," implied that the editors had spotted his ruse. An unruly but transparent hustler, Copeland got away with most things through the sheer force of his boundless boyish charm. He also managed to charm his way into a relationship with the group's sultry front woman, Sonja Kristina, and set up home with her and her young son, Sven.

Meanwhile, a web of connections drew the future Police men closer and closer together. They had, at times, even unknowingly crossed paths earlier. On returning to London, Summers had taken to hanging around the West London offices of Virgin Records, hoping to pick up some work. He was rewarded with a slot playing lead guitar in a live production of Mike Oldfield's *Tubular Bells*, the multimillion-selling synthesizer-pop record that had established Virgin as a major player in the music industry. The support act on the Newcastle run of the show (which took place in October 1976) was Last Exit. The newly established publishing arm of Virgin, which was run by a woman named Carol Wilson, had caught wind of the band and trooped up to Newcastle en masse (led by Virgin boss Richard Branson) to see them play live. A few months later, a songwriting deal was on the table. This would provide Sting with the hope that his career finally had forward momentum and that recognition might be around the corner. His Last Exit bandmates were duly convinced to make the long trek down to London in an attempt to establish further inroads into the music industry.

In the autumn of 1976, Wilson set up some showcase gigs for the band in London, including an appearance at Dingwalls, the club where the Ramones had made their feted London debut just a few months earlier. Last Exit appeared as support to singer-songwriter Isaac Guillory, playing to little more than a dozen people—and most of those were either employees at Virgin Music publishing, who had helped set up the show as a showcase, or friends and associates of the band. One of those was journalist Phil Sutcliffe, a Newcastle native like Sting and an avid fan of Last Exit, who had managed to get a commission from the weekly music newspaper *Sounds* to write a report on Last Exit's attempts at making it in London. The article was as upbeat as it could be, given that, as Sutcliffe conceded, no one in London knew who the band was and no one particularly cared.

Sutcliffe was the person who first introduced Sting to Stewart Copeland, whom he brought to see Last Exit in November 1976, when Curved Air came up for a date in Newcastle. Curved Air had by that time decided to split, and Copeland was playing out his tenure with the group in support of what was to be its final recording, a cover of the Big Joe Williams blues standard "Baby, Please Don't Go." The song had already been covered by everyone from Bob Dylan to Gary Glitter. Curved Air turned in a boogie-woogie version that sounded corny and outmoded. Stewart Copeland had already devised his exit plan.

2

CARPETBAGGERS

The name came first—the Police. It sounded aggressive and punky. Better yet, it was so commonplace as to be unforgettable. But the Police began as a one-man band that existed solely in the imagination of drummer Stewart Copeland. His idea: to form a power trio using Cream and Jimi Hendrix Experience as the template but tuned into the punk sound sweeping the UK.

By December 1976, punk had exploded onto the national consciousness to the extent that even the *Guardian* newspaper, that usually stolid bastion of the liberal establishment, was moved to acknowledge it. The article began with the ominous words, "And then there was punk . . ." and went on to describe the Sex Pistols as "insolent and violent," characterizing their music (and, by implication, punk as a whole) as the "anarchic rock of the young and doleful." The attitude of the mainstream press to this raucous and insistent new youth cult— snooty and dismissive, on the one hand; outraged and horrified, on the other—helped foster the impression that punk was a polarizing force, a groundswell revolt against the old order, pitting one generation against the next.

Stewart Copeland knew which side he wanted to be on. Despite having very little in common with punk on either a musical or a social level, he intuitively identified with and was swept up by the exuberance of it all. He even formulated a plan of action for the Police. "I wrote a manifesto which laid it all out," he recalled. "We're not interested in money. We're not into fame. We just want to follow our instincts. Which is kind of amusing when you consider that, in reality, the Police was entirely a fake punk band, wearing a uniform and flying a flag of convenience."

So enamoured was Copeland of his new band name that he sketched out a logo, crafted badges, and designed a potential record sleeve before writing one note of music or looking for other musicians to play with. He placed wanted ads in the music papers and even jammed with an existing band (called the Rockets) that he had toyed with the idea of renaming and remaking to suit his own ends, but both came to nothing. He did have one other player in mind, though: the bass-playing front man from Last Exit. *Sounds* journalist Phil Sutcliffe had been very insistent that they should meet when Curved Air had passed through Newcastle on tour a few weeks earlier, and he had personally taken Copeland and Sonja Kristina to see Last Exit play a show in the canteen of a local college, St. Mary's Teacher Training College.

The band was pretty crummy, Copeland thought, but the front man definitely had something and, when they were briefly introduced after the show, Copeland instinctively pushed his number onto Sting. Having settled on the idea of pursuing Sting to play in the Police, Copeland realized he had no way of contacting him and called Sutcliffe to obtain his number. Aware that the drummer's tenure with Curved Air was at an end and immediately suspicious of Copeland's motives, the journalist demurred, acting partly out of loyalty to his friends in Last Exit but also to protect his own interests. Sutcliffe had filed a story about Last Exit's attempt to crack the London music scene that was still awaiting publication.

Determined to bag his bassist, Copeland called up Sutcliffe's unwitting girlfriend instead and managed to pry the number out of her. Then, in the first week of January, Copeland phoned Sting in Newcastle. Reminding him that they had met a month earlier, Copeland raved about his idea of forming a new punk trio, with little in the way of tact or consideration for Sting's position with Last Exit. When Sting calmly explained that he would be in London within the week, Copeland assumed that his enthusiasm had prompted the move.

Sting had already come to the conclusion the previous summer that Newcastle was a "cul-de-sac," both too provincial for his ambitions and too removed from the hub of the music industry in London to facilitate them. With the confidence provided by his newly signed publishing deal and the encouragement of Carol Wilson, he had decided that his future in music, if any, existed down south, and he attempted to convince the rest of the band likewise. His wife, Frances, had an agent in London named Pippa Markham who offered them room in her flat while they looked for a home of their own.

Like Sting, Gerry Richardson also had nothing to lose. He was familiar with London and had even lived there for a spell several years earlier, operating a clothing stall in the Kensington Market fashion boutique that happened to be opposite the stall run by Freddie Mercury and Roger Taylor (later of Queen). In Newcastle, Richardson shared a house with Sting and led a bachelor's life, eking out a living as a musician-for-hire, playing the Hammond organ in working men's clubs.

Although committed to the group, the other two members of Last Exit, guitarist Terry Ellis and drummer Ronnie Pearson, wavered at the idea of uprooting themselves from their homes and families in Newcastle. Instead, they offered to commute to London when necessary, a situation that was far from ideal. Both were older, in their mid-thirties, and the prospect of an insecure future in a capital city that was already teeming with musicians did not sound particularly enticing—Pearson ran a drum shop in Newcastle, Ellis was a jobbing musician—but the agreed-to plan was that they would all make the move in January 1977.

Doubts were already beginning to creep into Sting's head as to whether this would actually happen, when Terry Ellis announced in mid-December (three weeks before their planned move) that he had accepted a nine-week gig playing in the house band for a children's pantomime. This put a wrecking ball to all of Sting's carefully laid plans. His own move to London with Frances and their newborn son, Joe, had already been finalized. "I want to strangle our guitarist," he confessed in a diary entry after hearing the news.

The call from Copeland, who seemed extremely eager to get Sting involved in another musical project, came at just the right time. It provided a fallback that allowed him to hedge his bets with one group or the other. Whether by accident or design, Sting left this phone call out of his memoir when he recounted the events that led up to his move to London, thereby preserving his good-guy reputation. But by this point, his loyalty to Last Exit was clearly faltering. Sting's bowdlerized account takes up the story in the first week of January, after he has arrived in London, where, worn down by a day of fruitless flat-hunting in Central London for himself, Tomelty, and their infant son, he dug Copeland's phone number out of his pocket and called it from a phone box, only to discover that he was standing at the end of the very street the drummer lived on.

According to Police lore, Copeland lived in a squat, a detail that was later used to help cement the band's credentials with the punk crowd. In the mid- to late seventies, the occupation of large swathes of derelict housing by groups of unemployed and disenfranchised youths (as well as by other more ideologically motivated groups of Marxist radicals) was commonplace in London. The practice was so widespread that it had led to violent clashes and standoffs between squatters, demolition crews, and police authorities. Sustained economic depression since the early seventies had hit the city hard. By 1976, unemployment in the capital had climbed to more than 7 per cent. Squatting was a means of survival for many, a way out of a system that clearly offered no future, but it also created a form of alternative society around socialistic living and values that were seen as more humane than those that drove mainstream society. And it was from this culture that the UK punk scene was spawned. Although less ideologically motivated, much the same thing had happened in New York around the same time.

The squat that Copeland shared with girlfriend Sonja Kristina and his older brother, Ian, had very little in common with this kind of living. By contrast, they lived in the palatial luxury of a duplex apartment on the top floors of a terraced Georgian house in Mayfair, one of the most exclusive areas in London. Inside, the décor was Middle-Eastern themed, outfitted with the kind of furnishings that were a shortcut to bohemianism for affluent city dwellers. Rooms were furnished with harem cushions, Persian rugs, and hookahs. Arabic swords and Islamic tapestries were mounted on the walls. Ian Copeland described the apartment as "magnificent."

The apartment was, in actuality, the London residence of an American woman named Marcia McDonald, who worked as the publicist for Muhammad Ali and was an acquaintance of Stewart and Ian's father, Miles Copeland II. Sting's recollection was that the actual owner was Michael Winner, the director of Charles Bronson's *Death Wish* movies. Its American tenant had, in turn, sublet the apartment to a friend while out of the country, one Lady Georgina Campbell, who had decided of her own volition to take up permanent residence there and had obtained a court order giving her the legal right to do so. The publicist had, in turn, asked for the expert assistance of Copeland Sr. to help evict Lady Georgina.

Although more experienced in staging covert operations in foreign countries, Miles Copeland II turned his hand to this domestic affair as a personal favour to his lady friend. The strategy he employed involved parachuting his two younger sons into the apartment and instructing them to behave as inopportunely as they wished in order to dislodge the sitting tenant. A full Tama Mars drum kit—which Stewart had somehow convinced the manufacturer to give him in return for a review in *Sounds* newspaper—was installed in an attic room on the second floor. Guitar amps were set up in other rooms.

After two weeks of late-night jamming, much playing of loud, tuneless electric guitars, and several rowdy parties, Lady Georgina remained unmoved. In fact, the Copeland brothers noticed, her visitors seemed even more louche than theirs. They soon discovered that Lady Georgina was neither a peer nor a lady: she was a transsexual. At this point, the game was clearly up. The Copeland brothers lost interest in trying to dislodge her but kept up the pretence in order to retain their own tenancy of the apartment. The flashy pad also provided Stewart Copeland with an impressive venue in which to hold auditions for potential band members. The bohemian atmosphere at 26 Green Street certainly impressed itself on Sting, although he admitted to being more taken by his first glimpse of Copeland's girlfriend, the "beautiful ingénue" Sonja Kristina. "I make a mental note to check her out on the way downstairs," he reported in his memoir. They ascended to the room where Copeland's drum kit was set up and began to play, feeling around each other at first, testing for musical connections. Sting later rhapsodized that the chemistry between himself and Copeland during the first time they played together was like "the sexual rhythms of natural lovers."

Copeland now also had a guitarist in mind for the group. Henry Padovani had arrived in London from his native Corsica in the second week of December 1976, carrying only his amp and a guitar as luggage and enthuiastic about the idea of throwing himself into the London music scene. Stewart Copeland was introduced to him just days after his arrival in the UK by a mutual friend, Paul Mulligan, in whose North London apartment the Corsican was crashing until he found a place of his own to live. Mulligan was an old friend of Ian Copeland's from Beirut. Padovani was the ideal candidate to join a punk band: he couldn't play a note. At the time, he looked like a stereotypical hippie with long hair and beard. Despite his lack of musical talent, Padovani also secured an audition with another drummer, Jon Moss (then of the Clash, later of Culture Club). Moss was starting a band called London, which was to be produced and managed by pop impresario Simon Napier-Bell. When Stewart Copeland heard about this, he immediately offered Padovani the gig before another band could snatch him. Padovani's inclusion in the initial lineup of the Police was also more a matter of expediency, a means to impress Sting that his punk trio was already a going concern and not just a pipe dream.

Copeland arranged an initial practice session for the trio at 26 Green Street, enjoining Padovani to dress more like a punk—"the hostile posture of the day" as Copeland described it—in order to impress their commitment on Sting. Both chopped their hippie locks down to a suitably "punk" length (Padovani even dispensed with his beard) and donned aviator shades and skin-tight trousers. To finish off his look, Copeland also threw on an imitation police bomber jacket and a police hat. But despite all their efforts, the studied cool they adopted was torpedoed the moment they opened the door of the flat to Sting. He was dressed in dungarees and held his infant son in a carrycot.

The new band started out by trying to work out the arrangements for several scrappy pop-punk songs the drummer had thrown together with his brother Ian. "The energy and the dynamism of the guy really affected me," Sting recalled. "I thought straight away—this is the bloke for me." He also instinctively realized that in Copeland he had found someone whose ambition, ego, and sense of entitlement equalled his own. Sting was not, however, taken with Copeland's choice of guitarist for the new band. Copeland usually attempted to mask Padovani's deficiency by coaching him on how to play the songs before Sting arrived for band practice. Nevertheless, the speed at which all three threw themselves into this new endeavour, despite barely knowing one another, gives an indication of just how hungry they all were.

Sting dates his first visit to the Mayfair apartment as January 9, 1977, two days after he drove to London with his wife and child in tow. Padovani had first played with Copeland earlier that same week. Copeland's last show with Curved Air had taken place just two weeks prior to this, on Christmas Eve. By mid-January, the Police were more than just a badge pinned to Copeland's jacket; the punk power trio he had dreamed up was a reality. And thoughts of Last Exit making it in London were beginning to fade from Sting's mind. By throwing his lot in with Copeland, Sting would leave his best buddy, Gerry Richardson, in the lurch. Richardson was the only other member of Last Exit who actually moved to London. Years later, Richardson would be quite pragmatic about the band's chances of success. "I think Last Exit would probably have cracked it, but our timing was diabolical because it was just when punk was just kicking in and we were as fashionable as a pool of sick."

The newly formed Police took part in a photo shoot in the last week of January, on the roof of 26 Green Street, recording their image before they'd even entertained the idea of recording their sound. The photos were taken by Lawrence Impey, an old school friend of Stewart Copeland's. They had met in English class while attending Millfield, a private boarding school near Glastonbury, in the late sixties. The son of a successful lawyer in Bournemouth—the seaside resort that had also been home to future Police guitarist Andy Summers—Impey dabbled in photography and played at being a rock manager. His talent as a photographer was passable at best, and, despite his enthusiasm, he was clearly too polite and too wet behind the ears to be a successful band manager.

Impey had also, in effect, already bitten off more than he could chew by attempting to guide the career of South London drug dealer turned front man Peter Perrett, whose talent as a lyricist and a singer was at least the equal of (but also at odds with) his debilitating heroin addiction. Perrett did manage to curdle his lifestyle into several albums' worth of songs with his band the Only Ones, which are chilling in their intensity and intimacy. Perrett also played with Glenn Tilbrook and Harry Kakoulli of the South London band Squeeze, who later took on Impey as their manager and thereby gained access to his then business partner, Stewart Copeland's older brother Miles. Impey later decided that he wanted to pursue photography instead and ceded the management of Squeeze solely to Miles Copeland, who had convinced the naive young band to sign 50 per cent of their publishing over to him.

That is the long and short of how Impey came to be on the roof of 26 Green Street on a wintry day in late January, snapping photos of the two-week-old band. Sting refrained from wearing his dungarees for the shoot, opting instead for a striped sailor's T-shirt and a Mod-ish pinstriped suit jacket. He threw Impey's camera a suspicious sidelong glance. Padovani had a raging toothache the day of the shoot. With his roughly hewn short black hair and small, wiry frame, he didn't have to try that hard to look "punk"; he just did. That Impey caught him open-mouthed, twisting his jaw in an agonized grimace, only added to the effect.

The drummer wore circular shades and hunched his body in an oversized leather jacket, looking like a knockoff Joey Ramone. If it looked phony, that's because it was. Just a few months earlier, Impey had shot Copeland inside the Green Street apartment, hanging off the banisters like a stick insect with a mop-top. He was dressed in his Curved Air stage gear: a preppy T-shirt emblazoned with the words "Air Control" and brightly coloured Spandex trousers with a stripe down each side, the ends tucked neatly into knee-high laced wrestling boots.

With the help of a loan from Paul Mulligan, a regular visitor to the Green Street flat, the Police recorded and pressed their first single before February was out. Mulligan is often described as the band's first manager, but he doesn't seem to have done much more than offer encouragement and cash to the nascent group. The amount they borrowed, which is variously cited as anywhere from £150 to £800, bought a day in the studio and a pressing of five hundred singles.

Both sides featured scrappy punk thrash renditions of compositions penned by Stewart Copeland (with assistance from his brother Ian). "Fall Out" was built around a lopsided two-line chorus that failed to conform to the most basic rules of metre and rhyme and grammar. The B-side, "Nothing Achieving," wasn't much of an improvement. Sting wasn't overly impressed with the songs, either. He described Copeland's musical ideas as "shit."

The record was placed in a rudimentary picture sleeve featuring one of Impey's photographs and a black stripe across the top with "The Police" stencilled on it. It looked DIY enough to pass muster as a punk single. With a single to their name, the Police were on the punk treadmill, despite never having played outside of Copeland's apartment. Copeland's enthusiasm had gotten them this far, but was the outside world ready for them? They stuck out as interlopers like a sore thumb—an American, a Frenchman, and a Geordie—and brother Miles saw through the scheme straight away. "Stewart always complains that I wasn't interested in the Police when they started," said Miles Copeland. "He forgets that no one was interested in them."

His younger brother's attempt to reinvent himself as a punk was so unconvincing as to be transparent. And Miles would know: he had been managing Curved Air up until their demise two months earlier. He was also a lot more clued in to what was going on in London than his younger brother was. It was his business to be so. Miles Copeland didn't get off on the energy of the music so much as on the idea of transforming all of the activity around it into a new business opportunity for himself. "Since when has music got anything to do with it?" he commented. "We're in the culture business, the *expression* business." Nevertheless, he saw a way to utilize the Police for his own ends and, in return, they would get a foothold in the London music scene.

While Stewart Copeland was still making homemade badges for his fantasy band, Miles had been busy plotting a stratagem to cut himself a piece of the punk pie from his offices in Dryden Chambers, a labyrinthine Victorian tenement building on Oxford Street. The prize he sought lay directly above his head, one floor up in the offices of Glitterbest, Malcolm McLaren's management company, where American photographer Leee Black Childers was trying to figure out how to get the band he managed, Johnny Thunders and the Heartbreakers, out of hock and back on the road.

McLaren had brought Childers and the Heartbreakers over to play on the Anarchy in the UK tour, the package of punk bands he had put together in December 1976 to give headline act the Sex Pistols more clout. But the tour was an unmitigated disaster. The Heartbreakers arrived in the UK the day the Pistols made their infamous appearance on Bill Grundy's *Today* show, during which Johnny Rotten was upbraided for uttering a dirty word ("shit") on live TV and guitarist Steve Jones called the host "a fucking rotter" for making a pass at Siouxsie Sioux. The appearance was followed by weeks of splenetic tabloid scaremongering about the horrors of the "punk rock cult" that took a sledgehammer to the Pistols' carefully planned tour schedule. All but seven of the scheduled nineteen tour dates fell apart while the bands—which also included the Clash and the Damned—were being shuttled around the country in a bus from one cancelled gig to another.

When the Anarchy tour finally ground to a halt toward the end of December, the resulting publicity found Childers fielding record company offers for the Heartbreakers, whose druggy reputation had previously made them lepers as far as the music industry was concerned. But the band members themselves were effectively broke and stranded in England. Meanwhile, the Pistols headed off to fulfil three dates in the Netherlands that had been booked for them by Miles Copeland.

The two Americans, Copeland and Childers, put their heads together and hatched a plan for their own all-star tour, pairing the new wave of New York City with the new wave of London. Copeland booked the dates. Childers provided the bands by putting in a call to his friend Peter Crowley, who booked the acts at Max's Kansas City in New York. Crowley also managed transvestite rocker Wayne County, the resident DJ at Max's. Another regular fixture at Max's, Cherry Vanilla, was roped into the tour as well. A strident "Noo Yawk" gal with flaming red hair, Cherry Vanilla had parlayed a talent for screwing rock stars into a career as a professional PR lady and performance artist. "I only hit a few of them," she said of her brief career as a groupie, "but I hit a few good ones who gave me jobs."

Childers, County, and Vanilla had history. They had participated in the scandalous 1971 London run of Andy Warhol's musical *Pork*. Childers stage-managed the show, while Vanilla and County performed. In London, they had befriended David and Angie Bowie and were all subsequently employed by his Mainman organization in New York. Childers became Bowie's personal photographer and the VP of Mainman's New York office, Cherry Vanilla did Bowie's PR, and Wayne County was signed to Mainman as an artist—reputedly to prevent him from competing with Bowie, who subsequently took County's amorphous-androgynous look as the basis for Ziggy Stardust.

Wayne County borrowed ticket money from Tommy Dean, the owner of Max's, and arrived in London at the beginning of January 1977 with Crowley and guitarist Greg Van Cook. They crashed on the floor of Childers and Thunders's Soho flat. Cherry Vanilla had traded her own apartment for plane tickets, and she turned up a month later with her entourage: guitarist/boyfriend Louis Lepore, Brazilian keyboard player Zecca Esquibel, and road manager Macs Macee.

"I sold everything I had to get us over there," she recalled. But she still couldn't afford to bring the rhythm section of her Staten Island Band, so Miles Copeland arranged one for her in the form of Sting and Stewart Copeland. It was also agreed that the Police would play support on the tour. The plan was to showcase all of the groups during a series of gigs in London and then send each band off on a rolling tour of the UK. And so it came to pass that a bunch of brash New York City rockers crashed the London punk scene, and the Police had their cherry broken in public by the world's biggest groupie and the first transgendered rock star.

"There are two places right now that are interesting musically and that is New York City and London," Miles Copeland asserted at the time. "London is twice as exciting musically as New York; mainly it's because the economic situation in London is more aggravated. . . . And it's much easier for a group to get a start here. In New York there are only a few clubs that a group can play in. There's CBGB's, there's Max's and one or two others. In London there's twenty or thirty clubs. All over the country there are clubs. So it's easier for a group to get in front of the people."

If this assessment of the musical climate sounds awkward, it's because Copeland's grasp of what was hot and what was not often relied on the judgment of others, as Andy Czezowski (the founder of London punk club the Roxy) would attest. He remembered being cornered in the Roxy one night by Copeland. "He was ear-bending me like an idiot and pumping me for information, and me being younger and naive I gave it to him," Czezowski said. "He kept asking me if things would work—such as putting Wayne County on at the Global Village [a London venue] under some ludicrous title like the US Package of Punk or something like that—a cash-in, basically. He kept saying, 'Do you think it'll work? Do you think it'll work?!' and I said I thought it would, yeah."

Czezowski wasn't the only person to question Miles Copeland's motives. "My first reaction to Miles was one of extreme suspicion!" said Jayne County (née Wayne). "I had heard all these weird things from Leee Black Childers. I was sort of half expecting the Beast! Soon I learned that he was kind of quiet but at the same time a 'real go get-ter' and very smart. He came off a bit like a computer programmer. His look didn't suit his involvement in Punk at all. But it really both-ered me that he wouldn't shave his neck! It drove me crazy! I would wonder to myself, 'Why doesn't he shave his neck? Ick!'"

Photographs of him from the time do indeed reveal that the usu-ally clean-shaven Miles Copeland did have a rather freakish-looking hirsute growth on his neck that was neither chest hair nor beard. While sharing their single-mindedness and independence, the nervy bespectacled American with the collegiate haircut and the leather jacket was a freak of a different stripe to the kids darting around the Roxy in their punk duds. He was a political animal equipped with a shrewd brain for business. Miles Copeland was enough of a figure on the local scene to make a cameo appearance in a feature article about punk rock in an April 1977 issue of *Sounds*: "Punk paranoia about 'Big Business taking over our scene' is poignantly underlined by the shadowy figure of agent Miles Copeland at every gig, terrified that something magically, supremely, quintessentially P-U-N-K might happen at the one gig he blew out."

When Miles Copeland wasn't cruising the Roxy and other venues for fresh punk meat, he was busy scheming in Dryden Chambers. With his tacit encouragement, the office had become the nerve centre for Mark Perry's Xeroxed zine *Sniffin' Glue*—the first and foremost punk fanzine in the UK but, it must be said, not the most astute or discerning. *Sniffin' Glue*'s chief stock in trade was a joyless enthusi-asm about everyone and everything it featured within its monotone photostatted pages. Its inarticulacy was worn like a badge of honour. "There's mistakes everywhere," proclaimed a strap-line on the cover of the March 1977 issue.

NME photographer Jill Furmanofsky, Copeland's then girlfriend, remembered the *Sniffin' Glue* crew jerry-rigging electricity and telephone wires through the window of Copeland's office from another unit in the building. It was a fair trade. Perry was a vital source of information about which bands on the scene were credible and happening. Copeland constantly plugged him for information and later ensured Perry's continued loyalty by giving him his own label, Step Forward Records, which would release early singles by Sham 69 and the Fall, that operated within the aegis of Copeland's umbrella group, Faulty Products. It was Perry who had originally suggested that Copeland check out the Roxy, and Perry also expressed admiration for the New York bands featured on *Max's Kansas City*, a 1976 compilation that eulogized the venue.

Of all the American bands, the Heartbreakers had the most kudos with the Brits. In a 1977 profile of Johnny Thunders, *NME* journalist Tony Parsons cited Thunders's previous band New York Dolls as the "major impetus" for British groups to seek out their own identity. Others though saw the invasion of the Americans, with their distinctly showbiz brand of rock 'n' roll, as a dilution of the ascetic and utilitarian ethic of UK punk.

The Dolls' only UK appearances in their brief career were on a short 1973 tour that was capped by the shocking death of drummer Billy Murcia from an accidental drowning after an overdose. On that trip, the band had supported Rod Stewart and the Faces at Wembley and also opened for a pre-Stewart Copeland incarnation of Curved Air in London.

While singer David Johansson was often compared to Mick Jagger, guitarist Johnny Thunders had no equal. A working-class hood from Queens, he wielded his instrument like a switchblade in a street fight, lunging and slashing as he unleashed great arcs of distorted electric guitar. And Thunders seemed all the more threatening as a preening pseudo-female with teased hair and stacked heels (the Dolls' statutory dress code), rather than wearing the leather duds of a regular street tough. So when he pitched up in England with his new band several years later, albeit without the makeup and the drag costuming, he was treated like a returning hero.

Consequently, Thunders's name lent a great cachet to American Week, as Miles Copeland's US Package of Punk became known. When the planned venue (Global Village) fell through at the last minute, Andy Czezowski graciously offered Copeland the Roxy on consecutive days at the beginning of March. Each of the US acts was paired with an up-and-coming British band as support. Cherry Vanilla played with the Police, Wayne County with the Adverts, and Johnny Thunders's band (which was billed as "the Heartbrakers" [*sic*]) with Siouxsie and the Banshees as support.

The concert series was trailered with posters and full-colour collaged Xeroxed fliers. Cherry Vanilla was featured on one, holding a rocket-red dildo up to her mouth like a microphone. In the bottom left-hand corner, a gaggle of miniaturized New York cops in helmets peered up at the sexually aggressive giantess towering above them, announcing the London debut of "The Police."

3

QUEENS OF
NEW YORK

The Roxy was the London mecca for punk rock. Despite having only opened its doors on New Year's Day 1977, it had already established itself as the premier punk venue in London. Previously, it had been a gay-fetish club called Chaguarama's (commonly referred to as "Shagaramas"), which had drawn a crowd of outlandish freaks wearing their own glam rock-inspired S&M creations—the progenitor of "punk" fashions. It was also frequented by the teenage rent boy runaways who plied their trade in the "meat rack," the nickname for the streets and amusement arcades around nearby Piccadilly Circus.

One of the habitués of Chaguarama's was a pretty boy singer (and part-time rent boy and gay porn pinup) named Gene October. He had scored a gig at the venue for his band Chelsea and subsequently turned his manager, Andy Czezowski, on to the idea of taking over the club. The Roxy was hired out from the owner on a nightly basis for the first month of operation. After Czezowski (along with partners Barry Jones and Ralph Jendrazyck) successfully promoted several nights during December, they extended their arrangement, hiring the club on a weekly basis for £350 from the beginning of the year. Outside of making cheap flyers, there was no need to advertise. The official capacity of the Roxy was only 150, but the club regularly drew double that amount on word of mouth alone. Punk scenesters and would-be musicians propped up the bar upstairs, while downstairs the audience pogoed like maniacs.

Cherry Vanilla and her band ended up at the Roxy the first night they arrived in London and immediately felt swept up by the energy of the place. "It was just exciting to walk into because it was so crowded," she said. "It had a cachet, it had an atmosphere. Everyone would hang around outside in the street."

The Police had also ventured down to the Roxy the month before they made their live debut, taking in concerts by the Damned and the Heartbreakers. While Stewart Copeland and Henry Padovani sucked up the atmosphere, Sting viewed the delinquent chaos that surrounded him with a smug superiority. He was almost ten years older than the average age of the Roxy crowd, and he had a wife and child. Every band he saw merely stoked his ire and fuelled his competitive nature. His antipathy only grew after watching the Heartbreakers, whose performance prowess seemed directly related to their collective chemical intake. Any sloppiness was largely overlooked by the crowd, awed by the presence of front man Johnny Thunders, the only bona fide rock star on the London scene.

"Sting hated them," maintained Copeland. "He'd see all these guys and say, 'Look at these guys causing all this media attention. They're shit! I can do better than this fucking lot.' He'd get wilder and wilder. He became very aggressive but also very determined."

A few weeks later, Sting would get a chance to prove himself in front of the same crowd. Playing at the Roxy provided the first real test for the Police to establish themselves on the London scene. It was only their second ever show. They made their live debut as a band the night before in Wales, supporting Cherry Vanilla, safely out of earshot of the cognoscenti.

They had built up a set that consisted of just ten songs—the majority written by Copeland, the rest by Sting—which, according to Padovani, they played straight through in seventeen minutes flat without waiting for applause. Padovani maintained that this was the punk style, and he, for one, embraced it. But playing with speed and aggression also served to mask the deficiencies in their material, which even Copeland later conceded was "pretty basic, crummy stuff." "Dead End Job," one of Sting's first contributions to the Police (for which Copeland received a cowriting credit), was inspired by his twice-monthly visits to sign on at the dole office in Lisson Grove, West London, a task he found humiliating and demeaning. It was, by chance, exactly the same dole office that had inspired Joe Strummer to write the sneering "Career Opportunities" for the Clash. By comparison, "Dead End Job" is an achingly traditional blues—certainly woeful, but far from anarchic. The songs Copeland penned were little more than a series of groaning clichés stitched together that seemed to desperately strive for punk authenticity and traded on barely literate lyrics that plugged directly into the ethos promoted by the *Sniffin' Glue* fanzine. But would they pass muster with the punks?

"I can't remember how the Roxy crowd reacted to them," said Jayne County. "But it was pretty hard not to go down well at the Roxy 'cause the kids were so starved for good music! And they were all extremely drunk and fucked up on sulphate!"

Cherry Vanilla recalled it slightly differently. "They didn't have the punk gear and I know that the audience gave them grief over that. I remember some people criticizing them and saying, 'You look like wankers.' Stewart and Sting did not have the bleached hair yet, and Sting was a little on the chubby side." But it might have also been Sting's insistence on playing bare-chested in dungarees that marked them out as interlopers. While playing sideman to Cherry Vanilla, he at least made an attempt to look the part, wearing a black T-shirt with the Max's Kansas City logo on it.

The shows at the Roxy inspired a round of articles in the UK music press that served to promote the tours that followed. *Zig-Zag* featured an illustration of Cherry Vanilla as Lady Liberty, brandishing a flaming torch at her crotch. She also appeared on the cover of *Sniffin' Glue* in black hot pants, alongside a headline heralding her as part of the "New York Invasion"; even if the text that accompanied it suggested an attitude toward women that was more reactionary than new wave: "All the females are jealous of Cherry especially all the dyke Patti Smith fans. They sit there passing their bitchy comments in her direction but she don't care a shit. She's great—a bird that's honest. I can't help admiring her and that's something from me 'cause I normally can't stand women rockers."

Immediately following the Roxy shows, Cherry Vanilla and the Police headed out on tour, travelling around the UK in a van provided by Miles Copeland. "We went out on the road with zero dollars," said Cherry Vanilla. "And I had to run the show with whatever earnings that I could make. Miles was just getting us whatever bookings he could all over the place. Sometimes we'd get there and it would be like a shack. Another city would be a cool place. There were a lot of new little punk clubs popping up, and Miles didn't go out and check them all out."

Along with playing backup to Cherry Vanilla, for which they shared the princely sum of £10 among them, the Police played their own set as well. Sometimes, both bands played two sets a night. The Police also doubled up as drivers and roadies on the tour, helping to lug Zecca's upright piano out of the van and into the venue every night and back again after the show. On a good night the Police might get paid twice. A promoter in Wolverhampton recalled paying Cherry Vanilla and her band £40 to play at a student night and throwing in an extra £12 to cover expenses for the Police. Other times, they'd get to a club to find that it was operated by shady management who paid whatever they felt the act was worth, rather than the fee agreed on with Miles Copeland. On those occasions, Cherry Vanilla said that she felt obligated to make sure that the Police got paid, no matter what.

"Sometimes that meant my guys and I went without," she said. "We might find ourselves five hundred miles from London in this van, which was such a rickety old thing, with all our equipment and no money for a hotel room. We used to have to ask people at the gigs if we could go home and sleep on their cold freezing floors, which we did many nights. . . . We barely had money to eat. Sometimes we ate chips and beer and that was our dinner."

Sting, she noted, usually came better prepared than everyone else. "His wife, Frances, used to prepare a little box of food for him, with sandwiches and apples and things in it. So he wouldn't need to spend his money on food and could bring that back to her."

Out on the road, Cherry Vanilla (who had almost ten years on the rest of her band) played mother hen, which was not easy because her chicks were constantly clucking. "My piano player Zecca was a little high-strung gay guy, and Louis, my guitar player, was an attitude-y Italian guy so, naturally, they were always coming back to me, complaining that Stewart didn't keep time well and Sting had an attitude. But what could I do? I had all these people out on the road that I was responsible for keeping alive. I could only keep going and just try to keep peace."

Padovani made the best impression on everybody. "He didn't actually play with us, but he was the friendliest. Stewart just reminded me of a college boy. He always had stupid jokes. . . . I thought he was corny. He reacted like a spoilt college boy. He was very attitude-y. Sting was pretty quiet, but he also had a big ego already—it wasn't attitude, just a big artist's ego."

Despite knowing that Sting and Stewart Copeland, respectively, had a wife and a girlfriend at home, Cherry Vanilla looked the other way when she saw them hit on girls. But when they imbibed stimulants other than alcohol, she felt compelled to say her piece. "They used to take these things, Benylin and Do-Dos," she said. "I used to criticize them for that, saying, You know, you're such a jerk, how can you take that crap and everything?"

Both of these over-the-counter cough medicines contained ephedrine and amphetamines, nothing that rock bands wouldn't regularly imbibe to keep them going through the long hours, lack of sleep, and irregular eating patterns that generally constitute a touring lifestyle. It was all pretty tame compared to the substances other bands pumped into their bodies to keep themselves going, and when the

Cherry Vanilla road show crossed paths with the Heartbreakers tour in Liverpool, they witnessed a stark illustration of that.

"We had a hotel that night," said Cherry Vanilla. "We were in the hotel room and Johnny [Thunders] was shooting blood from the hypodermic needle onto the walls. I liked Johnny, he was a good guy. I just felt sorry for him that he was so addicted to heroin. But I do remember being like, oh my God, I got to get out of here."

But they were tied to the Heartbreakers for three more dates across the Midlands before they could head back to London. There, the Police joined Wayne County and his Electric Chairs for their first foray into Europe. This time, the Police were relieved of their additional duties and simply played as support. "The Police were the most boring people I have ever met," said Jayne County. "Polite, charming, professional, but no fun. It was like playing with a bunch of old married men." Compared to her, though, anyone would seem boring.

Even before Wayne became Jayne (having sprouted breasts), she was the most outré performer the rock world had ever seen. Wayne sang about looking for "Toilet Love" and sometimes took the stage looking like a piece of trash that had been dragged out of one. She had toilet-paper rolls in her hair (instead of curlers) and empty product packaging piled on top like some couture creation by a high-fashion milliner. A pop art nightmare freakish enough to make even Warhol wince, she usually took to the stage in full makeup and drag but wearing not much more than fifties-style underwear (a girdle, a garter belt, a bra, and stockings) and a bouffant blond wig tinted with rainbow-coloured streaks. A living-dead beauty queen who wore place cards in her hair (instead of a tiara) spelling out the name of her favourite band, the Dave Clark Five. After hitting London, she (like Thunders) toned down her act considerably, dressing more conservatively in a one-piece flight suit but still wearing full makeup.

If the Police weren't much fun, she at least gave them their due for being a "pretty open-minded bunch." "Hey, they toured with rock's most notorious transsexual!" she said. "Most of the punk bands wouldn't even do that! I scared most people shitless, but the Police were very intelligent individuals and they understood . . . or at least seemed unperturbed!"

Wayne County was no Cherry Vanilla. She was more "Queen Bitch" than Mother Hen. "I could be a real bitch and get really fucked up," she said. Wayne and on-off bisexual junkie guitarist boyfriend Greg Van Cook fought like cat and dog in the back of the van. Jayne relishes telling the story of how she once opened the door of the van while it was hurtling along the highway in Holland and tried to throw Van Cook out. The poisonous atmosphere spread to the front of the bus, where Stewart Copeland and Wayne's manager, Peter Crowley, shared driving duties. "They bickered and fought in the van the entire time we were driving through Holland, France, and England together," she said. "Up and down on the motorway with those two trading insults like two fourteen-year-olds!"

Sting didn't take to Crowley either and began to call him "Aleister" (after the British occultist) in an attempt to get a rise out of him. Other than that, Jayne couldn't recall any of the Police indulging in anything that resembled bad behaviour: "I remember they went down to the river where all the prostitutes were. But everyone does that! Don't they?

"If I hadn't been so caught up with Greg, I would have done my darndest to get into Sting's pants, but unfortunately that did not happen. But somehow I think that if I had tried hard enough, I could have! Even before I started my hormones, I could look quite good in drag. And once a cute guy has a few drinks in him and all . . ."

The tour ended at a one-day punk festival in Paris at the Palais des Glaces. "Nuit de Punk" also featured Generation X, the Jam, and the Electric Chairs. French band the Stinky Toys opened the show. The Police were sandwiched between the Jam and Wayne County. Padovani recalled Patti Smith guitarist Lenny Kaye standing directly in front of him in the audience snapping pictures. "*Il est très cool!*" swooned the star-struck Frenchman, who felt that he had finally arrived. Where his bandmates were already more hard-nosed and snooty, Padovani seemed blissfully unconcerned with politics and ambition. He was just glad to be living out his dream of playing in a rock 'n' roll band.

Stewart Copeland would later boast of the backroom deals he cut to avert disaster when their gear (which they were sharing with Wayne County's band, all of whom had been detained by customs) failed to turn up for the gig. Copeland had the bright idea of convincing the other bands to change the lineup so that the better-known Jam played before the Police and Generation X played last. "Wayne County and the Electric Chairs were fantastic," Copeland reported, "and while Generation X were setting up and arguing and generally being total idiots, the kids all went home!"

But the improved pecking order didn't help the Police play better— "a bum sound and incomprehensible lyrics," was the blunt summation in the *NME*'s review of the show. Their attitude also didn't endear them to their fellow musicians. "The real punk bands hated them," noted Jayne County. The feeling, at least on Sting's part, was mutual.

As a front man, Sting wasn't just a knock to their credibility, he was a liability. His passive-aggressive stance made itself felt at one early performance in the Nashville Rooms (another famed punk strong-hold in London, located in a West Kensington pub). "Okay, we're a punk band and we're gonna play some punk now," he said, introduc-ing the Police's set. "That means the words are banal and the music's fast. So here's a punk song for you, you arseholes."

Given that the Police's handle on their material was tenuous at best, this awkward stab at the audience came off as more of a backhanded compliment to himself. Even his bandmates were embarrassed. "God knows what he thought he was up to," bemoaned the drummer. Sting's behaviour proved even more awkward given that the audience that night was crammed full of scenesters and taste-makers who could have helped further the band's fledgling career. They included the same *NME* journalist who would later give them the thumbs-down at Palais des Glaces and Mark Perry, the editor of the increasingly influ-ential *Sniffin' Glue*, whom Stewart Copeland derisively referred to as the "punkometer."

"In all honesty, I can't say a Police gig was high on the agenda of the *Sniffin' Glue* scene," said Nick Jones, Miles Copeland's second-in-command and a former PR man for BTM Records. "Mark Perry *had* to put them down. He was an honest guy. Just because he was receiving help and encouragement from Stewart's elder brother, he wouldn't endorse something he didn't believe in." And because Mark Perry didn't rate the Police, neither did Miles Copeland. In short, the Police had a credibility problem, but they were the only ones who couldn't see it.

Outside of the shows arranged for them by Miles the Police rarely made the bills of other punk shows. They did, however, play one show in May 1977—their first as a headline act—with another set of outcasts: a nascent lineup of neo-Nazi punk band Skrewdriver. Although details of the support slot have been whitewashed from official Police history, the gig has been accorded special status in Skrewdriver lore. Prior to their adoption of reactionary far-right politics, Skrewdriver was a regular common or garden-variety Oi! band whose lumpen odes to thuggery (which bore titles like "Anti-Social" and "Street Fighter") were fairly well-regarded by sections of the punk cognoscenti.

The night the Police played with Skrewdriver at the Railway Tavern in Putney, South London, Shakin' Stevens was playing with his band, the Sunsets, at a rock 'n' roll night in a nearby venue. At that time, the tabloids were awash with scare stories about the violent rivalry between the teddy boys and the punks, characterizing it as a replay of the mod and rocker wars of the 1960s. If truth be told, the reporting only fuelled further conflict, and the animosity was largely one-sided. The deeply conservative teddy boys, whose dress and lifestyle were based entirely on a romanticization of the 1950s, viewed the punks as an affront to their culture—particularly the punk fashion for taking razor blades to drape suits (the teddy boy uniform) and customizing them with safety pins.

Sting also debuted a new mode of dress at the show, wearing a grey flight suit given to him by Paul Mulligan. Prior to that, Sting had been prone to wearing loose-fitting shirts and flared trousers. Now, at least, he had an image. The flight suit would become his de facto stage gear for the next two years, eventually driving his bandmates to distraction with its sweat-encrusted stench.

Despite rumours of trouble from the teddy boys down the road, the Railway Tavern show went off without incident. Skrewdriver's self-aggrandizing singer Ian Stuart later maintained that "most of the people came to see Skrewdriver anyway." John "Grinny" Grinton, Skrewdriver's drummer, did think it strange how "near the end of the night the punks and the Police began to disappear rather quickly." But the Police didn't have any reason to stay. Guitarist Phil Walmsley recalled that they had used all of Skrewdriver's back line: "apart from the drums, Stewart Copeland would only use his own kit."

While loading equipment into their van, the members of Skrewdriver were surrounded by twenty or thirty teds who had just emerged from the venue down the road. They set about taunting the punks and egging one another on until the incident exploded into violence. Grinny was smashed in the mouth with a microphone stand that shattered all of his front teeth. The Police were nowhere to be seen when they were needed.

4

VIVE LE PUNK

He'd been circling around them for months. Watching from the sidelines. Making friendly overtures. Waiting for the opportunity to strike. Andy Summers had spotted an opening for himself in the Police, and he wasn't about to let it pass. His career as a jobbing guitarist provided a passable income, but he wasn't really progressing. He had been coasting for years. He thought of himself as a lead guitarist who had never gotten his dues, always playing second fiddle behind wilful and idiosyncratic front men. It frustrated and irked him.

"I've never really been a session man. That's a mistaken piece of history," he bristled years later. But Summers did play as a session musician on several albums in the period leading up to the time he joined the Police. In 1976, he played on albums by singer-songwriter Tim Rose, Deep Purple's Jon Lord, and keyboard player–composer David Bedford. Before that, he was a sideman and a largely anonymous one at that, taking on gigs with pop acts like Neil Sedaka and David Essex, as well as hipper and more credible performers such as Kevin Ayers and Kevin Coyne. Summers didn't have a whole lot of stage presence. A review of a 1976 Kevin Coyne show in London noted that "Andy Summers stands like a corpse, playing stark bare-boned licks."

One solid connection between Summers and the Police existed through Virgin Records. On his return to London from Los Angeles in the early seventies, Summers had manoeuvred himself into a social set made up of musicians on the label. Several were part of the so-called Canterbury scene of avant-garde rock bands, such as Soft Machine (which he had briefly been a member of) and Henry Cow (which he had flunked an audition for). Through this set, he had come to meet Mike Howlett, a former bassist with Gong. Howlett's girlfriend at the time was Carol Wilson, who had signed Sting to his publishing deal with Virgin.

Wilson had introduced Sting to Howlett earlier that year. "I had a demo studio in my loft," Wilson recalled, "and they started doing demos there." Summers recounted that when he went around for a friendly jam, Howlett played him some recordings he had made previously with Sting. "I'm not all that impressed but think the songs are okay," Summers recollected in his memoir. Howlett then proposed that Summers join him and Sting in a new group that he wanted to debut at a Gong tribute concert in Paris at the end of May 1977. Chris Cutler of Henry Cow was to drum. When he became unavailable, Sting suggested Stewart Copeland. And so the classic lineup of the Police came together.

At their first rehearsal session, Summers realized that he had crossed paths with both Sting and Copeland before, albeit briefly, and the comfort of familiarity softened his opinion. He began to feel more energized when they tackled a song Sting had written called "Visions of the Night."

The group recorded almost an album's worth of material under the name Strontium 90, a mix of songs written by Howlett and Sting, in a spacey hard rock style. Sting also contributed an early version of "Every Little Thing She Does Is Magic," which would later be reworked by the Police to become one of their biggest hits. But with two bass players in the band, the dynamic wasn't quite right. "The sound of a train wreck," was Summers's opinion of the recordings.

Following the Paris show in May 1977, Summers also became enamoured with the idea of forming a power trio and began to make overtures toward both Sting and Copeland about playing with them on a full-time basis. When Summers bumped into Copeland by chance on the London Underground, he seized the opportunity to further his ambitions by taking the drummer out for a coffee and making his wishes plain. In Summers's telling, this chance meeting is given pseudo-mystical significance (which also provided the title to his memoir, *One Train Later*). "One train later," he said, "and it might have all turned out differently." He went on to fantasize about the alternate unfulfilled lives that each member of the Police might be leading had they not heeded their calling. Sting might have returned to his teaching job in Newcastle. Copeland would have ended up working in the Middle East.

As it was, the Police were going nowhere fast. The advantage of taking Summers on was obvious. He was an established musician with a proven track record; in their eyes, he had already made it. If they could lure him into the band, it would legitimize both their ambitions and the view they held of their own proficiency as musicians. For his part, Summers saw a band with lots of potential and no clear leader. Although Copeland had formed the band, Sting was clearly the front man, but there was no one strong character— like Coyne or Ayers—who cast the rest of the band in shadow. If Summers could insert himself into Henry Padovani's position, they had the makings of a tight unit in which he could make his presence felt as a lead guitarist.

By committing himself to the Police full time, Summers would be foregoing his retainer as a member of Kevin Ayers's band, which he was also touring with at the time. But he could afford to take the risk. His wife, Kate, was then working as a copywriter at Young and Rubicam, one of the biggest advertising agencies in the world. They led a nice middle class life with a spacious flat in Putney, and no kids.

What did he have to lose? He was also possibly relieved at the thought of extricating himself from the endless drinking sessions that were part and parcel of being a member of Kevin Coyne's band, all of whom were subjected to excoriating put-downs by their leader. "I've spent too much time with professional musos who couldn't wait to get into a pub after rehearsal," Summers said later.

The Police began to rehearse together as a four-piece. Coyne even remembered seeing them playing at the same rehearsal space as his band, "and all of us laughing, because we thought, This is Andy's last shot to make something." They looked rather too old to be punks, Coyne thought, and they didn't really look the part, either. Playing opposite the less-experienced Padovani immediately caused problems for Summers. Their first gig together at the Music Machine in Camden was a disaster. "We arrive at choruses and verses at different times with different chords," Summers reported.

For the next two months, Padovani's future in the Police became the elephant in the room. Summers thought Padovani's lack of proficiency was holding them back, and, more pointedly, he did not want to share the role of guitarist. Rather than deal with the situation up front and ask Padovani to leave, they formed another parallel group without him. The Elevators were essentially a continuation of Howlett's Strontium 90 project, but now, instead of two guitarists, they had two bassists, and that wasn't satisfactory, either. After playing several shows in London as the Elevators, Sting, Summers, and Copeland told Howlett they wanted to carry on without him. And then there was the question of what to do with Padovani, who had just secured them a festival gig in France.

One of the first people Padovani had encountered in London was a fellow French ex-pat named Marc Zermati. A true believer in the primal power of rock 'n' roll, Zermati owned a record store in Paris called Open Market, which was known to have the best stock of import albums in Europe. He had been championing the terse and threatening twelve-bar boogie of British pub rock bands like Dr. Feelgood and Ducks Deluxe, the tumultuous delinquent blues of Johnny Thunders and the Stooges, and the more traditional R&B of Little Bob Story and

Flamin Groovies, helping to introduce them to foreign audiences by setting up tours.

Zermati saw punk rock as a continuum of the raw rock 'n' roll spirit he heard in the pub rock groups. In 1976, he set about organizing what would become the first European punk rock festival in Mont-de-Marsan, a small medieval town in the south of France near the Spanish border. It was the most unlikely setting for a punk rock festival, not least because it was also the location of one of the key military bases in the country: the 118th Air Force Base (later home to France's nuclear deterrent strike force).

By using a contact he had in the town's local government, Zermati managed to secure the town's nineteenth-century Andalusian-style bullring, a local monument, as the venue for his festival. The first festival had only one bona fide punk group on the bill, the Damned, but word of mouth about the event spread so fast that the second festival (which took place in August 1977) quickly became a prestigious event and drew support from some of the premier bands on the UK scene. The Clash was secured to headline the first day, and the Jam was due to top the bill on the second. The Damned also made a return visit. The rest of the bill was filled up by new wave French bands (including Bijou and Little Bob Story), as well as by Zermati's pub rock favorites, Dr. Feelgood and Eddie and the Hot Rods. The Brits all travelled down to Mont-de-Marsan together on a twenty-seven-hour bus journey.

The festival was even featured in a report on French national television that announced an imminent invasion by British punk rockers, accompanied by footage of British youths larking about on the King's Road, the punk hangout in London, and playing up for the camera. There was an interview with a barely sentient Captain Sensible of the Damned. France was on alert. The town was prepared for trouble—and they got it.

Soon after the Jam's arrival, its bandmates were arrested for trashing their hotel room and were promptly locked up in the local jail. Word of their arrest spread to the crowd back at the bullring, causing thousands of kids to rally to their cause. The mob surrounded the police station, demanding the release of the band, then went on a rampage through the town and looted the supermarkets. Despite all of this chaos and destruction, Zermati still maintains today that the powers that be in Mont-de-Marsan remained unfazed. They'd seen worse. Every summer the town also hosted a traditional bull-fighting fiesta, an excuse for a drunken street party that regularly got out of hand.

As one of the lesser-known bands on the bill, the Police played early in the afternoon on the second day. They were well-received by the crowd, despite the glaring arrogance of Sting's introductory comment to the crowd: "We're gonna play some songs you won't understand." The set they chose to play—a grab bag of original material, interspersed with cover songs that lent themselves to the punk idiom—reflected the lack of direction in the band. Summers picked the Animals' "It's My Life." Copeland chose Curved Air's "Kids to Blame." Their performance was overshadowed by a rather unseemly spat between Summers and Padovani that set the stage for the latter's ejection from the group.

To keep transportation costs for the festival down to a minimum, Zermati had hired enough back-line equipment to ensure that the bands didn't need to bring their own. On their arrival at the festival site, Summers and Sting went for a swim in a nearby river, while Padovani wisely went to check out the gear. He secured himself a Hiwatt amp, the same model used by Pete Townshend of the Who. By the time Summers arrived, all of the amps were gone. When Padovani showed off his Hiwatt, Summers blew up like a petulant child, insisting that he should use the amp because he was playing all of the solos.

At Copeland and Sting's behest, Padovani begrudgingly agreed to keep the peace. He gave the amp to Summers and went off to search for one to use himself. He ran into the Maniacs, a band he was friendly with, whose musicians offered to let him use one of their amps, a Marshall. Pleased as punch, Padovani returned to the group with his find. Summers was apoplectic with rage. "That's not fair," he whined. "Henry always has a better amp than me!" Summers glossed over all mention of this incident in the account of the festival contained in his memoir. But there was worse to come.

Two days after returning from Mont-De-Marsan, the four-piece Police prepared to record their second single. The band's debut single had sold steadily on Miles Copeland's Illegal Records imprint since its release in May, causing him to take a more active interest in the group. He had secured John Cale to produce the session for the second single, something of a coup for such a young band. As well as being a founding member of the Velvet Underground, Cale had produced some seminal rock albums—by the Stooges, Patti Smith, and the Modern Lovers, to name just three—alongside his own idiosyncratic solo output. With the exception of Padovani, who was delighted at the idea of working with this legendary figure, the Police were not impressed.

Miles Copeland had a long-standing association with Cale. He had even, according to Lou Reed and Patti Smith biographer Victor Bockris, apparently been in the running as a potential manager for the Velvet Underground. Their initial connection had come through Jane Friedman, a New York publicist whose company, the Wartoke Concern, had handled publicity for Woodstock. Friedman was also Patti Smith's manager. Emboldened by his success with the US Package of Punk, Copeland sought more New York acts. This time, he turned to Friedman, who suggested Television and Blondie. Copeland brought both bands over for a successful double-headlining tour of the UK in May 1977 that helped break both acts into the British market. (In 1978, Ian Copeland would share office space with Friedman in New York, from where he launched his own booking agency, FBI. His brother used the same office as an American base for his management activities.)

Miles Copeland returned the favour by bringing Friedman's boyfriend, Cale (whom she was also managing), in to work with some of the acts in his Illegal Records stable, thereby hoping to secure some of the cachet that Cale had lent to the New York bands he had produced. Cale would produce singles for Menace and Sham 69. Copeland also released an EP by Cale, "Animal Justice." But the first band to benefit from the association with the producer was Squeeze. Their debut EP,

Packet of Three, released on yet another label setup that Copeland called Deptford Fun City, went on to sell twenty-five thousand copies and paved the way for Copeland to broker a record deal for the group with A&M. Cale's services were retained to produce their self-titled debut album. At that time, Cale had something of a substance-abuse problem that was rapidly spinning out of control. Members of Squeeze recalled him gripping a bottle of brandy during a rehearsal session and taking liberal swigs from it until he drank himself into unconsciousness.

The sessions with the Police also got off on the wrong foot when Cale arrived at Pathway Studios both drunk and late. While the two guitarists struggled to get the right balance between them, Cale sat reading a newspaper. His apparent lack of enthusiasm immediately rubbed Summers up the wrong way. "He couldn't take us on our own for what we were," Summers later sneered. "He just wanted us to be an imitation punk band."

But, in effect, that was exactly what they were. The Police were not to discover their "sound" until several months later. It's just possible that Cale was bored, not seeing much promise in their selection of material and faced with a band whose members thought they knew better and treated every suggestion he made with outright hostility.

There was almost certainly an element of professional jealousy in Summers's attitude toward the producer. Cale had been successful both as a member of a band and as a solo artist and a producer in his own right. But Summers, just nine months younger than Cale, had been consigned to playing the sideman for his entire career. Within the Police, he had the advantage of both age and musical experience, and his pride got the better of him. Yet there was also something else going on that served to create an uncomfortable atmosphere in the session. Stewart Copeland, Summers, and Sting had already decided that Padovani had to go. The discomfort they evidently felt about this boiled over into their resentment toward Cale.

"Cale knew during the sessions that we were going to fire Henry, and he flipped," Copeland said. "He said, 'Whaaat? This new guitarist [Summers] you've got is a load of crap!'" The producer then put

Summers's nose further out of joint by asking Padovani to play a solo on the single. Summers protested that they had already agreed among themselves who was going to play the solo. "Okay, you want to play the solo?" Padovani recalled Cale saying to Summers. "Play it on Henry's guitar!"

Summers's response was to knock out a Led Zeppelin riff. "That's it," he reported Cale saying, excitedly. "Let's record that." At that, said Summers, they called it a day. "The truth is, we are more serious than he is and we simply don't need him," Summers concluded smugly in his memoir.

It wasn't only Summers who had borne the brunt of Cale's chaotic working methods. After Sting ran through what he considered a near-perfect vocal take of "Visions of the Night," his work was given a curt dismissal by the producer, who ordered him to try again. "He was taking the piss out of us," Sting raged to Padovani immediately after the session. Cale was notoriously tough and overbearing toward the bands he worked with, in order to get the results he was after. The Police got off lucky.

When recording Squeeze's debut album later that year, Cale locked the group in the studio and made them run through "Amazing Grace" over and over again until they could play a note-perfect rendition. He also threw out all of the material they had written for the album and told them to write new songs on the spot. "He was an intimidating man and came with this huge reputation and ego," said Squeeze lyricist Chris Difford.

Padovani had his own view of the method in Cale's madness. "He was just trying to bring up the adrenaline." And Cale himself acknowledged as much in his own memoir. "As a producer," he said, "you've got to be a catalyst, an ally, a co-conspirator. Sometimes you have to introduce conflict in order to resolve it. You have to make one position or other untenable."

Recordings from the aborted Cale session have never seen the light of day, not even turning up as a bootleg among Police fans, which suggests that nothing usable ever resulted from it. The fallout from the humiliation they felt finally spurred Sting, Summers, and Copeland into action. Padovani was given his marching orders later that night.

Sting was ordered to do the dirty work, a role he evidently did not cherish. As Sting stammered excuses, Padovani already knew what he was trying to say and accepted the decision gracefully. An authorized 1981 biography published about the band (*The Police: A Visual Documentary*) offers up a mischievous morsel of misinformation as a rationale for the split: "Henry Padovani's worst suspicions were confirmed when he came across Andy experimenting with a flattened thirteenth chord. He left the band in disgust." It was a line so loaded, it could have been written by Summers himself.

Three decades later, Summers, still clearly peeved at the widespread perception that he had engineered Padovani's ejection from the group, dropped another bombshell in his autobiography. He related an incident (secondhand) that had occurred before he had even started playing with the Police. While on tour with Cherry Vanilla, Copeland and Sting had taken her guitarist boyfriend, Louis Lepore, aside before a London show and told him in no uncertain terms that there was a place for him in the Police if he wanted it. "When I read that [in Summers's book], I just stood in the bookstore and cried," said Cherry Vanilla. "How could they do that to me?"

It's possible this was a preemptive strike on the part of Copeland, who was well aware during the first six months of the Police's existence that Sting's commitment to the group was wavering. Copeland was horrified to watch the Police fall apart at the seams (musically) during their final rehearsal before the Cherry Vanilla tour: "Henry had forgotten all the chords and stuff. Sting was going 'Oh Jesus *Christ*' because the Cherry Vanilla band was really quite good. I was thinking, 'Oh no, now my band's going to get stolen by Cherry Vanilla!'" The implication of the story about their attempt to recruit Lepore was that prior to Summers's involvement in the band, Copeland had already taken the initiative to dump Padovani in order to appease Sting.

As far as Summers was concerned, it was a simple case of "do unto others." The guitarist had been given short shrift from his two-month tenure with Soft Machine in exactly the same fashion. "Kevin does not want either me or a guitar in the band," was Summers's sober take on his sacking. "The Soft Machine as he sees it is a trio."

The only person who seems to have been largely unaffected by all of these machinations was Padovani himself. The phlegmatic guitarist took the sacking in his stride and, sensibly, sped off to spend time with his family in Corsica. On his return, he was recruited by Wayne County to join the Electric Chairs. At the time, it seemed as if he had lucked out. Wayne County was far better known than the Police and was much in demand as a live performer. Unlike the Police, County appreciated Padovani's talent.

"Henry has a huge monster cock!" Jayne screeched. "And you always knew when he had a girl in his room, cause you could hear her screaming all the way down the hallway of the hotel, 'No no, it's too big!'"

While on tour with the Police around Europe, Jayne had ample opportunity to get the measure of the rest of the band too. "Andy was small framed but kind of cute. He was always quiet and polite. A real gentleman. Stuart came off like a nerd. But still really smart and an incredible drummer! Although he seemed a bit naive in sexual matters!

And Sting . . . well, Cherry Vanilla had already told me that she thought Sting was a real sexy bastard . . . Sting was well mannered and highly intelligent. I often wondered why he wanted to be in a band instead of working at the British Museum! Sting always had a nice smile on his face. I used to hide and then peek at him when he was changing his clothes. I often wondered if he knew I was watching him undress. Hmmm, what a body!!"

While their sex appeal was apparently without peer, the financial status of the group was in dire straits. Gerry Richardson, Sting's former bandmate in Last Exit, had landed on his feet by securing a job as the musical director for Billy Ocean. Richardson knew that his old friend was struggling and offered Sting the role of bassist in Ocean's backing band, a position that paid the not inconsiderable sum of £80 a week. If Sting had taken the gig, he would have almost certainly split the Police. Summers intervened by arranging for Sting and Copeland to accompany him on a series of outstanding dates that Summers was scheduled to play in Munich with a German composer named Eberhard Schoener.

Summers had connected with Schoener during sessions for former Deep Purple bassist Jon Lord's third solo album, *Sarabande*, a symphonic prog-rock project that Schoener conducted. Summers had struck up an unlikely rapport with the German over that three-day recording session in Dusseldorf.

With his shock of red hair and penchant for bow ties and crushed-velvet jackets, Schoener looked more like a krautrocker in his Sunday best than a classical composer. He was often cited as part of the new wave of German prog-electronic composers, alongside Amon Duul, Klaus Schulze, and Popul Vuh. Schoener's stock in trade was an eclectic but not particularly exciting mash of musical styles—Balinese gamelan chanting with Moog synthesizers, a classical boys' choir with hard rock and liberal doses of symphonic rock. Summers would record three albums with Schoener between 1976 and 1980. On the latter two, he was joined by the other members of the Police.

For their first collaboration with Schoener, the Police were employed for a week of rehearsals and live dates in Munich; the production was housed in a circus tent and featured an odd supporting cast that included trapeze artists and an opera singer. After the shows, the band went into the studio with Schoener for two weeks to record the material for an album, *Flashback*, that was to be released on EMI's progressive rock label Harvest. "The purpose of all my journeys is the return. The album *Flashback* is about a return," was Schoener's rather vague explanation of his concept album. They worked for three weeks in total, all expenses paid. Sting later recalled that the money they earned was so good it kept the Police going for the first two years of their existence. But money couldn't buy them love. And as 1977 drew to a close, no one loved the Police.

5

PAGING DOCTOR ROCK

At the beginning of 1978, Sting found himself back where he had started out in life: above a dairy. Only now he was taking counsel from a country doctor. Nigel Gray had trained as a general practitioner but was also a keen music hobbyist who had set up a studio in a village hall above a milk depot in his hometown of Leatherhead. Gray was almost the same age as both Copeland and Sting and also had a young family. He was clean-cut, sensible, and, above all, practical.

Gray and his younger brother, Chris—nineteen years old and just out of college—built the studio with their own hands over the course of two years. The lobby of the hall became a reception area. The auditorium, a large room with a high vaulted roof, wooden floors, and natural-sounding acoustics, became a studio space with walls damped down by egg cartons. And the stage area was converted into a control room. Gray gave the studio a grandiose name, Surrey Sound, after the county Leatherhead was located in. At first, he hired the space out as a rehearsal room and recorded 4-track demos for local groups, teaching himself and his brother how to be sound engineers at the same time. At the beginning of 1977, he decided to make the studio a going concern, borrowed money to upgrade it to 16-track, and placed advertisements in UK music papers.

Sting would later describe Surrey Sound as "a cruddy, funky studio with egg cartons on the walls"—a rather uncharitable description, given the role that the two albums the Police recorded there would play in launching their career. By the time Sting came to write his autobiography, tact had tempered his recollection of the studio to a description that was purely functional: "spacious, homely and inexpensive." At the time he had little choice in the matter. The Police could not sustain themselves as a band on the meagre number of live bookings they had secured, let alone pay for enough studio time to record an album. Based on the sales figures for their first single, which had been healthy for a new band, Miles Copeland figured that an album by the Police was probably a sound investment, so he offered to foot the bill for the studio time.

Up until then, Miles Copeland had been using major label-owned studios in London (namely, Columbia, Polydor, and EMI) to record the bands on his Faulty Products labels, often scoring free demo time from the labels. Mark Perry's band, Alternative TV, had cut a demo for EMI, and when the label passed on it, Copeland was able to put it out himself while off-loading the recording costs to someone else. Surrey Sound was dirt cheap at £10 an hour and cheap was Copeland's style. The Police were not the first group he sent to Surrey Sound. Jools Holland had recorded a solo single there. Alternative TV recorded both their "Action Vision Time" single and their debut album, *The Image Has Cracked*, in Leatherhead.

The Police began their sessions at Surrey Sound in January 1978. According to Sting, basic tracks were laid down quickly, in the first ten days, but the album itself wouldn't be completed until August. Prior to Surrey Sound, there had been an abortive attempt to record at Matrix Studios in London, with a different engineer. "I can't tell you how dreadful they sound," said Nigel Gray, who still has the tapes stashed in his attic. "Just a noise, it's a mess."

"Miles was quite canny," said Chris Gray, whose apprenticeship in the studio had involved engineering some of the other Faulty Products bands. "He knew that Nigel was the main man and did the engineering, so he insisted that Nigel work with the Police; otherwise, being the punky young brother, I probably would have done it."

The only downside to this arrangement was that Nigel Gray was still working out his own apprenticeship as a junior doctor and was required to attend to patients twice a day. "I was doing morning surgery up to about eleven," he said. "I would go on a couple of home visits, then go to the studio and record the band, still wearing my doctor's shirt and tie. At four o'clock, I had evening surgery, so I'd say to the band, 'Have a cup of tea for a couple of hours and I'll be back.'"

To further cut costs, Miles Copeland had given the band some old two-inch tape to record on that he had found stored in his garage. They contained the masters for an album by Caravan, a band he had managed in the early seventies. The Police set about recording over it, initially cutting the songs they had rehearsed for their live set. "We thought the music was something else," said Chris Gray. "We would actually play it after they were gone."

The Gray brothers' enthusiasm for the band's material and, more important, Nigel's technical know-how would prove invaluable to the group. The engineer knew exactly what kind of sound he wanted to achieve. *Punchy* and *clean* are the two words he used to describe the Police sound, an approach that reflected his own (extremely conventional) tastes in music. "I liked rock music, not heavy rock," he said. "I liked the Beatles, the Stones, and I love Roxy Music . . . good quality pop-rock music. I also used to listen to J. J. Cale and that sort of stuff."

Recording progressed in fits and spurts for the first three months, in blocks of two days at a time, but without any clear sense of direction. One of the first tracks they recorded was a throwaway spoken-word piece about a blow-up doll, written and recited by Andy Summers in an exaggerated country bumpkin accent. On hearing it, Miles Copeland, who turned up periodically at Surrey Sound to check on his investment, denounced it as "hippie crap." He still wasn't convinced the Police had much to offer on a creative level. In turn, his lack of approval weighed heavily on the group.

The recording of "Roxanne" proved to be a turning point for all involved, but it was no simple task. The song had a stop-start structure with a sustained guitar figure running underneath the vocals at the end of each verse that marked time before the next verse came in. Although they had practised the song over and over, they found it impossible to get the timing right when playing without the vocals to guide them.

"I remember recording 'Roxanne,'" said Gray, "because I had to actually conduct it. We never used click tracks and time codes and that kind of thing in those days, because they didn't exist, so I had to go out into the studio and stand on one of the loudspeakers so they could all see me. And I conducted them like a conductor: one, two, three, four; just waving my hands around so they all came back in on time. And because there was only me in the studio, I had to press play and record on the tape recorder, run out into the studio and jump on the box, then run back in to turn the tape machine off at the end. It wasn't very sophisticated, but it worked! We all thought 'Roxanne' was the best thing that they'd done. But they didn't have the confidence."

The next time Miles Copeland came down to check on their progress, he sat reading a magazine while they ran the tapes. "Is that it?" he said at the end, unimpressed by what he had heard. The band admitted that they had one more song but prefaced it with excuses. The song was quite different from their usual stuff, jazzy even, and didn't at all conform to the punk standard they had set for themselves. Sting recalled watching Copeland's ears turn red while the song played, half-expecting him to explode with rage at any second. He did explode but with unbridled enthusiasm, telling them something to the effect that it was "a fucking smash." Finally, they had produced something that Copeland approved of and felt had commercial potential.

Copeland took a tape of the song away with him and the next day marched into A&M, determined to bag a deal for the Police. This wasn't simply bravado. He was on very good terms with A&M. Squeeze's first single for the label, "Take Me I'm Yours," had been released at the beginning of February and climbed into the upper reaches of the top 20. (It was still bubbling just under the top 20 nine weeks later, at the beginning of May.) Copeland knew to strike while the iron was hot and turn the goodwill he had with the company into another deal. He quickly wrangled a verbal agreement out of A&M to release "Roxanne," a deal that mirrored the one he had already secured for Squeeze: namely, a commitment to release the single in the UK and the States.

The band members were elated, especially Sting, who realized he could finally hope to see an end to the financial instability he and Frances Tomelty had endured for the last year. But his joyous mood was tempered by the news that back in Newcastle, his mother had run off with her longtime lover, taking Sting's younger sister, Anita, with them. This all came as a terrible shock to his father, Ernie, who had been given no indication at all of his wife's plans. To Sting, it was the inevitable culmination of something he'd been aware of for a long time. He remembered when, as a child, he had accidentally caught his mother in the arms of another man. Instead of confronting her directly about the hurt that she had caused and the damage she had wrought on her family, he wrote her a letter to say that he wanted nothing more to do with her. His failure to deal with this event would rend his emotional life in two and have much more dramatic consequences further down the line.

If the recording of "Roxanne" helped establish the musical style of the Police, another event that occurred shortly afterward contrived to lend them the visual identity they lacked. Since moving to London, Sting had also been working as a magazine model and an extra in commercials to supplement his income. It was a far more lucrative line of work than playing gigs with the Police. On average he earned £150 a day, often with residuals from repeat fees on top. Frances Tomelty's agent, Pippa Markham, had sent him out on several auditions that resulted in his appearing in a series of TV ads for companies like Brutus Jeans and Triumph Bras. Now she arranged for Sting to audition for a Wrigley's Chewing Gum commercial that called for him to play a member of a punk band. One apocryphal story, possibly fabricated by Sting himself for a gullible biographer, has him jumping onto a desk and "gobbing" at the casting director to demonstrate his punk credentials.

Sting admitted employing what he described as a "basic chancer's psychology" during these auditions to give the impression he didn't care about getting the part. He recalled one such audition in his memoir, during which he was faced by a panel of advertising agency creatives who, after discovering he was a musician by trade, handed him a guitar and asked him to play a song. "I tell them, 'Fuck off!'" he reported, "and saunter out of the oak-panelled office with a look of such confident disdain and nerve that they immediately call my agent to hire me."

Although Sting didn't identify it as such, this sounds suspiciously like the audition for the Wrigley's ad. If so, it provides an illustration of his "chancer's psychology" at work. Had he performed one of his own songs, say "Roxanne," he would in all likelihood have blown the audition. In any event, he got the part and promptly managed to get the rest of the Police hired as well. The one catch: they all had to dye their hair blond. Sting would later claim that the Wrigley's ad was directed by Tony Scott (who was then working for his brother Ridley's agency RSA), but there is nothing to verify this. The commercial was shelved and never screened.

That an ad agency was looking to shoot a punk-themed commercial for a major brand in January 1978 gives some indication of how quickly the punk look had been appropriated and assimilated by commercial interests outside the music industry. An all-male, all-blond punk band was the kind of pop fantasy that could only be dreamed up in the insular environs of ad land. If the Police ever considered that pretending to be a punk band in a TV commercial was not only a bad idea but a credibility killer, they never let on. Instead, they embraced it as a commercial opportunity. They were left with these achingly conspicuous blond 'dos. As a man in his mid-thirties (albeit a young-looking thirty-six) with a peroxide dye job, Summers must have looked particularly out of place, especially in the mid-1970s.

He acknowledged being harassed about his new image. "I looked like some old whore!" he admitted. "It took a fair bit of getting used to and, of course, the people I'd known before were all sniggering at me."

Punk rock was about individuality. Here was a band whose members set themselves apart from the pack by making themselves all look the same. "It unified the group," offered Summers. Sting's spiky platinum-blond crop, combined with his air force jumpsuit, lent him an aggressive look to match his attitude. Summers began to dress differently, too, discarding the flowing scarves and flares for skin-tight trousers, a T-shirt, and a leather jacket. Even Stewart Copeland managed to look less camp in the quasi-military garb that was his favoured stage gear. They now had a uniform. Just like the real police.

Miles Copeland sensed that unlike most of the bands he was working with at the time, the Police had a real chance at commercial success, and he took the opportunity to put his management of the band on an official basis. A deal was agreed to, even though the management company itself wasn't registered until November 1979. Unlike the fifty/fifty agreement Miles Copeland had with Squeeze, he cut himself in for only a quarter share of the Police's earnings, effectively making him an equal shareholder in their financial affairs. Although it was, in part, an egalitarian solution to the thorny problem of percentage splits, it was still a cut above the 15 to 20 per cent industry standard for management agreements. What it did was effectively make Miles Copeland the fourth member of the Police—a cliché, in most regards, but in this case absolutely correct. It was a role he would fulfil in every respect, save for actually playing an instrument. Miles was certainly as much of a showman and a performer as any other member of the band, and the methods he used to promote them and their interests would become increasingly creative.

Now that Sting was beginning to emerge as the chief songwriter of the group, a similar arrangement was struck among the band members. To ensure that the spoils of their industry were not unevenly weighted toward one person, the bassist was convinced that for the future harmony of the group, it was in everyone's best interests to divvy up some of his songwriting royalties among them. In fact, this would have the opposite effect, sowing a seed of resentment that would take root and then fester in years to come.

Miles Copeland also sought to strike a deal with Nigel Gray. Having tried and failed to convince A&M to fund the recording sessions for the album, he offered Gray a percentage point on the record in lieu of the studio time the Police needed to finish recording their album—with the promise that Gray would also be paid the full amount once the album had been picked up by the record company. Gray relied on the semi-regular income he was getting from the studio to cover his expenses and continue paying off the loan he had taken out to upgrade the equipment to 16-track technology. He knew the Police had potential, but there was no guarantee that they would succeed. In his eyes, he was essentially being offered 1 percentage point of nothing, and it was a gamble he was not prepared to take. He turned down the offer, a decision he would rue in years to come. In any event, Miles Copeland simply ignored the mounting studio costs until the album was complete and A&M had agreed to release it. Then he arranged for the label to settle the £1,500 bill they had racked up.

"That was classic Miles," said Nigel Gray. "He wasn't going to pay whatever. Eventually, I got paid by A&M. By that time, it was over a year later and 'Roxanne' had been a hit [in April 1979]. So I lost and lost; I didn't get the money and just had to scrape through, and I didn't get the point."

Emboldened by the response to "Roxanne," the band began to record more songs in the same vein, weighting the album toward the lighter-sounding material that Sting had brought to the table. The singer even remembered writing the lyrics to some songs on the drive up to Surrey Sound in the mornings. Most of their original set was elbowed off the running order, one by one, and later relegated to B-sides. Copeland received a songwriting credit on only one cut that would end up on the completed album, a song called "Peanuts." That, too, featured lyrics by Sting: a bizarre moralistic rant about a sell-out pop star, inspired by Rod Stewart, of all people.

If the change in material marked a shift in the dynamic of the group, the Police were also feeling their way toward a style. Summers had acquired a vintage Echoplex Maestro tape delay unit that he used as a filter for his guitar. Although Summers claimed otherwise, the Echoplex (whose exponents included Jimmy Page and Brian May) was a shortcut to a classic rock sound. "There was no thought about using it as a tool to create my own sonic identity," he said. "I just thought it was cool."

This seems a little disingenuous on his part. Rock guitarists generally distinguish themselves through their sound, as well as their mode of playing, and Summers was more studied than most. Indeed, he seemed most comfortable when discussing music in terms of technique and talking in an arcane language that consisted solely of guitar figures, tunings, phrasings, and chords (whether open, flattened, major, or minor). "I explored a much cooler, sort of disinterested chord style that utilized sacked fifths or an added ninth to get the harmony moving without the obvious sentimental associations of major and minor thirds," was how he explained the Police sound to one interviewer. His relationship to music seemed similarly cool and disinterested. He rarely, if ever, talked about what it meant to him on a personal or emotional level.

Yet Summers also ached for acceptance as part of the body of hallowed musicians and more often than not described his own music in relation to others. "From an instinctive and unself-conscious [sic] journey," he said, eulogizing the moment he felt the Police had arrived, "we discover a sound for which there is no previous formula, a space jam meets Bartók collage with blue-eyed soul vocals."

He made it sound as if they had reinvented the wheel, but there was one very good practical reason they drifted toward the reggae rhythms that became their hallmark. "At that time," said Chris Gray, "Sting couldn't really sing and play bass at the same time so well. Either the bass would be good or the singing would be good, but not so much at the same time."

Even Sting himself copped to this. "The other nice thing about playing a reggae groove in the verses was that you could leave holes in the music," he reflected. "I needed those holes because, initially, I had a hard time singing and playing at the same time."

"The Police weren't sure about reggae or what reggae should sound like," furthered Nigel Gray. And so they invited Joe Sinclair, a house musician and engineer for reggae label Trojan Records, down to Leatherhead for one session. "They got him in to see if he could help me with it. He was just hanging out, and I didn't know why he was there. I didn't really speak to him. When we came to mixing, the only thing I can remember him saying was, 'I need to check the frequency, mon.' I thought, Check the frequency? What are you talking about? Eventually, he just went."

Chris Gray also recalled Sinclair "playing a bit of piano" on two tracks that ended up on the finished album—"Masoko Tanga" and "Hole in My Life." Sinclair was rewarded with a credit of "thanks" on the finished albums, but the tracks themselves were the weakest on the set. "Hole in My Life" was cloying sentimentality, with an ersatz reggae skank that sounded like the Beatles' "Got to Get You into My Life" spliced with the Gerry Rafferty AOR staple "Baker Street." "Masoko Tanga" employed a revolving groove over which Sting recited nonsense lyrics. To absolve himself of blame, he later insisted he had sung the words under hypnosis.

In April, the Police took a break from recording to play two shows in London in support of the single release of "Roxanne." For the first, a headline gig at the Nashville Rooms in West London, they were supported by a band called the Crooks—a bill that must have seemed like a jape at the time but did little to dissuade anyone from the general feeling that the Police were nothing more than a gimmick band.

Five days later, the group supported British roots reggae band Steel Pulse at the Camden Roundhouse, alongside Stiff Records artist Wreckless Eric and Liverpudlian "punk poet" John Cooper Clarke: a bill that seemed gauged to cash in on the fad for reggae sounds among punk fans. The Police used it as an opportunity to plug their single. Faux headlines (such as "Latest News: Police Release Roxanne") were dotted around the stage on sandwich boards, while two ample-sized women dressed as stereotypical French whores emerged onstage and flounced around them as they played.

PAGING DOCTOR ROCK   63

Britain was in the grip of the Yorkshire Ripper. He had struck twice in January of that year. The body of his eighth victim, a 21-year old prostitute from Bradford called Yvonne Pearson, had been dumped underneath an upturned couch and only discovered two months later on Easter Sunday, March 26. A&M released "Roxanne" on April 8. Given the climate of fear surrounding the Ripper murders, it might not have been the optimum time to release a pop song about a man's fixation on a prostitute.

"Roxanne" is generally perceived to be a song about romantic obsession (and referred to as such by its author), but the lyrics could equally suggest jealousy that has tipped over into madness. The mannered sentiment of Sting's vocals—which, despite the keening pitch of his voice, seem emotionally flat—gave no indication one way or the other. There is a cold, moralistic tone to the lyrics that could be perceived as threatening, especially during the song's bridge, which differentiates itself from the insistent pleading that characterizes the lyrics in the rest of the song. Sting makes it clear that he will not share his woman under any circumstances and has made up his mind to take a course of action in order to prevent this happening (what exactly we are not told), and that he views Roxanne's profession as a "bad way."

"Roxanne" didn't make the playlist at BBC Radio One, and without that, airplay was almost nonexistent. Neither did the Police have the grass-roots support of a fan base that could promote the single by word of mouth. One profile described their popularity at the time in the starkest terms imaginable: "empty seats at a Police gig were about as common as falling leaves in November."

Once the Police had tasted success, the band would offer another reason for the failure of "Roxanne" the first time around, taking the line that the song had been banned because of its subject matter. It made a good story and one that was repeated ad infinitum, lending the Police a kind of edgy credibility that was clearly not reflected in their music. "We got a lot of mileage out of it being supposedly banned by the BBC," Stewart Copeland admitted twenty-three years after the fact. "In fact, all that really happened was that we didn't make their playlist, so we turned that into 'Banned by the BBC.'" A&M even printed up posters that announced the banning.

Sting continued to play along with this ruse even after "Roxanne" had become a chart hit the second time around (in April 1979), affecting an air of hurt and pomposity while lambasting the BBC for setting itself up as "the arbiters of poetic metaphor."

"I felt very strongly about 'Roxanne' because that was a serious song about a real relationship," he said. "There was no talk about fucking in it, it wasn't a smutty song in any sense of the word. It was a real song with a real, felt lyric and they wouldn't play [it] on the grounds that it was about a prostitute."

But there was nothing "real" about the song at all. It was inspired by a trip the Police had made to Paris a year earlier, where, while the band stayed in a hotel behind the Gare St. Lazare, Sting's imagination and curiosity had been pricked by the sight of prostitutes soliciting punters in the doorways of a dark alley in the Pigalle. A fantasy blossomed in his mind. "Roxanne" was a figment of Sting's imagination—not simply the heavy-handed literary reference to *Cyrano de Bergerac* implied by the title, but also the rather naive notion on which the song was based: that love could save a prostitute. If anything, it merely reinforced an old-fashioned and moralistic view of the world's oldest profession. It was Sting's Catholic upbringing talking through him.

There was nothing so radical in the song's sound or execution that would warrant a ban by the BBC. Compared to, say, "God Save the Queen" by the Sex Pistols—which had been considered so offensive that the BBC refused to even acknowledge that it had reached number one in the charts—"Roxanne" sounded as middle of the road as Gerry Rafferty's "Baker Street" (also a fixture in the charts that April).

"Roxanne" sold just eleven thousand copies, only marginally more than the Police's "Fall Out" single a year earlier, and failed to even crack the top 40. Summers took the snub personally. "Despite the classic pop brilliance of 'Roxanne,'" Summers wrote in his memoir, "the myopic party line concerns of the hacks override the ability to hear the incisive edge and ultimate staying power of the song."

To add insult to injury, two months later, a frothy novelty single called "Don't Care" that Stewart Copeland had recorded as a side project under the name Klark Kent became a surprise chart hit: "surprise" because the vocals were flatter than Table Mountain and the lyrics were so asinine they made the Bay City Rollers sound like Robert Burns. In the song, Copeland assumed the persona of a bratty adolescent to declare himself the "neatest thing in town." Copeland's grammar clearly hadn't improved a whole lot since he'd written "Fall Out," but his arrogance had grown in leaps and bounds.

Copeland roped Nigel Gray in to engineer the song at Surrey Sound and played all of the instruments himself. The song was originally intended for (and had been rehearsed by) the Police, but Sting could not come up with a convincing vocal. "Stewart's forte in his songs is a dry wit, which I don't perform well. Some of the things they write just aren't applicable to me," was his tactful appraisal of his bandmates' songwriting contributions.

Sting was simply being kind. The humour of "Don't Care" was more witless than dry. Copeland's off-key vocals proved the perfect fit. The single was released on Kryptone Records, yet another label set up through Miles Copeland's ever-expanding Faulty Products empire. The initial pressing sold so quickly that A&M was persuaded to license the song and re-release it. Stewart Copeland also concocted a convoluted comic book origin for his alter ego that was sent out as his official biography.

The record had barely hit the shelves when a sly piece of detective work by *NME* journalist Paul Carr revealed the true identity of Klark Kent. It didn't take a genius to make the connections, though. Klark Kent not only shared a record label with the Police, he also recorded in the same studio and used the same engineer. Desperate to keep the ruse going, Copeland called the paper to deny any involvement, but the game was up. The single was now a joke without a punch line. Yet it achieved a chart position just shy of the top 40, prompting a booking on *Top of the Pops*.

The Police camp (including manager Miles Copeland and roadie Kim Turner) turned up at the studio wearing Halloween masks. The producers at the BBC—who had evidently not yet cottoned on to Klark Kent's true identity—balked at the idea of an act performing in scary masks on a show whose audience was primarily made up of children. As a compromise, Copeland wore shades and a slash of lurid green face paint. The band members, who looked like groovy ghoulies in leather jackets, were allowed to keep their masks on. Because Copeland wasn't able to drum and sing at the same time, Florian Pilkington-Miksa from Curved Air was drafted in to mime the drum parts.

Stewart Copeland later joked that A&M only signed the Police to get Klark Kent. There was a grain of truth to this, though. The modest chart success of Copeland's novelty single would have given A&M faith that there was at least potential in continuing its relationship with the group. The Police were given a stay of execution and an extra length of rope, which they proceeded to hang themselves with.

The cover of their second single, "Can't Stand Losing You," featured an image (by British photographer Peter Gravelle) of a man doing just that—hanging from the neck, his toes barely touching the surface of a large block of ice that was being melted by an electric heater placed on the ground beside it. Stewart Copeland modelled for the suicide himself, gripping a promo photo of the Police in his right hand. Although a neat visual joke, it was a clumsy ploy to court controversy.

Like "Roxanne," the song dealt with a serious subject in a frivolous manner; it was a witty ditty about a guy who threatens suicide when his girlfriend dumps him. The song is notable for the first appearance of a linguistic trick that Sting would use repeatedly in some of the earlier songs he wrote for the Police. The chorus unwound the title of the song phrase by phrase and only revealed itself at the end. In one stanza, the subject of the song ("you") is excised entirely. Rather than a piteous plea for attention from a lovelorn male, the song suggested that the protagonist was a bad loser, given to petulant and destructive behaviour. Or maybe it was simply the author's competitive streak cutting through the flippant tone of the lyrics. Sting was trying to say that he can't stand losing.

This time, the treatment of the subject matter really did make radio stations uncomfortable—the photo that graced the cover didn't help—and they shied away from playing "Can't Stand Losing You." The song peaked at number forty-two, one notch higher up the chart than the position achieved by Klark Kent. And it would be the relentlessly upbeat and dumbed-down Klark Kent who provided the model for the band's public image from then on. The title that Miles Copeland came up with for their debut album helped reinforce this idea: *Outlandos d'Amour*, a faux-Franglais concoction formed from the contraction of the phrase "outlaw-commandos of love." It sounded exotic and meant nothing at the same time and fit their music to a Tee. It was certainly more appropriate than their manager's first suggestion, *Police Brutality*.

When the album was released in November, it fared about as well as their first two singles. The Rolling Stones were said to be fans, but patronage from a national institution only worked against a group who were still trying to prove themselves as the new gang in town. *Smash Hits* posted a succinct (if functional) description of the album contents—"Loud and energetic rock-n-roll but short and catchy tunes with great playing and tight, interesting arrangements"—its mannered enthusiasm a forebear of the pop success to come.

The dogged Phil Sutcliffe gave his pals their dues in a review for *Sounds*, while attempting to strike a note of impartiality, but he also filled his article with all sorts of insider information that suggested a depth to the group that might not have been apparent to the casual listener. "These guys have got ideas and a future," he surmised. But the *NME*, the arbiter of modal fashion, was not so convinced that these "outlandos" had much chance of making it to the front line of the music industry. Writer Paul Morley concluded that "the Police have no ambition and too much complacency." He was right on the second count but way off on the first. It was ambition that had sustained them thus far and would propel them even further. If the folks at home were indifferent to their music, the Police would simply seek a more receptive audience elsewhere.

6

WELCOME TO AMERICA

They were their father's sons. Gung-ho thrill-seekers. Guys who relished the rough and tumble of life. And they applied this philosophy to their respective business enterprises. From now on, the success of the Police was in the hands of the two older Copeland brothers, Miles and Ian. Without their involvement, it's safe to say that the group would have languished in obscurity. Miles Copeland was not prepared to take the lukewarm critical and public reception to *Outlandos d'Amour* lying down. Having gotten his hooks into the group, he was determined to push the band as far as he could.

"In order to make anything happen, you need an infrastructure," Miles explained. The Copeland family had more than an infrastructure; they were a force unto themselves. Their father, Miles Axe Copeland II, a gentleman spy from Birmingham, Alabama, was clearly something of a sharp operator, shrewd and resourceful. His wily analytical nature had made him an indispensable authority at the CIA and an indefatigable foe. Their mother, Lorraine Copeland (née Adie), born in Scotland and privately educated in England, had also been a spy (for British intelligence). While her husband meddled in Middle East affairs, she became an expert scholar in the field of Palaeolithic archaeology. They passed the qualities that brought them success in their respective fields on to their sons, all of whom were driven by a combination of savvy entrepreneurialism and wily opportunism. (A daughter, Lennie, became a filmmaker but shunned the limelight.) Yet despite sharing similar outlooks on life, the brothers were all quite different.

Stewart was a typical youngest child: bratty, privileged, and self-centred, driven by a mixture of insecurity and an overweening sense of entitlement. He felt that the world owed him something. His father once referred to him as "the genius of the family," but this seems to have been said with the kind of affection a parent reserves for his youngest child rather than any specific ability in which he excelled. In many respects, his two brothers both excelled and surpassed him in their chosen fields, while the baby of the family reaped all of the attention.

Ian was a roustabout character who seemed to succeed at anything he set his hand to. Before entering the rock business, he had a moderately successful career as a petty criminal, stealing cars in Beirut. He threw himself into numerous reckless adventures—hitching a ride on a cargo plane to Europe as a teenager, riding back to Lebanon by motorbike, and serving in Vietnam as a marine—but always managed to land on his feet. When he entered the music industry as a booking agent, he had already experienced a lifetime of adventure but faced the challenge of his new endeavour head on, with a similar disregard for the established way of doing things.

Miles, the most conservative of the three brothers, had an ascetic personality that drove him to extremes. Ian Copeland recalled that his brother's youthful obsession with judo encompassed not only mastering the sport but also adopting Shinto philosophy and a toxin-free diet consisting solely of yogurt, carrots, and tomatoes. As an adult, he had an unwavering disdain for drugs and drug taking that seemed at odds with his immersion in the rock world, which was awash with the encouragement of narcotic excess. It was Miles whose business acumen and single-minded determination to succeed drove the efforts of the other two. But he had learned business the hard way, succumbing to the bravado inspired by his initial success as manager of British prog-rock band Wishbone Ash and losing his shirt in spectacular fashion.

In 1975, Miles initiated the world's first touring rock festival—Startruckin' 75—conceived as an attempt to revive the fortunes of its headline act, Wishbone Ash, whose popularity was then on the wane after their early seventies success. "In concept, a success" is how Miles Copeland described Startruckin' in his official biography, but "a financial quagmire." That's putting it mildly. Instead of going supernova, Startruckin' fizzled and died, saddling Copeland with a huge debt and wiping out most of his business interests in one fell swoop.

The concept was this: seven headline acts, playing seventeen dates in eleven European countries. Using connections Miles had acquired through his company British Talent Managers (BTM), he put together a motley assortment of groups for the tour, four of which were already part of his client roster. The bill included Wishbone Ash, Lou Reed, Mahavishnu Orchestra, Soft Machine, Caravan, Renaissance, and the Climax Blues Band. (Copeland managed the last three acts on the bill.) The entire festival was a huge undertaking that involved transporting more than sixty people, as well as twenty-five tons of equipment (including a 25,000-watt P.A. system).

In the grandstanding style for which he would later become known, Copeland chartered a sixty-seven-seater DC-4 plane to fly the entire troupe and their equipment over to Holland for the first date on the tour. The Startruckin' logo—a groovy-looking space-man illustrated in the style of American artist Robert Crumb—was emblazoned across the nose cone of the plane. Once in Europe, the groups travelled around by coach while the plane was kept on standby. The tour was to wind its way around to Germany, at which point the plane was to fly the whole operation back to England again, where the Startruckin' lineup would feature on the last day of the Reading Festival. The extravagant travel arrangements alone contributed to an outlay of £100,000, even before they'd set out on the road. But with an estimated audience of three hundred thousand, Copeland looked set to easily make his money back and more. That was the theory, anyway.

According to legend, the tour was effectively scuttled by one phone call at the eleventh hour from Lou Reed's transvestite lover, Rachel. She called Copeland from New Zealand on the eve of the tour to say that Reed was in the closet (of the hotel room they were shacked up in) and wasn't coming out. The truth is a little more prosaic. Reed had just fired his booking agent, William Morris Agency, and found himself booked on an extensive tour alongside acts with which he had absolutely nothing in common. He had just released *Metal Machine Music* to almost universal critical opprobrium. And that's to say nothing of his health at the time, which had been affected by a chronic addiction to prescription drugs and heroin.

"Where the hell is Lou Reed?" journalist Charles Shaar Murray wondered aloud at the start of the report on the Startruckin' tour he filed for the *NME*. Reed was conspicuous by his absence. His slot was filled by Ike and Tina Turner. But the rest of the lineup didn't hold much appeal for Shaar Murray, either. It was already a bad sign when the opening act, Climax Blues Band, was considered the most "consistently entertaining." Caravan was written off as "dithyrambic shy-guy student rock," while Soft Machine were judged as well beyond their prime on the basis of their performance. Workmanlike headliner Wishbone Ash was "hardly the kind of group to bring a lump to your throat in mute testimony to the beautiful savagery and splendour of rock and roll." They were, Shaar Murray contended, "the Shadows of the 70s." Little wonder, then, that Lou Reed went missing before the bus left town. Tina Turner, however, saved the show with "star quality" and "galvanic funk energy," but that didn't last long, either. Ike and Tina suddenly jumped ship after the third date, leaving Miles Copeland's monsters of rock tour to lumber to its grave like a dying elephant for the next few shows without a star turn. The tour eventually collapsed under the weight of its own anticlimax.

Concert promoters felt cheated by the absence of the two headline acts and refused to pay the contracted booking fee, despite largely selling out the shows. Miles Copeland was left £80,000 in the red and forced to declare himself bankrupt. A month after the tour ended, he flew to the United States to finalise recording arrangements for Wishbone Ash's first album with Atlantic Records, a contract Copeland had negotiated for the band himself. On arriving, the band summarily fired him as their manager. Renaissance followed next. "[They] told me 'You've got no money any more so we don't want to be with you,'" Copeland recalled. "That was their exact words! My talent didn't mean anything to them. There were a lot of people wandering round the business saying, 'Well, that's it for Miles.'"

A good businessman learns from his mistakes. A driven individual never gives up. Copeland was both. For a time, he was reduced to hawking posters and badges around London's Oxford Street, all the while looking out for the next score. Then punk hit him, not just the music but the attitude. The "do-it-yourself" element of the culture immediately appealed to his sense of bootstrap individualism. But it was the frugal business model that really changed his idea of how to do business in the music industry. No more needless spending of money, no more expensive studio bills, no more mollycoddling spoiled rock musicians. From now on, the bottom line was God.

When interviewed in his office at Dryden Chambers for *Punk in London*, a 1977 documentary by German filmmaker Wolfgang Büld, Copeland was canny enough not to voice his enthusiasm in strictly monetary terms but spoke instead in the language of rock 'n' roll: youth. "Most of the groups I've been dealing with were groups who were getting over thirty years old, almost forty. It was very difficult to work with them, because you start having success and they wouldn't be able to follow through because of their home life."

This was meant as a sly dig at the Climax Blues Band, which had also just left Copeland's managerial stable. They split after backing out of a European tour he had booked to promote their hit "Couldn't Get It Right," a bland white-boy boogie that topped the charts in the UK and the States in 1976. Given the financial loss he had sustained, Copeland now dispensed with niceties when making the remaining bands he managed aware of what it was going to take for them to survive in this new musical climate. Geoff Richardson of Caravan recalls that the band was told to "shape up or fuck off." Looked at this way, Miles Copeland's initial reluctance to get involved with his brother Stewart's new band can be easily explained. After all, his previous group, Curved Air, was exactly the kind of act that Miles now wanted to avoid working with. They, too, had squandered their career by clocking up huge bills through needless self-indulgence in the studio.

By the end of 1978, Miles Copeland had successfully applied his new business model to build up a network of small independent labels—including Illegal Records, Deptford Fun City, and Step Forward (all of which fell under the Faulty Products umbrella)—releasing cheaply made records by bands from the UK punk scene. The bands themselves were low maintenance and low cost. It didn't really matter whether they were even any good. Copeland knew that such was the excitement and buzz around the punk scene, he could sell several thousand copies of any single he released. In that way, he kept the labels profitable and minimized any risk of debt.

The Police, however, required a different strategy. Copeland was undeterred by the group's lack of success in the UK and decided to send them off to the land of opportunity: America. The US wing of A&M had other ideas. "We arrived in America [in October 1978]," Copeland said. "And A&M actually told us: 'Go home because you're not here under our auspices.' They said, 'We're not supporting you, we're not financing you. So why are you here?'"

He informed A&M that the Police were there to play music and build an audience and that's what they intended to do, with or without record company support—his confidence buoyed by having achieved much the same thing with Squeeze, several months earlier.

Almost all of the strategies that he used to promote the Police were road-tested by Squeeze, which Copeland had accompanied on its first tour of the United States. The deal he had put together for Squeeze with A&M mirrored the one he would later negotiate for the Police. It guaranteed an American single release on the proviso that the band toured the States to support it. Then Miles gave his brother Ian, the booking agent, the not-inconsiderable task of booking a club tour for an unknown British group as a headline act. Ian managed to achieve this by booking the group into venues traditionally used by record companies to showcase new acts.

A&M released "Take Me I'm Yours" as a single in February 1978, and Squeeze hit the States from the end of May 1978 through to mid-July. On that trek, Miles performed his usual trick of plugging anyone and everyone he encountered for information. He even quizzed unsuspecting members of the audience to find out what the best local radio stations were, the names of their favourite DJs, and the locations of the coolest record stores and venues. He then checked out the stores himself, while pasting up posters around town as last-minute advertising for the shows. He also called on radio station contacts he had acquired from touring the States with Wishbone Ash six years earlier, browbeating them to come and see his new act.

"When we got to a town," said Chris Difford, "Miles would take us straight to the local radio station, give them our record, and say, 'Get that ELO crap off of here and start playing Squeeze.' He did that on the whole tour, and it paid dividends because later on when the Police came around, all the radio stations knew Miles and would play whatever he had in his hand."

The Police tour, though more modest in execution, refined this strategy further. The band played twenty-three dates in twenty-seven days on a route that largely confined itself to northeastern and midwestern states, with a brief foray into Canada for a date in Toronto. Now Copeland had a notebook full of people and places to target at every stop.

The Police set off on their first US tour at the end of September 1978, but there would be no customized aircraft to jet them around.

The band flew from London to New York on Laker Airways' no-frills Skytrain service—flights cost £60 one-way—toting their instruments as carry-on luggage and packed lunches for the journey. They arrived at JFK with just ninety minutes to spare before their scheduled midnight stage time at CBGB's.

Jet lag notwithstanding, Andy Summers seemed to have been not at all impressed by the legendary home of punk rock, describing it as "not much more than a filthy hole." But he reported that the Police, determined to transcend their environs, "cut through the tawdry atmosphere like a knife." Slim though the numbers were, the Police were greeted by an enthusiastic audience in the dressing room afterward. After the indifference they had experienced from UK audiences, being accosted by enthusiastic fans came as something of a relief, and Summers decided that American audiences "get it on a gut level."

The US tour was, in effect, the band's first-ever tour as a headline act. And it was a formative experience for them, not least because they now had to conceive of how to stretch the meagre amount of original material at their disposal into a full set. The trio fell back on a tried-and-tested solution: they jammed. Writing about the change this made, Summers elevated their live performances into a hallowed sphere: "We are able to hit a place where with a combination of tape delay, Trenchtown beats, dissonant harmony, and Sting's soaring tenor over the top, we start sounding like a punk Weather Report."

From New York, they travelled around the Eastern seaboard states. Miles had arranged for his brother, Ian, to purchase a Ford Econoline van, reducing costs on the tour to little more than gas, food, and lodging. The van was driven up to meet them in New York from Macon, Georgia. Their British road manager Kim Turner, the brother of Wishbone Ash founder Martin Turner, handled the driving duties. The band shared motel rooms two apiece to further cut costs. But drumming up an audience to come and see this bunch of unknowns was another matter entirely.

"We did a show in New Haven, Connecticut—in Toad's," recalled Miles. "There were four people in the audience. But one was a DJ. And the group went out and killed that night. They played to those four people like there were fifty thousand. And that DJ was so impressed that this group could walk out and deliver. He thought that was so great that the next day he started playing the record."

Copeland wasn't there himself and is a little off on the facts, but the sentiment he expressed is part of the Police mythos—that, initially at least, the band broke the States person by person. The show in question was actually in upstate New York at Frivolous Sal's Last Chance Saloon in Poughkeepsie, a bar-cum-restaurant in a rundown former vaudeville theatre.

One of those in attendance was a radio DJ named Jane Hamburger, who worked the weekend graveyard shift at a station called WPIX in New York. Hamburger had first met Copeland during a Squeeze show at CBGB in July 1978. She remembered being given an import copy of "Roxanne" and told by Copeland that his new band would be coming through town next—suggesting that the plan to bring the Police to the States was already well in place by then.

When booking the Police, Ian Copeland had sent out cassettes of "Roxanne" to prospective venues. Larry Plover, the owner of the Last Chance Saloon, had already heard about the Police on a recent visit to the UK, and booked them sight unseen. "The reality was, 'Roxanne' did have something," said Miles. "The Police music did work. It did sound different. It stuck in people's heads. If we'd had crap music, it wouldn't have worked."

As Ian had done previously with the Squeeze tour, he made it clear that the onus was on the club to promote the show. On his own initiative, Larry Plover contacted Stan Bernstein, the sales manager at local radio station WPDH. By hitting venues on the showcase circuit, Ian Copeland knew that club owners would already have relationships with local radio stations and newspapers. He was, in effect, simply tapping into an existing network and rewiring the connections.

Bernstein, a regular customer at the Last Chance Saloon, recorded a commercial for WPDH advertising the "arresting sounds of the Police." He was a little crestfallen to find the venue virtually empty on the night of the show and even more bemused to see Stewart

Copeland and Sting fooling around inside like "ninth-grade kids" prior to their first set.

When the curtain rose, there was one paying customer: a sales manager for Marlboro cigarettes who had spotted flyers for the show posted up around town and turned up on a whim. Two regulars moved on to another bar when it became apparent that they would be unable to watch Monday night football without paying a door fee. That left Plover, his business partner, Marc Chiamatti, Jane Hamburger and Bernstein to watch the show.

"One of the things that impressed me the most was that these guys played both sets like they were playing to a thousand people," Plover recalled, echoing Miles Copeland's account. "I think they really believed in the dream."

When the tour curled back up to New York City for two final shows at CBGB, Hamburger interviewed the Police for her show on WPIX. They put on a brave face about the turnout for their debut jaunt. "Gigs haven't all been empty," Stewart remarked defensively. "In Boston we played four nights at the Rat Club." Sting seemed in a more jocular mood. "We are celebrities in Boston," he joked—at least, they were to the table of overenthusiastic A&M Records personnel who turned up at the Rat in costume, sporting police uniforms and sheriff badges. Summers had more important things on his mind. He longed to get home to his nine months pregnant wife, Kate. His daughter, Layla, would be born just hours after he touched down in England following the final CBGB's show.

On that first tour, the Police played more to a record-selling public than to a record-buying public, a canny strategy on the part of Miles Copeland to get people in the industry working on their behalf to generate hype and excitement about the band.

Ian himself often used a tried-and-tested formula to book the shows, promising a bigger act if a club would put the Police on sight unseen. Two nights after the show at the Last Chance Saloon, the Police were booked into the Shaboo in Willimantic, Connecticut; Copeland offered the club's promoter, David "Lefty" Foster, an Iggy Pop date six weeks later as incentive. Foster knew that he was going to take a hit with the Police show, which coincided with a Yankees-Dodgers World Series baseball game. The door price was lowered to a dollar and the band played after the game. Incensed at playing second fiddle to a sporting event, Sting paced around the bar in a fit of pique. "He was driving everybody nuts," recalled Foster, "so finally, I say, 'Look, what's your name? Sting? Sting, look, we're all going to watch your band, but it's a tie game; it's the World Series. Wait until ten o'clock, and then go on.'"

The show made a straight $12 on the door again. "Two days later," said Foster, "all of a sudden, 'Roxanne,' every two minutes on the radio. WHCN [a Hartford, Connecticut, rock station] was all over it."

The Copeland strategy was evidently beginning to pay off. "Roxanne" started to pick up regular radio play across America, and because it had not yet been released domestically, *Outlandos d'Amour* crept into the Billboard import album chart. By January 1979, the Police were starting to become a cult act. And the record company had been caught unawares.

"All of a sudden it showed up in something that they all recognized: *Billboard*," said Miles Copeland. "I got a call from Jerry Moss saying, 'Shit, I think we got a hit record here. Is this an A&M act?' I said, 'Well, yeah. We've done one tour and we were told to get the fuck out of America by your head of New York office but . . .' He said, 'Well, we better get behind you.' And I said, 'That's great.'"

A second US tour was put into place for March 1979, by which time A&M, now fully committed to the band's success, had released "Roxanne" as a single and had scheduled a release date for the album. A&M artist relations man Bob Garcia admitted that at first "there were an amazing amount of doubters at the label." It's safe to say they didn't get the Police on a gut level. Garcia reported that one A&M promo man scornfully described the Police as "three bleached blonds singing reggae." But crucially, the boss was behind the band. "It was a Jerry Moss go," said Garcia. "He loved the band. He felt that they could be very big." Slowly but surely, the A&M machine swung into action behind the Police.

"It was a snowball thing," said Miles Copeland. "A huge snowball at the bottom of the hill started as a small one at the top. And all we really did was figure out how we could create a bunch of different snowballs."

At that time, Copeland said, record companies could not conceive of alternative strategies to break a new unproven act: "They want to start with the big snowball. They want to get their record on the radio. They only think about radio. They only think about that one big gain. And then three weeks later it doesn't get on the radio, it's over. So it's all or nothing. Whereas, our strategy was more like, let's get a little bit going here, a little bit going here . . . chipping away at it. And then finally you find out that, 'Shit! Something's happening.'"

"Roxanne" broke in Houston, Texas, first and was then picked up by other stations dotted across the US (including KHJ, the key station in Los Angeles). AM radio was not accustomed to playing "new wave rock", but "Roxanne" changed all that—largely, it must be said, to counteract the licentious appeal of disco.

During the first half of 1979, disco was firmly entrenched at the top of the Hot 100. Donna Summer, the Bee Gees, and Gloria Gaynor all scored number-one hits in succession. Disco fever had hit America. But antipathy toward the music was also reaching fever pitch. In July, popular Chicago shock jock Steve Dahl became the cheerleader for the anti-disco fervour when he hosted a "Disco Demolition Night" dressed as General Patton during the intermission of a double header between the Chicago White Sox and the Detroit Tigers at Comiskey Park. Cut-price tickets were offered to those who turned up to the game clutching a disco album.

A record crowd of 50,000 (in addition to a reported 15,000 teenage rock fans milling around outside the stadium) turned out to watch Dahl blow 20,000 disco records to smithereens with dynamite in the middle of the field. Then, fired with "anti-disco" ire, the crowd proceeded to tear the park apart themselves, destroying the pitcher's mound and setting a bonfire in the middle of the diamond. Baton-wielding police were sent in to clear the field, and they arrested thirty-nine people. The second game of the night was postponed, and the event passed into local legend. July 12, 1979, became known as "the day disco died."

Dahl had been fired by his previous employee, WDAI, at the beginning of the year after the station moved to an all-disco format. When his contract was picked up by rival hard-rock station WLUP (known as "the Loop"), Dahl took his revenge by starting a popular campaign to eradicate and eliminate the "dreaded musical disease known as DISCO." Dahl even issued membership cards for his "disco army," the Insane Coho Lips, and riled up listeners by destroying disco records on air—most notably, demolishing a copy of "The Hustle" to "celebrate" the death of Van McCoy. He also recorded a parody of Rod Stewart's "Do You Think I'm Sexy?" called "Do You Think I'm Disco?" under the name Steve Dahl and Teenage Radiation.

More than just a silly radio promotion gimmick gone awry, Disco Demolition Night has been cited as an example of how "white male America" rallied to contain the advance of the flourishing gay liberation and black pride movements.

"The real reasons for rock fans' denunciations of disco were almost surely racial and social," John Rockwell wrote in the *New York Times*. "Disco came, at least at first, from outsider labels like T. K. and outsider cultures like gay, black and Latin. They represented disturbing big-city mores to a heartland that had only recently accepted (and coopted) rock-and-roll. . . . Disco disk-burning was the revenge of the white majority against threatening armies at the portals."

The tide began to turn in late August when the Knack became the first new wave band to score a significant number-one hit with "My Sharona." Blondie had hit the top spot back in April with "Heart of Glass" but were displaced by soul duo Peaches & Herb a week later. At the beginning of 1979, the Police had inadvertently found themselves leading the groundswell against disco. Even their own record company saw them as the great white hope to stave off the threat posed by urban music.

"Radio is really desperate for rock product," A&M's senior vice president of promotion Harold Childs told the *Los Angeles Times*.

"It's scarce out there. The top 40 stations are being deluged by disco. They're all looking for some white rock-n-roll." And rock 'n' roll couldn't really get much whiter than the Aryan blond Police men and their radio-friendly reggae-rock.

As "Roxanne" started to take off, resources were rallied at A&M to give *Outlandos d'Amour* the push it needed to break the Billboard chart. An April 1979 profile on the band in the *Los Angeles Times*— their first piece of mainstream press in the United States—and the "huge promotional campaign" behind them, reported that A&M was prepared to spend up to $250,000 to secure a hit record. For that expenditure, A&M expected it to hit the top 10. (It peaked at 23.)

Having made the decision to turn the Police into a priority act, A&M suddenly became anxious that the band's image would scare off Middle America. "Their music sounded perfectly mainstream rock and their album looked new wave," reasoned A&M communications director Mike Gormley.

The blue-and-grey-tinted portrait that graced the album cover did not scream "pop music." It resembled an Andy Warhol silk-screen, flat and emotionless. The blank stares of the three peroxide blonds looking out of the sleeve, as a cavernous tunnel loomed behind them, was evidently perceived as too threatening for Middle America. A&M requested a softer redesign. But Miles Copeland fought tooth and nail to maintain the image he had already established in the UK: "A&M Records says to me, 'You can't have the Police on the front cover because they have short hair. We just want the word *Police* on the cover.' I said, 'Well, the fact that they have short hair is *why* I want them on the front cover! I want to show they're different.' Big argument."

A compromise was struck over the back sleeve, which was changed from a collage of graphics that aped the design of punk fanzines like *Sniffin' Glue* to something less assaultive—a plain black sleeve with white text. The front cover was also toned down. The tunnel was airbrushed out of the photograph entirely and the Police logo rendered in red not blue. This version, Copeland says, A&M accepted "with much reservation."

Copeland also vetoed press ads that read, "The Police are not punk." Instead, the campaign struck a tone that was both roguishly authoritarian and completely in step with the need to reassert macho rock values, using the slogan, "Support the Police."

Having ironed out these minor difficulties to get the record company on-message, Copeland now had to deal with an overabundance of enthusiasm on the part of the promotion team. "If anything, we have to hold them back. They get carried away with gimmickry," he told the *Los Angeles Times*. All manner of crass marketing gimmicks and "rock junk jewellery" (including police whistles and bumper stickers) were wheeled out to raise the profile of the band. In Boston, the same record company people who had turned up in costumes at the Rat arranged for a local radio station to pay listeners' parking tickets as part of a promotion to announce a return trip of the Police to Boston to play the Paradise Rock Club.

The hype was so overwhelming that it grated on one local journalist who was sent to review the show. *Boston Phoenix* music critic Kit Rachlis suspected that beneath all of the rah-rah and the hype, the Police were contrived to be "stylistically ambiguous enough to be all things to all people." It started with their incongruous stage gear. Take away the blond hair, and these guys didn't look punk or new wave. They didn't have any kind of style. The drummer wore lurid green running shorts, the guitarist was squeezed into skinny pink Levi jeans, and the lithe blond "beach boy" bassist-singer wore a baggy grey-green mechanic's jumpsuit. On record, Rachlis conceded, the Police were "masterful pop manipulators," but onstage at the 650-capacity venue, they committed "the one sin pop fancy doesn't allow: they were dull."

The band's predilection to jam through their more serious-minded pop songs made them seem "even more ponderous," Rachlis decided. Extended to twice its length, "Roxanne" was turned into "an interminable piece of self-righteousness, with Sting sounding more like a prurient parole officer than a sympathetic companion." But at that early stage, Rachlis was in the minority. Naysayers in the press were few and far between. The A&M machine was cranking out a promotional campaign targeted to inspire radio station bombast, rather than fickle critics in the print media.

In Atlanta, another marketing gimmick was employed. A concert staged at the Agora Ballroom was advertised as a Police Ball that incorporated a Roxanne look-alike contest. Summers claimed this was organized without the band's knowledge by a local radio station in Atlanta, which they were compelled to appease in order to get their music played. But there is no mention of the station on the flyer, which prominently displays the A&M logo. Bob Garcia recalled the contest being "the result of adventurous promotional people" at the label.

The upshot was that the band members were there to be on hand as judges, poring over the scantily clad Southern belles in order to decide which one best exemplified Sting's fantasy whore. According to Summers, British reserve melted in the face of all the pouting pulchritude presented before them: " 'Okay, so we're sexist pigs,' we say to one another, as we stroll up and down in front of the line of giggling girls, our eyes roving over the Roxanne wannabe flesh."

And what did the winner get? "I think it was cash," said Garcia. "Maybe a hundred bucks or something like that." Not a bad take for a single trick. But the winner wasn't only paid for her services. She also had her portrait taken while handcuffed to a bed in a hotel room. She wore a slip, stockings, and not much else, other than a tattoo on her shoulder—the word "Roxanne" written through a heart pierced by a dagger dripping blood from the tip. Behind her, the Police stared out from a framed album cover hung on the wall.

"In a funny way, you didn't really need gimmicks to sell this band," Garcia muses now. But it evidently helped. By spring 1979, the Police were poised to take America.

7

LADIES AND GENTLEMEN, THE SENSATIONAL NEW BLOW WAVES

Three musicians sit on a fence at the side of a road, looking to hitch a ride. They have detoured off the highway and found themselves stranded on a deserted country lane, but look distinctly out of place. They are dressed like exceedingly camp punk rockers— one wears a red beret, another, a mohair sweater, the third a green string vest and lots of makeup.

An open-topped red sports car cruises to a halt beside them. The driver, the drummer from the Sex Pistols, and seemingly lost himself, leans out to ask directions. The trio approach the car, affecting an air of menace. The bass player, a familiar-looking character with a spiky blond mullet, speaks first.

"Be advised, drummer boy," he sneers, "we are the Sensational New Blow Waves and we know how to sell more records than Malcolm McLaren." He hoists himself into the backseat of the car and continues to hector the driver. "We believe in rock 'n' roll and we don't need you, sex-piss-toll. The record companies know that our music means more to them than your sick anarchy ever did!"

The red beret positions himself behind the wheel as the driver is manhandled into the back by the other two Blow Waves, who then begin to paw and grope him. "Get out of my car, you arseholes!" the drummer barks. But his protest comes too little, too late. As the car speeds off, the bass player tears down the drummer boy's pants and proceeds to rape him.

Sting's first-ever screen appearance, as the Blow Wave's bass-playing rapist, was a shocker. His victim, the drummer boy, was Paul Cook of the Sex Pistols. The scenario was shot as part of *The Great Rock 'n' Roll Swindle*, the feature film in which Malcolm McLaren attempted to recast the history of the Sex Pistols in his own image. Much to Sting's relief, the scene ended up on the cutting-room floor (until director Julien Temple retrieved it many years later to use in his Sex Pistols documentary *The Filth and the Fury*). The ham-fisted analogy it presented of a musician getting reamed by the music industry contained at least a grain of truth. The speech that Blow Wave Sting delivered to Paul Cook mirrored the attitude of the Police towards the punk scene. They looked down on punk for its lack of musical discipline and viewed its sloganeering as cheap radicalism. And their contempt had paid off.

By 1979, punk had died on the vine, descending into farce and self-parody. The Sex Pistols now consisted of only guitarist Steve Jones and drummer Paul Cook, and existed solely to promote *The Great Rock 'n' Roll Swindle*. When Sid Vicious died of a heroin overdose in New York City on February 23, 1979, a single from the soundtrack was rush-released a week later as a cash-in—a Vicious cover of the 1959 Eddie Cochran song "Somethin' Else". It shot up to number three, then remained on the charts until the end of April. It was followed by the release of another Cochran cover by Vicious in June. The Pistols had backpedalled into irrelevance, leaving the door wide open for a new wave. The music press had also moved on, championing the anodyne power pop of Elvis Costello, Squeeze, and the Boomtown Rats. The climate had clearly shifted in favour of the Police.

But the band had little indication of this on returning to the UK at the end of November 1978. The Police had broken even on their first US tour, but only just. Sting recalled returning home to Frances Tomelty and handing her £10, his take from the entire tour. To keep the band afloat, Miles Copeland set them up with a support slot, a short three-week tour of UK colleges leading up to Christmas, playing second fiddle to a comedy band called Alberto y Lost Trios Paranoias.

The Albertos' stock in trade was lame rock parody that was an unquestioning hit with student audiences. Their biggest hit took the melody of the Sex Pistols' "Holidays in the Sun" and reconfigured it as the kind of four-bar boogie performed by British rock stalwarts Status Quo. The title of the track said it all: "Heads Down No Nonsense Mindless Boogie." The B-side was an even more direct swipe at punk rock mores, called "Fuck You." Subtlety was not the Albertos' strong point.

At the very first show on the tour, the Police were bemused to encounter a horde of teenagers who had come to see them play. Andy Summers wrote of leaving the stage to "a mob of screaming, hysterical girls calling out after us," a scenario that was repeated on every date of the tour. Stewart Copeland included a scene in his 2006 documentary *Everybody Stares* that illustrated the kind of hysteria they faced when they attempted to leave the venues. Crowds of expectant teenagers were packed into a loading bay outside the stage door. When the Police emerged, the fans began to cry and howl with delight. There was a moment of panic when the Police and their crew realized the car they have just gotten into was trapped behind the swarm of kids, who then pounded on the windows and chased after it as it drove off. The Police had inexplicably gone from having no following at all to being full-blown teen idols in less than six months.

Sensing that the band was now certain to break, A&M hustled the Police into the studio to record a second album. The sessions ran over two 2-week blocks, the first in mid-February 1979 and the second in late July, interrupted by a second (longer) tour of America. During the first two weeks, Nigel Gray was on notice that he could be replaced at any time by a more experienced engineer.

"A&M were adamant that the Police weren't going to work with me," Gray explained. "They didn't want to entrust the recording of an album by a band who were potentially going to do quite well to somebody with no track record. They didn't want it done by a doctor in Leatherhead. But the Police were adamant that they liked working with me and liked the sound. A&M eventually said, 'Okay, go down there and see what happens,' because we were still cheap and it didn't cost much to do it."

Chris Gray maintained that at that point, the band felt comfortable working with his brother. "The persona of the engineer makes a lot of difference in allowing people just to be themselves in a studio and not have to get through the engineer. That way the engineer is really working with them and creating a very safe space. Nigel was credited as coproducer on the second album because they were so delighted with the sound. It was exactly the sound that they wanted. That's what Nigel was good at."

The Police returned to the studio just six months after they had completed their debut album, with most of the intervening period spent on the road. This meant that they had only a handful of new songs at their disposal. Some had already been incorporated into their live sets. One of these was a song written by Sting called "Message in a Bottle," a high-concept pop ditty that revolved around the idea of a Robinson Crusoe castaway stranded on a desert island with only his isolation for company. Desperate to communicate his situation to the outside world, he vainly tosses a bottle into the ocean. The song's pat resolution finds him waking up one morning to find a "hundred billion bottles" washed up on the shore.

"As a narrative, it had a beginning, middle and an end," Sting explained. "The story actually developed. It wasn't just 'I'm lonely, isn't it terrible!'—which is what a lot of my other songs were about. If I'm lonely but I realize everybody else is, too, I feel better. I think the Germans call that *Schadenfreude*—enjoying the misery of others."

The self-reflexive means by which Sting sought to alleviate his own suffering dovetailed with the conceit behind the song, which seemed to be founded on the projection of his own alienation and self-pity onto the entire population of the planet. In and around the narrative and a Morse code chorus that was a telegraph for audience participation, were shoehorned lines of such plastic profundity that the song seemed tailor-made for mass acceptance.

Other songs selected for the recording sessions were culled from demos that each individual member of the band had made on his own. Stewart Copeland had, by that time, moved into a house on Goldhawk Road, in Shepherd's Bush. The attic was converted into a makeshift home studio, filled with an array of instruments—drums, bass, guitar—mini amps and effects pedals and a reel-to-reel machine on which to record them all. One of the walls was plastered with photographs of the Police, along with posters, flyers, and album covers of Copeland's favourite bands. The Police at times also rehearsed there.

"Stewart would play a demo from a cassette that he had done in his house," said Nigel Gray. "The band would listen to it and that was the first time they'd ever heard it. They'd learn it there and then, practise it, find a way of playing it, get a style for it, and then we would just record it straight off. So the recordings would be one of the first times that they had ever played it. They were quite fresh in that way. Sting wasn't that keen on doing Stewart's songs, but he did, because they didn't have any other songs."

Copeland wrote (or cowrote) six of the eleven songs on the second album. But it was the last time he would contribute that much material to any Police album, because the dynamic of the band was about to undergo the kind of dramatic shift that is part and parcel of popular success and adulation.

While they worked on the album, another group entirely was engaged in its own clandestine activities at Surrey Sound under cover of night.

The Homosexuals were fucking with the Police, making a mockery of them without either their knowledge or their consent. The Homosexuals were the shadow residents of Surrey Sound studios. A bunch of reprobates from Deptford, South London, tweaked by chemicals, possibly touched by madness, and following their own arcane path through music, they recorded through the night at Surrey Sound with Chris Gray.

One night, while attempting to lay down some tracks and getting nowhere, they unearthed the master tapes for "Roxanne" and decided, of their own volition, to remix it. They found three completely different vocal takes on the masters. There was, according to Gray, "one jazzy and smoochy, one rocking out and one in the middle (which was the one on the release)." The Homosexuals mischievously set about making their own dub mix of the song, layering the different takes on top of one another and turning Sting's mooning vocals into a keening lament. "We had three Stings going on in really heavy dub," said Gray.

After that session, Lepke Buchwater of the Homosexuals took the tapes home with him, and the track never saw the light of day again. "Quarter-inch tape would cost a lot of money for people living in squats," said Gray. "People would record over stuff for their home 8-track recordings, so that got recorded over. Almost all the Homosexuals' master quarter-inches got recorded over by [singer] Bruno Wizard in his smacked-out home-recording phase." And so the world would forever be denied the guilty pleasure of hearing "Roxanne (the Homosexuals' remix)." But the group made its presence felt on the Police in other ways.

The Homosexuals were everything the Police were not: chaotic, abstruse, absurd, and inspired. They were a subculture unto (and of) themselves, spurning any kind of engagement with the music industry at all, pressing up limited-edition albums in homemade sleeves under myriad different identities. Everything about them, from their name on down, was "awkward." The nocturnal activities of the Homosexuals grated in other ways, too. Typically, said Gray, "the Homosexuals would skulk in about midnight. It was alright as long as we were out by seven in the morning, but you couldn't really control those people very well. My brother would come by in the morning, furious!"

Their presence was driving a wedge between the two brothers. "Nigel hated the Homosexuals," said Chris. "They took the piss out of him. Because now he was dropping into the lifestyle." Since record-ing *Outlandos d'Amour*, Nigel had started to work with ex-10cc duo Godley & Creme. Flushed with success, he had upgraded Surrey Sound to a 24-track studio and, according to his brother, had acquired a taste for other accoutrements of the rock 'n' roll life that included a Ferrari and a pair of leather trousers.

The Homosexuals also thought Nigel was stealing their ideas and passing them on to the Police. "There's a repeat echo on the bass drum for 'Walking on the Moon,'" said Chris. "The Homosexuals vainly assumed that Nigel had nicked their idea. But Nigel was always into echo. He had two Revox amps, and he used them to bounce back and forwards and get stereo echo on the guitar, which we thought was really out of sight. So he was always actually into bouncing echoes around the room."

"Walking on the Moon" was the nearest the Police ever got to approximating the breathy, living rhythms of dub reggae. But, as Chris recalled, the Police guitar sound "was a bit of luck." The storeyed guitar style that Summers unveiled on that song was based on the kind of arpeggio picking that came naturally to an experienced player; then it was funnelled through a studio effects unit to give the sound some depth.

"We had this thing called a Scamp rack," said Chris. "It's modules of processors. You get different ones that fit into the racks (echoes and flangers) and there was one in particular that was a sort of phaser/chorus/flanger/close echo/double tracking module. When those guitar chords come in on 'Walking on the Moon,' that is purely the sound of that Scamp rack. They used that one a lot."

Despite the band's newfound confidence and elation at having finally made it, on occasion, arguments began to flare up among the Police in the studio. "In those days they were flushed with being in a successful band so it would just be good-natured arguing," recalled Chris. "I'd be engineering and they'd say to me, 'Don't worry, we fight all the time.'"

Summers confirmed this. "We fight about the music but are a locked unit," he said. Yet however good-natured this jockeying for position seemed to be, it had a tiring effect on the combatants. "Sting was definitely always detached from the other two," observed Chris. "He'd muck in and be the lad and swap insults and stuff. But he told me once that he had a trick where he'd pretend to be ill. He'd pretend to be a hypochondriac because then he could just lie down and have some peace."

The sessions were interrupted by a second American tour that would take in new markets to capitalize on all of the interest generated by the first. It included a three-night stand at the famed Whisky A Go-Go, attended every night by A&M's Jerry Moss and new wave luminaries like Ric Ocasek of the Cars.

While the Police were in the United States, Miles Copeland employed a British husband-and-wife filmmaking team, Derek and Kate Burbidge, to fly out and produce a couple of promotional clips for the band. One clip was to accompany the US single release of "Roxanne"; the other would be serviced to TV channels coinciding with the release of "Walking on the Moon," which had only just been recorded.

The music video would not become common currency as a promotional tool until the August 1981 launch of MTV, but promotional films had been used to provide a visual component to hit songs since at least the late 1950s. Primarily filmed on 16mm, they were destined for use on a device called the Scopitone, an early form of video jukebox that was installed in bars and clubs. Scopitone clips were frequently broadcast on *Top of the Pops*.

The clip that was shot for "Roxanne" was simple but effective. The band was filmed performing the song in a set that was empty, apart from their kit, and the surroundings entirely painted fire-engine red. The first notes of the song played out over a shot of Sting sitting on the ground, head bowed, microphone in hand, overlaid with the flickering of a flashing police light. They proceeded to play the song straight through, selling the band on its performance alone. At the end, the video cut to another shot of the trio lined up in front of three microphone stands like a vocal group, japing around like the Monkees.

When the tour hit Florida, the Police made a detour to Cape Canaveral and filmed the video for "Walking on the Moon" in the shadow of the huge booster rockets of one of the Apollo spacecraft. All three band members were decked out in sunglasses, looking for the first time like rock stars. Sting and Summers mimed along to the song with their guitars. Copeland hit out a rhythm on the side of the rocket. From this point on, the Burbidges were kept on as the band's main image makers, and they filmed clips and promotional films for the Police for the next four years.

While the band was in Florida, "Roxanne" made its debut on the UK pop chart on May 5. The date was significant for another reason. It was also the week that Margaret Thatcher was elected as Britain's first woman prime minister, marking a return to power for the Conservative Party. The Police began to cement their position in the pop firmament during the opening months of the Thatcher administration. Under Thatcher's watch, British society would undergo momentous change. The country would be dragged through the greatest period of modernization since the Industrial Revolution. It would become wealthier. At the same time, the divide between the social classes would open up like a fissure, never to be healed again, creating a permanent underclass in British society.

Thatcherite philosophy emphasized the benefits of a free market economy and fostered a climate in which entrepreneurial businesses could thrive. Miles Copeland, who was not only an anglophile but also an enthusiastic adherent of the Conservative leader's policies, would utilize the same methods in his attempts to break the Police. They were, in effect, the first Thatcherite pop band. This did not sit easily with Sting, who still publicly maintained his adherence to true socialist ideals.

On their return from the United States, the Police immediately set out on a two-month UK tour. "Can't Stand Losing You" was scheduled for re-release next and, with the head of steam building behind them, looked set to storm the charts. The band would return to Surrey Sound toward the end of July for a final two-week session to finish off the album. Now they had been given new impetus and strove to complete their second album with worker-bee efficiency.

Their lives had shifted dramatically. For Sting, in particular, it was a stark contrast to the year before, when, desperate to pull in some sort of income to help support his young family, he had decided to turn his hand to acting. Pippa Markham, Frances Tomelty's agent, had secured him an interview with Franc Roddam, the director of a screen adaptation of the Who's 1973 concept album *Quadrophenia*. It was a step up from chewing gum and bra commercials. "I didn't think there was a hope in hell of getting the part," Sting recalled, "so I strolled into the Who's office on Wardour Street in filthy overalls, looking like a garage mechanic."

This sounds less like insouciance and more like studied cool, another example of Sting's "chancer's psychology" at work. He also walked into the audition carrying a copy of a Herman Hesse novel, a weighty existentialist tome titled *The Glass Bead Game*. Sting was, by all accounts, a voracious reader. This was the kind of book that conferred the idea on an unwitting observer that the reader possessed an insatiable intellectual curiosity. It seemed to work. Sting immediately struck up a rapport with Roddam. The two men recognized each other as fellow Geordies. Sting was offered the role on the spot.

Quadrophenia recreated the notorious events of the summer of 1964, during which pitched battles between affiliates of two opposing youth cults, the Mods and the Rockers, and the police authorities erupted at English seaside resorts along the south coast. Sting played a central character in the film, "Ace Face," the imperious leader of a Mod gang in Brighton.

The introduction of Ace Face is long and drawn out. At first, Roddam circles around the character, who is only seen in glimpses; a steely blond youth in a knee-length grey-leather overcoat, leading his gang down the Brighton promenade on his customized moped. The bike is tarted up with all manner of chrome fixtures that indicate the man's status—mirrors, lights, and, for some strange reason, a broom fixed to the rear that sweeps the street behind him.

Ace Face's big scene takes place inside a disco. "Louie Louie" is playing on the sound system. Roddam's camera zeroes in on Sting. Dressed in a tight-fitting grey suit, he struts and swivels and snaps his fingers to the music, glaring into space and defiantly chewing gum like a square-jawed hoodlum. Not a natural actor, Sting appears stiff and unconvincing, trying too hard to appear menacing. And neither was he a natural dancer. He looks like Pee Wee Herman geeking out to the surf instrumental "Tequila" during his *Big Adventure*.

The big payoff at the end of the film occurs when the main character, Jimmy (played by Phil Daniels), spies Ace Face's moped in the street and determines to steal it, having just totalled his own bike. He looks up and, to his surprise, spies Ace Face dashing out of a posh hotel. He is dressed not in his sharp grey suit but in a bell-boy uniform, complete with hat fixed to his head by a strap that reaches around his chin. The discovery that the suave gang leader lugs bags for the bourgeoisie causes Jimmy to let out a howl of angst. But Roddam's dramatic denouement is so ridiculous, it feels like unintended comedy.

Quadrophenia has acquired cult status since its release, perhaps owing to its association with the Who. But it feels more like a hackneyed after-school special than a gritty portrayal of youth culture. Nevertheless, it opened to great fanfare in September 1979, with a red-carpet premiere in the centre of London. The same week that "Message in a Bottle" was scheduled for single release, posters for the film went up all around the city. They featured a lineup of all the main characters standing against a wall. Sting stood dead centre and head and shoulders above the rest. Suddenly, his severe countenance and platinum-blond crop were everywhere you looked. "The Police did a lot for that movie," Sting maintained. But more likely it was a little bit of both. The "Face" sold the film, and the "Face" sold the band. Everyone wanted to know what was behind that harsh, inscrutable look. Sting enjoyed the attention. It stoked his ego.

When the microphones were turned on him to discuss his role, he made the most of it, exploiting the fascination of his unknowable façade but revealing only enough about his true character to fuel further interest. "Ace is very much part of my own character. I have a very, very strong ego," he told one reporter, adding to another, "I'm not an 'actor'; looking good on screen is just a matter of intelligence." Two years later, he had apparently tired of being mistaken for Ace Face. "That wasn't me in *Quadrophenia* at all," he explained. "I was nothing to do with Mods. When that whole Mod revival happened we exploited it."

Just as the Police had used punk to launch themselves, now Sting shamelessly milked a tenuous connection to the brief Mod revival sparked by *Quadrophenia*, despite admitting that he had no affinity with it at all. He even swapped his flight suit for a parka (the signature garment of Mod fashion) when the Police played live.

The Police, who had at first been rejected as bandwagon jumpers and, more pointedly, as an anachronism, would soon come to be seen as the vanguard of the new wave in music. A band that had started with no identifiable image at all was now being feted for a lead singer who had the "look." If the other two band members felt uneasy about all of the attention foisted on their front man, they did not voice it in public. Summers maintained that they were just happy to be along for the ride, and all three benefited from the mania that began to surround the band. From this point on, the band's image would be rigorously defined, fiercely controlled, and exploited by Miles Copeland.

A large part of that job would be carried out by Keith Altham, a former rock writer for the *NME* who churned out reams of celebratory profiles in the sixties about rock and pop idols. Altham operated in the years before rock criticism became an art, before rock writers affected to become stars themselves. He was part of the old school, when a music journalist was only expected to turn in the kind of perfunctory prose that helped grease the wheels of industry. In those days, music papers in the UK were little more than an adjunct to the PR industry, and the journalist pretended to be the rock star's friend and fan.

Altham was a man who bought into the myth of rock stardom and later made it his business to help maintain the illusion that created it. In the early 1970s he formed his own PR firm, K. A. Publicity, and represented many of the top pop and rock acts of the day. The Rolling Stones, the Who, the Kinks, Rod Stewart, and Marc Bolan were just a few of his clients. He was once described as "the godfather of music PR."

In the introduction to his memoir, *The PR Strikes Back*, Altham provided an astute (if wordy) assessment of the position pop artists found themselves in during the second phase of their careers: "The second album is often inferior to their first—which the new artiste may have taken years to hone as he or she learnt their trade, as opposed to the few months it took to record the follow-up so that the record company can capitalize on the initial success."

What this meant, concluded Altham, was that the second time around, "you are now buying the publicity not just the music—never mind the quality, feel the face." There was only one solution to counteract the law of diminishing artistic returns: exposure, exposure, exposure. Celebrity inures the rock star to critical opprobrium. Fame enables him or her to transcend the faddish time limit on pop success and join a firmament of established stars. A good PR strategy protects not only the stars' public image at the height of their success but provides them with a bankable investment for the future.

There was constant pressure, said Altham, for more and more publicity and bigger press scoops from Miles Copeland. "I found Miles Copeland's combative and aggressive American style of management impossible in the early days of my representing the Police," Altham recalled in an open letter to Sting, written for his book. "After just a few weeks I informed you that much as I liked the group, I could not put up with any more GBH of the ears from Miles." Altham's solution was to open the drawer of his desk, place the receiver inside, and close it until Copeland had finished barking his commands or had hung up, thinking the line had gone dead.

Altham dutifully presented Sting to the tabloids cloaked in "super punk" camouflage. The newspapers had begun to pick up on the Police in the middle of June 1979. By that time, "Roxanne" had already spent seven weeks lodged in the top 40, hitting its peak at number twelve. Following that came the run of singles that assisted the band's breakthrough, fired off like a battery of heavy artillery from June to December. Just as the chart position of one song began to wane, another was released. Between May 1979 and the end of January 1980, the group had a single in the top 40 for twenty-eight weeks out of thirty-seven. Had the first album achieved greater success initially, this clearly would not have been possible. The decision to re-release the band's early singles ahead of the two lead tracks from the second album gave the impression that the Police were made of hits.

"Can't Stand Losing You" was re-released in the last week of June and hit the number-two spot by mid-August. Three weeks after it dropped out of the top 40 came "Message in a Bottle," the first new Police single in a year. It reached number one in its second week on the chart, holding that position for three consecutive weeks and paving the way for the release of their second album, *Reggatta de Blanc*, which went straight in at the top of the album charts. At that point, Police mania erupted all over the country. But it wasn't the music alone that drove interest in the Police. A large part of their appeal was sex.

In 1979, the largest slice of UK record sales garnered by the Police was not accounted for by young male music fans—the natural audience for an all-male rock band—but by teenage girls. The group had far more cachet as a boy band than as a rock band. The Police had turned into the Sensational New Blow Waves: three blond men sitting pretty in the charts, even if they didn't fit the stereotypical mould for teen idols. Copeland and Sting were both twenty-eight—although the latter would sometimes slice two years off his age. Summers was old enough to have sired many of their teenage fans. By taking the path of least resistance, they got an easy ride. Sting was the first to admit that was the case: "It's very satisfying that girls do follow us around. I think there would be much more pressure on us if they didn't."

There was clearly less pressure on the Police because teenage girls were not too discerning about the music they latched onto. All they desired was candy pop music presented by delectable, sugar-pop idols. Even so, Sting liked to think that his age and experience lent something extra to the usual relationship between fan and idol: "I am married, I have a kid—what girls get with the Police is real sexuality. The Bay City Rollers was jerking off. Kiss me quick. With the Police you can actually get fucked." Given that the majority of fans were largely underage, it was a rather awkward analogy, but the comment passed without further inquiry.

When the Police graduated from the teen mags to the tabloids, they were crowned the new golden boys of British pop. Sting became "beefcake du jour": an alpha male pop star whose bare chest and nipples were frequently plastered across tabloid newsprint, just like the topless models on "Page 3." He was not merely a willing participant in the strategy to sell him as a sex symbol; he was an active proponent of it. An April 1980 profile of the singer in the *Daily Mirror* used a quote from Sting as its banner headline: "In this business everything is for sale. The looks are just part of it."

The article ran next to a full-page photograph of Sting posing bare-chested, hands gripping the top of a low wrought-iron spiked fence, as he stared coldly into the camera. The caption for the image made note of Sting's "raw sex appeal." But it was a peculiar kind of sex appeal, one that didn't appear to offer any sex at all. As much as he was evidently an exhibitionist, he also appeared aloof and remote.

In the accompanying article, Sting admitted that he was "very aware of anything I do." This, of course, included the manner in which he presented himself. There was little precedent for a male pop star being willing to display his body like a *Playgirl* pinup. But there was a precedent in another forum altogether that goes some way toward explaining the appeal.

In the early seventies, a performance artist, photographer, and porn star named Peter Berlin had embarked on a one-man art project to remodel himself as a self-regarding sex symbol. Known as the "Garbo of gay porn," Berlin cruised up and down the Castro, in the heart of San Francisco's gay community, dressed in a very particular uniform: a cowboy hat perched atop a Dutch pageboy haircut, a denim shirt unbuttoned to the navel, and either skin-tight jeans or leather chaps whose singular feature was a large cartoonish bulge at the crotch. He wanted to be admired. He wanted to be looked at. He wanted to be desired. But this was not the kind of sexual attraction that was fuelled by an exchange of glances. It was purely one-way. Peter Berlin was a black hole for sexual desire—sucking it up, absorbing it, and giving nothing back. "Every guy I meet is in competition with myself," he said. "I get into my persona. I look at myself; I have sex with myself."

Sting seemed to be doing exactly the same thing: exhibiting and having sex with himself. He had an overweening desire to be looked at, to draw observers in through his vanity. His stern, unfeeling look demanded that you take notice of him. But he did not return the favour. "He knows he is capable of churning up a chapter of day-dreams with just a flicker of that sensual, almost cruel smile," cooed Pauline McLeod, a pop columnist for the *Daily Mirror*. But Sting inspired more than one chapter of dreams. He would inspire a whole genre of fantasy fiction devoted to his sexual persona.

The phenomenon of fan-written "band fiction" has been around in some form or other since the late 1970s, initially as an under-ground phenomenon involving stories passed around among female groupies. It became more widespread with the introduction of the Internet in the nineties, when female fans of the British pop group Duran Duran began to write their own stories about the band and publish them in *UMF*, a webzine devoted to the group.

A bizarre subset of this genre is "slash fiction," homosexual fan-tasies largely written by heterosexual members of the opposite sex. In the shadow world of the slash-fiction writer, the staunch hetero image of the Police is imbued with a homoerotic subtext. The tension driving the band is sexual, rather than creative, and it eventually (and inevitably) boils over into frenzied sex sessions—either in the back of the tour bus or in the studio while the band is recording—during which its members consummate their love for one another. A collec-tion of Police slash fiction was self-published in 2007 under the coy title *Internal Affairs* by a long-term fan of the band (using the pen name Sidewinder), illustrating the kind of wild fantasies the band's sexualized image inspired:

Everything soon dissolved into a blur of exploring touches and hungry caresses, lingering kisses and playful bites. . . . They fit together, in this, just as they did on-stage. Together they were always so much more than they were apart, and it should have been no surprise that the same chemistry that electrified their music brought magic to this union as well. Sting's cool sensuality, Stewart's fire and energy, all smoothed over and sealed by Andy's ethereal touch—whether it was in sex or rock and roll, they blended together perfectly.

In reality, there was no room for horseplay, and the Police were staunchly hetero family men. By the close of 1979, the Police could justifiably claim to be the biggest band in the UK. They had sold five million singles and two million albums in one year. They celebrated their success with a publicity stunt that reeked of macho triumphalism. Miles Copeland had arranged for the band to play two shows in one night at venues in close proximity. The first was at the legendary Hammersmith Odeon, the second at the nearby Hammersmith Palais. He had also arranged for the band to parade between the venues in an open-topped US military truck. As they travelled slowly up the road, they were surrounded by thousands of cheering fans. It was the kind of showboating event that Copeland loved. "Anything paramilitary seems to get him going," Summers noted.

Copeland was also given to introducing the band onstage wearing a tight-fitting green military jacket adorned with medals. Footage of their final show in 1979 (at a venue in Lewisham) shows the trio lined up just behind the stage curtain. Miles stands in front of each band member like a general inspecting his troops: primping the hair of one, straightening the collar of another, and giving the shoulder of the third a reassuring grip. Then he steps out onstage to announce the band's arrival, "For the last time in 1979," he barks triumphantly above the howl of the crowd. But the conquering ambitions of the Police's master and commander had only just begun.

8

THE ORGANIZATION

Strike while the iron is hot. That was the thinking when Miles Copeland hit A&M boss Jerry Moss with a proposal in the middle of 1979. He wanted backing to set up a rainbow coalition of distributed labels in the United States that paralleled his Faulty Products operation in the UK.

"The Police were beginning to happen," said Copeland, recalling his initial pitch. "I went to Jerry Moss and said, 'Look, I think there's a whole movement of music happening. And I would like the opportunity to put it out in America.'

"He said, 'Well, okay, give me some of the music. Let me hear it.'

"I said, 'No . . . no. I'm not letting you listen to any of the music. All I want you to do is put it out. I'm not going to ask for any of your hard-earned money. Don't pay me a penny. I'll deliver the records. You get your sales people to go out into the marketplace, go to the stores and say, "Hey, how many do you want?" The records are pressed based on the orders that the stores place so you're not at risk! I don't ask for any of your money, you don't ask to listen to any of my music.'

"He said, 'Deal!'"

It wasn't the first time Copeland had tried to score a label deal in the United States, though. Sire Records boss Seymour Stein recalled Copeland offering him a clutch of bands two years earlier. Sire was already the American home for the Climax Blues Band and Renaissance, Copeland's former management clients, both of which had done very well for the label. He offered Squeeze to Sire but only on the proviso that he be given a label deal to release other bands.

"I didn't want to do it unless I knew what the other acts were," Stein said. "One of the other acts was a male prostitute—he was horrible, had no talent!" This would have been Gene October of Chelsea. But Stein wanted to sign Squeeze so badly, he was even prepared to sign a rent boy to get them. Copeland included one other group in his pitch to Stein.

"Miles told me, 'My brother just started a punk band and they're all in Germany now.'" This would date the meeting to October 1977, when Andy Summers, Sting, and Stewart Copeland were recording with Eberhard Schoener in Munich. It shows that Miles Copeland was more involved in promoting the interests of the band at an earlier stage than their official history lets on, perhaps to allay the obvious charge of nepotism. When Copeland told Stein the name of his brother's band, the mogul balked. "I said, 'I don't want 'em!'" he recalled. "We all make mistakes."

Copeland evidently learned from this, too, which is why he offered Jerry Moss his new label sight unseen on the proviso that there would be no veto over the bands. Copeland already had a name for the operation, the International Record Syndicate (commonly known as IRS). "We had the Police, CIA (my father), FBI (my brother); it was a name you remembered," he said. "We picked a name that was very establishment—the fucking tax man, how much more establishment than that can you be? But we tweaked it."

He was essentially asking Moss to offer him a manufacturing-and-distribution deal. Copeland would cover all of the recording costs himself. In return, he was given the use of an office on the A&M lot. The *Los Angeles Times* described the deal as "unprecedented"—"a multi-label umbrella company representing seven grass roots British new-wave record companies," all of which Copeland himself owned.

The deal was even more unprecedented given that A&M was about to lay off around two hundred of its staff. "It must have happened in early December," said Bob Garcia, "because every year A&M had a huge Christmas party on the sound stage, and right after this particularly huge layoff there was no huge Christmas Party. It was someone delivering sandwich trays to the various departments. That was a very dark day."

Copeland remembered the layoff occurring around three months into the IRS deal. He took advantage of the situation by scooping up several of the younger and hungrier members of the A&M staff and employing them himself. "About four of my staff were college promotion guys who had just gotten fired," he said. And one of those ex-A&M staffers was a preppy and ambitious twenty-one-year-old named Jay Boberg, who had proved himself by helping to break the Police on the college radio circuit. Copeland immediately made Boberg the president of IRS Copeland did much of the signing himself, but the younger man acted as another pair of eyes and ears and strategized promotion of the label.

The success of the Police had blessed Copeland with "golden boy status," and the bigwigs at A&M didn't have enough good things to say about him. "There's a whole new infrastructure evolving and he understands it and knows how to use it," label president Gil Friesen told the *Los Angeles Times*. "The media, the music, the venues, the way he manages his group—he just generally knows how to get things done."

In the US music industry, which had an entrenched way of doing things, Copeland's laissez-faire approach to releasing records was a breath of fresh air. Garcia contended that IRS, building on Copeland's now proven flair for generating interest in an act from the ground up, developed the first street teams used by the music industry.

"I think Miles laid the groundwork for that sort of street team hustle that was used to break rap records, long before anyone began acknowledging it as an art; making a certain demographic or age part and parcel of the entire campaign. It was a unique way of making everybody feel a part of breaking whatever artist it might have been."

In the case of IRS, it was college kids and college radio stations that were used to build the buzz for IRS acts. Photocopied posters were sent to be pasted up around campuses prior to an act arriving there. "I can't remember how many times the Police played cafeterias in schools at ungodly hours," said Garcia, "merely because the cafeteria was closed down after a certain hour, so that this was an open big space. Nothing was taboo in terms of where you played. And I found that fascinating."

The Police would become the vanguard in a two-pronged assault on popular culture. IRS brought up the rear. The label would become synonymous with new wave music. When Copeland first approached Jerry Moss, new wave was already fairly well-established in the United States and had been since at least the mid-seventies. But most of the bands—including the Talking Heads, Television, Blondie, and the B-52s—were on the East Coast and had been signed by New York-based labels such as Sire and Elektra. Out on the West Coast, A&M was distinctly out of touch with what was occurring in its own backyard.

Los Angeles had its own vibrant underground music scene centred around bands like the Germs, X, and the Screamers. While New York punk was all about image and attitude, the L.A. scene was weirder, off-kilter, and theatrical. But A&M's roster was still stocked with dinosaurs from the seventies. Blodwyn Pig, Joe Cocker, the Carpenters, Styx, and Waylon Jennings were the A&M cash cows at the time.

The British arm of the label, headed up by Derek Green in London, was almost solely responsible for bringing in all of the acts that would drag A&M into the new age: the Police, the Stranglers, Squeeze, and Joe Jackson. Even the cartoonish L.A. band the Dickies, whose gimmick was throwaway power-punk covers of hits by Black Sabbath, the Moody Blues, and the Banana Splits, were signed only because Green insisted that Moss go to see them play.

Miles Copeland also used his connection to the UK to leverage influence with Moss. At that time, US record companies had been carefully watching what was going on across the pond. The punk scene had shaken everything up in the British music industry and provided the labels with a raft of new bands. Initially, Copeland used the IRS banner to put out albums by acts he was already working with in the UK. Still being largely based in London, Copeland didn't really have much of a clue what was going on in Los Angeles either. But he did have one crucial link to the American music scene: his younger brother Ian.

Ian Copeland was employed by Paragon, a booking agency based in Macon, Georgia. When he started working for the agency in 1977, its roster exclusively featured high-profile Southern rock bands—Lynyrd Skynyrd, the Charlie Daniels Band, and the Allman Brothers. Paragon had also booked dates for Miles Copeland's Climax Blues Band. Powered by an enthusiasm similar to his brothers' for the new sounds coming out of the rock underground, Ian—whom Seymour Stein described as "the only good one of the bunch!"—started to build up a network of connections across the United States. Pretty soon, he had his own roster of acts at Paragon, a mishmash of British and American artists who didn't fit in easily anywhere else—Iggy Pop, Siouxsie and the Banshees, Ultravox, and the Cure, to name a few—alongside the acts he had managed to secure through his brother Miles: the Police, Squeeze, and John Cale.

In August 1979, Ian Copeland left Paragon to form his own company, Frontier Booking International (F.B.I.). He took his client list with him and all of the contacts he had built up within the American tour circuit: record company promotion people, club promoters, and radio DJs. At first, F.B.I. shared office space in New York with Jane Friedman, John Cale's partner and manager.

Cale's split album *Sabotage/Live* (on his own Spy records label) would be the second release put out under the IRS banner. The first was a no-brainer. Miles Copeland licensed *Singles Going Steady*, a singles compilation from Manchester power-punk band the Buzzcocks, who were stars in England but had yet to make any inroads in the United States. The album went on to sell twenty thousand copies, although the band themselves claimed to have never seen any of the proceeds. "Miles Copeland produced it," Buzzcocks bassist Steve Garvey said in a 1996 interview, "and he ripped us off."

Copeland had a keen eye for a safe bet, cherry-picking acts that already had a substantial amount of success in the UK and that he figured would also find an audience in the States—bands such as the Beat (known as the English Beat in the US), the Buzzcocks, and Magazine. Like any sharp businessman, he also had one eye on the competition. Two of the US-based acts signed to IRS had debuted with singles released by UK label Stiff Records, which aside from being home to Elvis Costello and Madness was also the label that had inspired Miles to start Faulty Products in the first place. Those two groups were Wazmo Nariz and the Go-Go's; the latter would provide IRS with its first and greatest taste of commercial success.

It's probably just as well that Copeland's deal kept artistic decisions at arm's length from A&M. If Jerry Moss had caught wind of some of the acts Copeland intended to release, he might have balked at devoting A&M's resources to the label. The first domestic act to be signed to IRS was Skafish, a band named after its leader, Jim Skafish (pronounced Skay-fish), the new wave Tiny Tim. He elevated ugly to an art form and inspired extreme reactions with his music, a form of intensely personal psychodrama that was painful in its honesty. In a song called "No Liberation Here," Skafish even implored to be abused, misused, and tossed around the room. Any time he performed in public, usually wearing a dress or a tube top, he often got what he wished for.

Compared to Skafish, Wazmo Nariz looked normal. And that was exactly the point. Nariz didn't look weird at all. He was clean-shaven, neatly coiffed, and dressed in a suit. But he also wore two neck ties side by side, and the cover of his debut album on IRS, which featured a photo of Nariz illuminated only by candlelight, seemed to be misprinted, with the back cover intruding on the front. Everything about Nariz was contrived to be slightly off-kilter, and the title of his album, *Things Aren't Right*, made it plain. Like Skafish, he had emerged from the Chicago punk scene.

The third artist signed to IRS, a fellow called Root Boy Slim, was even more out there. He was once described as a "250-pound emphysemiac [sic] who descends into an Animal House alcoholic stupor on stage." Offstage, Slim (né Foster Mackenzie III) was the wayward son of a well-to-do Washington family and a Yale alumnus who later claimed to be a fraternity brother of George W. Bush. His group, the Sex Change Band, had already acquired a cult following. Root Boy Slim's dry-humoured blues had been given a previous airing on an eponymous 1974 album released through Warner Bros., which contained songs with titles like "Boogie Till You Puke" and "I Used to Be a Radical." The starting lineup at I.R.S was the most motley bunch of musicians imaginable.

Copeland resumed the narrative: "After one year, we had the Buzzcocks that did about twenty thousand. We had five, six, seven, eight records out. Nothing had really happened. [Jerry Moss] said, 'Nothing's really happening with the label. I don't know if we should continue.'

"I said, 'Well, let me ask you a question. Did you lose money on any one of the acts?'

"'No, but we didn't make any.'

"'Okay,' I said, 'Let's look at your signings for the last couple of years. How many acts did you make money on for the first album?'

"'Well, none.'

"I said, 'Well, in our first year, you have actually made money— although you've said it's not a lot.'

"'Yeah, but you've had seven albums out.'

"'Yes, but the first album of each act! I've had seven albums out and you made money! I'm already unique!' [Copeland is yelling, as he recalls this.] I said, 'Give me another year.' So he did. And the Go-Go's went to number one."

This exchange is as good an illustration as any of how Copeland did business: whether negotiating with a musician or with the head of a record company, he would state his case plainly in terms that seemed to possess an irrefutable logic. If the chips were down, as in this case, he would find a positive way to spin the situation to his advantage. Brave is the man who would take issue with his reasoning, built as it was entirely on appealing to the logical outcome desired by the party he was negotiating with. It was a whip-smart hustle, and it seemed to get results. As it was, only two out of those seven acts—Buzzcocks and the Cramps—that IRS worked with in that first year would get the chance to release another album on the label, proving that Copeland was as likely to drop an unprofitable band as any of the major labels.

A 1981 profile on IRS in the *Wall Street Journal* put a positive spin on the label's business, which it described as the equivalent of a "baseball farm club," seeding new talent in the hopes that they will grow into bigger things. Part of the conditions for A&M's financial backing gave it the option of signing groups that were released through IRS to the main label. Oingo Boingo, formerly a musical theatre group that specialized in a kind of abstruse surrealistic humour inspired by the Firesign Theater, was one of the first acts to benefit from this arrangement. John Cale, too, was offered a deal on A&M.

IRS was able to operate because its overhead was low; the firm typically spent no more than $20,000 to record an album and often considerably less, whereas a major label might spend five times that. Copeland also expanded on some of the ideas he had used to help break the Police in America. He invested in the purchase of a fleet of vans that became a means of providing cost-effective tour support.

"Gee, I can't remember how many he actually bought," said Bob Garcia, "but long before some of his bands were on planes and buses, they were definitely trading the proverbial van around town. In other words, when one band was finished touring, another would pick up the same van to go out on tour in. It was that kind of no-frills type of touring situation. Very low overhead and, obviously, cash and carry."

The *Wall Street Journal* noted the apparent eccentricity of IRS and its recording artists in the title of its profile on the label: "How the Weird Can Get Started in Recording." Copeland apparently possessed a sincere belief that the weirdos of today were the stars of tomorrow. He was convinced that psychobilly band the Cramps, one of the second wave of acts he signed to IRS, would be as big as KISS: "I have no doubt in my mind that acts like the Cramps and Alternative TV will eventually draw mainstream audiences. You have to remember that it took Fleetwood Mac ten years to break."

"Miles loved the Cramps," said Garcia. "You must remember that in addition to being a manager, this is a guy who was on stage throwing fans off stage if they menaced his band. If somebody tried to grab Ivy [Rorschach, the Cramps guitarist] or menace anybody in the Cramps he'd be right there to throw them off the stage. That's why I compare him to [Led Zeppelin manager] Peter Grant. Definitely that type of person but at a younger level and, obviously, with a completely different sort of circumstances."

Whether the acts Copeland had marked for greatness were pre-pared to march into battle with him toward this glorious future was another matter entirely. But initially, at least, Copeland did everything he could to provide them with the opportunity to break out of the limited markets they had established for themselves. The label would be heavily promoted through its association with the Police and, to a lesser extent, vice versa. In this way, explained Copeland, "the Police benefited from the fact that they seemed to be part of a movement—which made them seem more important. And, of course, the move-ment benefited from the fact that the Police were fucking happening. So everybody benefited. Every act in the movement benefited by the fact that somebody is big in the charts."

"Miles would always book IRS acts with the Police," said Bob Garcia. "Almost all of the Police dates Stateside had one or two open-ers, whether it was Wazmo Nariz or the Cramps or the Buzzcocks or the Go-Go's. These were your standard openers."

In the case of the Cramps, this arrangement—which resulted in a slot as a support for the Police on a May 1979 UK tour—also served as an opportunity to "demonstrate his commitment" to the group. Guitarist Kid Congo Powers, who joined the Cramps in 1980 for the recording of their second IRS album, *Psychedelic Jungle*, and would also tour the UK with them, recalled that Copeland's largesse toward the group was such that he let them stay in the Copeland family resi-dence in London, a grand townhouse near Regent's Park.

"Miles was out of town," Powers recalled. "It was a nice big house and there were all these Middle Eastern artifacts in it—statues and things. I was always wondering where they came from. Maybe they just picked them up from somewhere, because they looked like they should be in a museum! And certainly not fake.

"I remember that we all had crazy, weird dreams and experiences while we were staying there. We were all in different rooms in the house. I remember waking up in the middle of the night and the door was opening and closing. I went out into the hallway and it seemed like the whole thing was tipping on its side. It was really crazy. Lux and Ivy said they had similar crazy stuff happening. We just figured it was because of all those artifacts in there. The house was haunted by all the Middle Eastern ancient artifacts gods! Obviously not happy to be in the Copeland manor in Maida Vale."

Out on the road with the Police, it was the general public that was spooked by the presence of the Cramps. So spooked at times that people were moved to violence. On the very first date of the tour, in Glasgow, Cramps front man Lux Interior, sensing the fear emanating from the audience, antagonized and goaded the Police fans further. When he leaped into the crowd, they retaliated by repeatedly kicking and spitting on him. He took his revenge later in the set by hurling a bag of trash from the backstage area onto the audience.

Despite seeming to have nothing in common except Miles Copeland, the Cramps and the Police proved to be surprisingly amiable tour mates. "It was such a thrill for us," reported guitarist Ivy Rorschach, "and the Police were incredibly nice and hospitable, and let us have sound checks, which I've heard is not typical at all."

But behind closed doors, the warmth was evidently not reciprocated. Andy Summers implied that the Cramps' ghoulish presence on the tour gave him a case of the heebie-jeebies; in other words, he feared he was about to be upstaged, just as the Police had upstaged Alberto y Lost Trios Paranoias six months earlier. "After a while their stage act palls," Summers recalled of the Cramps. "What they are selling is an attitude, what you are supposed to come away with is uncertain."

More than likely, this seems to be a case of score settling on Summers's part, due to the fact that the Cramps garnered the lion's share of critical acclaim on that particular tour. In June 1979, both leading music papers in the UK, *Melody Maker* and *NME*, ran cover stories on the band. The Police had not yet been featured on the cover of either, despite their growing profile. They had even lost out on a cover story to the Cramps in September 1978, when *Melody Maker* editor John Williams opted to run a story on the garage rock ghouls over a puff piece on the Police written by journalist John Pidgeon that eventually ran under the servile title "The Best Rock 'n' Roll Band I've Seen in Years."

Summers's public persona was of the cheeky chap with an aching dry wit, but he was also extremely competitive and did not take well to criticism of any kind. When the Cramps took top billing in the music press over the Police, to whom they were playing as support, Summers took it as a personal slight. "Compared with [the Cramps], we are normal," he fumed in his memoir, "and a number of the British rock press try to make a meal out of this, preferring to cast their lot with no-chance weirdness than with anyone who puts an honest song across—and we are criticized for playing too well."

Despite their position as one of the top bands in the country, the Police still felt like underdogs and outsiders in their own country. But their ambitions would not be stifled. They were determined to succeed and to be acknowledged, even if that meant taking their music farther afield than any band before them.

9

POLICE THE WORLD

The Police seemed to be ubiquitous, in all places, at all times, and that was almost certainly the intention. Countries previously immune to the freedom march of rock 'n' roll fell, one by one, to the wail of the Police. At least, that's what they wanted you to believe. The band's PR machine was so persuasive that in effect the Police became the biggest band in the world by default.

Just two albums into their career, they had already established a foothold in both the UK and the States. Now the Police prepared to embark on their most audacious endeavour yet, one by which, potentially, they would stand or fall: a world tour of countries that were largely virgin territories for Western rock acts. Initially, their itinerary would take them on their first trips to Japan and Australia, then they would detour through Thailand, China, India, and Egypt, before finishing the tour in Greece.

"The idea to play in these countries was originally mine," Andy Summers claimed in his memoir, although he failed to explain how or why he came up with it. And Miles Copeland would probably beg to differ; the scheme smacked of the lateral thinking through which he had accelerated the rise of the Police.

Up until that time, Western rock and pop acts rarely, if ever, ventured outside the prescribed and established routes for concert tours. Cliff Richard was one of the first Western stars to perform in the Soviet Union, playing twenty sold-out dates in Moscow and Leningrad in autumn 1976. He was followed three years later by Elton John. The Rolling Stones announced their 1975 "Tour of the Americas," which was to employ an elaborate theatrical stage show, with great fanfare by playing a gig on a flatbed truck down New York's Fifth Avenue. The tour was meant to visit Mexico, Brazil, and Venezuela, but those were quietly dropped from the schedule. Political and financial instability in the region was cited as the reason, along with concerns about the security of the band itself.

Rather than taking a huge production out on the road, the Police tour would adopt the same no-frills approach that had allowed them to tour America without the backing of record company support. Miles Copeland and Sting each had their own reasoning for why the Police's brand of rock 'n' roll deserved to be delivered to far-flung corners of the globe. Copeland saw Western music as a liberating force. "The thing you have to understand about Miles," explained Sting, "is that he has this very laissez-faire rightist attitude in which he sees rock 'n' roll as bringing freedom to all these obscure places we've gone and played in."

Sting, on the other hand, just wanted market penetration for his songs. "As far as I'm concerned, though," he said, "the reason we've done them is because being a world-class group shouldn't just be restricted to being big in the Western world—the popular conception of it. It should mean you're a force everywhere."

Copeland denied that market forces were ever an impetus for their idiosyncratic take on a world tour: "The drive initially was 'How do I make this group the most interesting group in the world?' They gotta be doing the most interesting things in the world. They've got to be doing things like, 'What the fuck? You played in Egypt! You were the first rock group ever to play India? What was that like?' That's a good hour on a radio show."

"We didn't go to India to make money," he continued. "Or Egypt to make money. There's no money to make there. Egypt's not a market. Neither is India. They're piracy markets. Why would we open up a market for pirates?"

In effect, the tour was routed and planned so that the grandstanding gigs in places like Bombay and Cairo—shows that would also be the hardest to pull off, logistically—could be played for free, with the band shouldering the cost from the proceeds of dates in Japan and Australia. Copeland also knew that any financial liability they incurred would be offset by the extraordinary amount of publicity the shows would garner.

"Here's the other great reality of business," he offered. "The media needs something to write about. Every day, fucking *Melody Maker* or *NME* (or whatever the newspaper is) gets a photograph of a group. There they are in their spandex trousers, long hair with a guitar. Same fucking photograph I saw fifty times in the last three weeks. What makes them different?

"All of a sudden they get a picture of these three guys by the Taj Mahal in fucking India, all dressed up as Maharajahs, looking like they're out of their fucking minds. What the fuck is that!? All of a sudden they listen to the music, they see these guys, it looks glamorous."

After servicing the press, they had so many photos left over that Copeland initiated a Police magazine in order to drip-feed new images to their fans every month. *The Police File* also served as the official organ for the band to relate their newfound adventures.

"What you're dealing with here," asserted A&M artist relations man Bob Garcia, "is that taking the place of instant mass media exposure or satellite broadcast was the live appearance, or appearances."

In the absence of MTV, which would not begin broadcasting in the States for another eighteen months (in August 1981), or anything similar, they not only created their own media events but also created their own media. "Wisely or not," noted BBC Radio One DJ Annie

POLICE THE WORLD 115

Nightingale, "the Police film, photograph and record everything that happens to them."

Copeland had by this time begun to capture everything that happened to the Police on a portable tape recorder, preserving it for posterity. His brother Stewart had invested in a Super-8 camera that seemed to be permanently attached to his eye. But now Nightingale, an early supporter of the group, was surprised to find herself inadvertently foisted in front of a Police camera crew while attending an event as innocuous as an A&M presentation of discs commemorating gold record sales in December 1979. Two months later, she would travel with the band for several months—ostensibly to make a documentary for the BBC titled *Police in the East*—as they undertook their first world tour beyond the reaches of the traditional rock circuit.

In something of a coup, Miles Copeland managed to insert his own film crew into the project (namely, Derek and Kate Burbidge), rather than a BBC crew. The Burbidges worked in concert with Michael Appleton of the BBC (the producer of the *Old Grey Whistle Test*), who also joined the rest of the entourage in Japan for the first two-week stretch of the tour.

As well as the BBC show, the Burbidges were tasked with making a promotional film for "So Lonely," which A&M had hastily scheduled for a February 1980 re-release to cash in on the band's popularity. Although not particularly happy at having singles from their debut album shilled out to the public—"It stinks," opined Stewart Copeland—the band had little choice in the matter and dutifully mimed along to the song, singing into walkie-talkies borrowed from their minders, while they paraded through trains and stations in the Tokyo subway.

Miles Copeland also commissioned the Burbidges to make another separate documentary film that covered the entirety of the world tour. The finished document, *The Police: Around the World*, was an efficient piece of propaganda, even if it played out more like a tourist video than a rock 'n' roll tour film. Crafted to relay the message that the world was now at their feet, it opened with a crude graphic of a world map with Sting's, Summers's, and Copeland's faces superimposed over each hemisphere.

The film was coolly edited to excise anything that might disrupt the image that the Police were anything but a harmonious, fun-loving bunch on a wild adventure around the world. In one brief sequence, though, there is a slight hint that this was not the case. Stewart Copeland is singing out of tune in a hotel room, in what (it becomes apparent) is meant to be an imitation of Summers's guitar playing. "You're panic-stricken every time you play it," Summers sneers in retaliation, tearing into Copeland for his inconsistent drumming. "You were fucking diabolical!"

"Don't attack me!" Copeland whines defensively. But Summers isn't finished. "Because I think you're a wanker!" he snaps. Then the film quickly cuts away from the remainder of the altercation, providing neither context nor resolution, to show a Benny Hill-style skit involving Sting hailing a rickshaw on a Hong Kong street, then removing his shirt and hauling the cart himself.

On their days off in between shows, they mooned around like starstruck tourists in whatever country they were visiting, stacking up footage that could be used as set pieces and cutaways in the various films the Burbidges were working on. Summers was filmed engaging in a wrestling match at a sumo training school outside Tokyo. Clad in a sumo nappy, his scrawny thirty-eight-year-old body looking like that of a sickly and malnourished child, Summers clearly has no chance against his meaty opponent, who is at least double his size in both girth and height.

In their eagerness to talk up the adventures of the all-conquering *Übermensch* pop trio in alien lands, even the English music press reported on the titanic bout between Summers and the sumo wrestler. But the jocular tone of the introduction to the article that ran in *Record Mirror* did little to disguise its apparent xenophobia:

> Picture that lean streak of Police meat Andy Summers. He of the bleached barnet and jarring guitar figures. Consider his angular attractiveness, accentuated by him standing amidst a beach-load of indigenous Nips. For indeed, Mr Summers is currently basking in the Land Of The Rising Sun and I can't imagine any sallow-skinned Jap kicking sand in his face. Can you?

This kind of talk wasn't limited to the reporter, though. In a quote contained within the same interview, Stewart Copeland revealed his own attitude toward his hosts to be equally unenlightened. "I've bought a million things here," he enthused about the consumerist frenzy inspired by his trip to Tokyo, "tape machines, clocks, accessories for movies, the lot. Everything's so small and efficient. Just like the people. I guess that's why they call them Nips. They never stop nipping about all over the place."

Sting, who was less prone to these types of gaffes than his drummer, chose to express his enthusiasm for Japanese culture in visual terms that were certainly more rarefied, if no less clichéd. He was photographed wearing a lily-white ceremonial kimono with billowing shoulder pieces and glaring defiantly into the camera, while holding a tanto (seppuku dagger) firmly to his gut—a pose no doubt inspired by the ritual suicide of Japanese author Yukio Mishima. But pop idols are not meant to feign suicide. The photos only ever appeared in a special edition of a popular Japanese music magazine, *Music Life*. The shoot was also filmed (for possible inclusion in the BBC documentary or as a cutaway in the video clip for "So Lonely"), but the footage was never made public. This was perhaps wise. Sting was still scaling the heights of teenybopper adulation, and his teenage girl fans would probably have been extremely distressed to see photos of him in the act of suicide, no matter how valiant and sexy he looked.

In Japan, gaggles of giggling girls followed the Police everywhere they went, snapping pictures and crowding around them with autograph books, forming welcoming committees when they stepped off the bullet train, and stalking the corridors of the hotels they stayed in. The band members travelled in a pack but weren't hard to spot. Miles Copeland had outfitted them all with black bomber jackets emblazoned with "Police" on the back and mock police badges on the front.

Their entourage had now swelled to include the BBC camera crew and several burly-looking minders (provided by Japanese promoter Mr. Udo), who were instructed to shadow the band's every move. Summers admitted to being a little unnerved at the militaristic efficiency with which they operated—and described the ever-present and infallibly cheerful Udo as an "Al Capone character"—but was nevertheless impressed that all of this muscle had been deployed on their behalf.

From Japan, they moved to Hong Kong and played in a tiny club called Today's World Disco to a crowd of largely Anglo ex-pats. Sting, afflicted with a throat infection, was ordered to rest, forcing the cancellation of planned dates in Taiwan, Singapore, and Thailand, the latter to be played in a Bangkok bar-cum-whorehouse called the Kit Kat Club. Instead, the Police moved back onto more familiar territory for their first tour of Australia, where they were already huge stars, having notched up a number-one album.

Although the publicity for the tour appeared to be slick and run with corporate efficiency, the logistics on the ground were a nightmare. As the booking agent, Ian Copeland had the unenviable job of organizing events in far-off countries that had neither the infrastructure nor the equipment to put on a show by a rock group, let alone one with the stature of the Police. But these obstacles did not always make themselves apparent until the group had already arrived in the country with one or two days at most before they played the show.

The Police found this out the hard way when they got to Egypt and all of their equipment was put into storage until after the weekend they were due to play. Summers claimed in his account that this was because the gear arrived after the office had closed for midday Friday prayer (which he describes as the "Arab Sabbath," exhibiting his irreverent grasp of Middle East affairs). Not to be outwitted by jobsworth officials (or even God), Miles Copeland called on one of his father's old friends to help pull some strings—a man named Hassan Touhami, whom Ian Copeland described as former President Nasser's bodyguard. Touhami was much more than that, though. He was an English-speaking member of the Mukhabarat (Egypt's secret service) and the key contact between the Nasser regime and the CIA. Copeland II described Touhami as "fanatically patriotic, intensely religious, impeccably honest." In 1952, Copeland II had arranged for Touhami to visit Washington to be schooled in CIA techniques. At a topless bar in Maryland, Touhami poured Coca-Cola over a "hostess" who tried to sit in his lap. And when one of his new CIA pals offered him money and suggested he have some fun, Copeland reported that Touhami put his gun to the case officer's head and said, "With my diplomatic immunity I could plaster your brains against that far wall and wouldn't get so much as a parking ticket."

Miles Copeland II brought his young family to Egypt in September 1952 (when Stewart was barely a couple of months old), just two months after the July 23 coup headed by Nasser. At that time, he was ostensibly working for Booz Allen Hamilton, a private management consulting firm with long-standing ties to the CIA that has been called the "shadow intelligence community." He was really there to advise the Nasser regime, having initiated the CIA project two years earlier that would parachute Nasser into power. Police manager Miles even remembered going over to Hassan Touhami's house (which neighboured the Copeland residence) as a child and playing with Touhami's guns while the adults talked.

When the Police came to play Egypt in March 1980, Touhami was deputy prime minister. He took a call from Miles Axe Copeland III, thinking that his old CIA buddy was on the line. (It's quite possible the Police manager was even counting on this case of mistaken identity.) Copeland explained what had happened to their equipment, and Touhami kindly agreed to grease the wheels, even though smoothing the path for a pop group was probably the least of his problems at that precise moment. The Shah of Iran had been spirited into Egypt just three days earlier. Protests against his presence in the country had erupted outside Cairo University, where the exiled leader was about to undergo an operation to remove his spleen by Michael E. DeBakey, a top American cardiovascular surgeon, who had been flown in especially for that purpose.

In the middle of this political unrest, the (musical) Police arrived. They were playing at a university, too, but at the American University in Cairo, safely across the Nile from all of the turmoil. Caught up in their own little bubble and indifferent to the political chaos, the band members were filmed racing horses across the desert dressed like Lawrence of Arabia and larking about on camels in front of the Great Pyramids of Giza for the Burbidges' camera.

"This is my brother Ian, who is our agent in New York," Stewart Copeland announced for the camera, pointing up at his older brother, who sat atop a camel swathed in a kaffiyeh (Arab headdress). "He's our tame Arab. In fact, he's more Arab than human."

"It's all very well playing around on the camel," Ian Copeland responded, playing along with the gag, "but we've got lots of problems with this gig. The roadies are all refusing to carry the equipment."

Word of Touhami's intervention had evidently not reached the roadies. There were other problems, too. The P.A. system that had been flown in from Greece for the show wasn't powerful enough to push the sound out much farther than the first few rows of the auditorium. And of the six spotlights trained on the stage, only one had a working bulb. To top it all, the audience had already been let into the auditorium before the P.A. had even been set up. A sound check seemed out of the question. Sting's guitar tech, Danny Quatrochi, was losing his mind. "I hope abortion is legal," he muttered to the camera, "because we're about to witness one tonight."

As it happened, it was Sting who almost aborted the remainder of the tour by inadvertently telling the chief of police in Cairo to "fuck off" during the show. Seeing a man attempt to forcibly pull down an American kid who had climbed up onto his friend's shoulders, while the band was playing, Sting verbally lashed out at the policeman (who was dressed in plain clothes) from the stage, then instructed the kids in the audience: "See him. Fill him in."

"Sting almost got arrested and put in jail in Egypt because he insulted the chief of police," admitted Miles Copeland. "A lot of fast talking on my part kept him out of jail." The fast talking he employed was as much to convince the front man not to inflame the situation further while Copeland mollified the top cop. Sting refused to apologize and instead stared the police chief down in the dressing room, then petulantly stormed out. "I had to eat the shit for him," Copeland recalled.

Compared to this, the previous stop on the tour (Bombay, India) had been a breeze. The show had been organized by a group of well-heeled retirement-age Parsi women who ran a charity called the Time and Talents Club. Copeland had been referred to them after putting out word that he wanted a nonprofit organization to host the show in Bombay, but he hadn't realized exactly who they were until he met them on a reconnaissance trip to organize the event. The upper-crust ladies of the Time and Talents Club had never promoted a rock concert before, and they didn't have any idea who the Police were, so Copeland also roped in a twenty-three-year-old journalist (and Police fan) named Vir Sanghvi. He was the editor of the newly founded *Bombay* magazine, an Indian equivalent of *Time Out* for the hip moneyed set in the Indian capital. By involving Sanghvi, Copeland was canny enough to secure an influential media contact to stir up interest in the show.

While Copeland thrashed out the details of the Police gig over lunch at the Victory Stall—a fashionable snack bar run by the Time and Talents Club on Apollo Bundar, overlooking the Gateway of India—Sanghvi politely explained the finer points of rock 'n' roll to the Parsi women, who were more used to staging society evenings of piano recitals. He remembered having to reassure them that Sting did not actually have a second name and neither did he need one.

The show was advertised by huge banners that were hung around the city to announce the band's arrival. "The Police—Not Cops but Pops" they said, calmly allaying any fears the population of Bombay might have had that they were about to be invaded by foreign para-militaries. The only foreseeable problem that the band would encounter was the arrival of an enemy journalist.

At twenty-two (going on twenty-three), Paul Morley was considered one of the senior writers at the *NME*, Britain's most influential music publication. A cocky but keyed-up Northerner with a tendency to self-flagellate his psyche in prose, Morley had made no secret of his antipathy toward the Police, describing them as "motley mercenaries" in his review of *Outlandos d'Amour* for the *NME* a year earlier. Morley thought the band was silly and utterly transparent in the affectations (of pose and rhythm and image) they adopted to win appeal. After joining

Ted Nugent on tour to write a story, the journalist even upbraided the rebel rocker in print for praising the band. The Nuge, Morley thought, should know better.

"His [Nugent's] way of appealing to me was to say how much great music there was coming out of Britain: 'That Police record is fantastic.' He'd responded to Stewart Copeland's drum sound," said Morley. "Said that it was like chopping trees. And in the piece I had sort of scoffed at this notion that what appeared to us to be bland music actually had any aggressive quality. But for Ted Nugent it did."

When the offer to go to Bombay to cover the Police came through, the *NME* put Morley forward, thinking (in the way that music magazine editors do) that it would make a more interesting piece to send someone less disposed to their charms. Summers gave the impression that the band was already on the defensive in anticipation of Morley's arrival. "We are not sure what to make of his appearance," Summers brooded, "other than the fact that if he has been flown at great expense to India, he will be nice to us if he wants to live."

During their three-day stay in Bombay, the Police resided in the Taj Mahal InterContinental Hotel, a tower block camouflaged with faux minarets that overlooked the Gateway of India and served as an annex to the Taj Mahal Palace hotel next door, which was a far more resplendent colonial-style building. Their entourage had swelled even further to include several other journalists. Morley recalled there being a *Melody Maker* journalist, who was due to travel on to Egypt with the band, a reporter from the *Daily Mail*, and a photographer named Brian Aris from the *Sun*.

The *NME* had its own stable of eminently capable rock photographers—including Joy Division photographer Anton Corbijn and Clash photographer Pennie Smith—but were instructed that they had no other option than to use glamour photographer Aris, who was more accustomed to shooting topless models for "Page 3" of the *Sun*. In any event, he did find a topless model to shoot in Bombay, too: Sting posed bare-chested by the hotel pool for the *NME* cover.

This might have been an attempt by Miles Copeland to reassert his control over the music paper after having a hostile journalist imposed on him, thereby making sure that even if the text was negative, the Police at least had approval over the photographs. "It was an early sighting of that celebrity nonsense that became a lot more apparent later," Morley maintained. "[That kind of thing] didn't really happen at that time but clearly it did with the Police."

The other downside to this arrangement was that Morley also had to share a room with Aris. "He was always arguing with me about the fact that, bizarrely, the *NME* only had a circulation of 200,000 while the *Sun* had a circulation of 3 million."

Although his close confinement with Aris was an irritation, Morley did begin to enjoy a rather more challenging relationship with Sting that allowed him to experience the full force of the singer's personality at close quarters. Sting, by his own admission, had specifically set out to win Morley over. This charm offensive had begun a full seven months earlier, in August 1979, at a Who concert in Wembley Stadium. Morley remembered "nattering away to some friends" in the backstage area after the show when he was approached by Sting, who was carrying his infant son in his arms and who made a point of discussing Morley's article on Ted Nugent.

"Whatever you thought of Sting at the time," said Morley, "by then he was a pop star, and it was incredibly flattering, you know? He came up to me and said 'Hello' and talked to me. And of course, this made me look incredibly important in front of the people I was talking with. He said, 'Hi, Paul. How are you doing?' And that was incredible for a number of reasons: that he took the time to do it, but also took the time to do it on the back of me having been, obviously, hating on his group."

Morley was also secretly flattered that Sting had evidently taken notice of his writing. And so, shortly after this initial encounter, he felt moved to pass his regards on to Sting when a colleague was given an assignment to photograph him. Sting later told Morley that this was the moment he realized, "I've got him." (Later still, he told another journalist that this was in fact a lie, and he had said it only to impress Morley of his cunning.)

In Bombay, over breakfast at the Taj Mahal InterContinental the morning Morley arrived, Sting let the journalist in on his ruse. "I went up to you at Wembley with the sole purpose of introducing Sting," he explained, revealing the extent of his own self-regard by referring to himself in the third person. "I didn't think that Paul Morley had ever thought about Sting," he continued, "and it was a good opportunity to get you to."

By saying this, Sting simultaneously gained the journalist's confidence while continuing to ruthlessly apply the charm. "He's trying to camouflage his true nature by confessing to it," Morley offered, reflecting on Sting's modus operandi. "'Yeah, I am that cold and manipulative but, by the very act of saying it, perhaps I'm not.' But it's just a part of the game. And he was quite good at that, double-bluffing." Morley further speculated that Sting probably engaged in the same kind of political game-playing within the group, too, thereby hastening its swift demise.

Morley, who admitted he was, by this point, completely in thrall to the pop star, further pressed the singer to reveal the secret of his "immense cool." "I care about how I look, and I care about how I present myself," Sting revealed, before uttering a line so cold in its narcissism that it would come back to haunt him. "Like this morning when we met, I cared very much what you thought of me at breakfast," he said. "Maybe it's vanity. I feel that I'm being watched and I enjoy it; therefore I have a task to do it at all times, I mean. It's no great burden on me. If anything I find that it's a pastime, just to maintain that kind of cool."

The simple truth behind what is usually termed *star quality* or *charisma* is contained within the extraordinary efforts made by an individual who wants and (more to the point) desires to be liked at all costs and attempts to effect this through little more than force of will and personality. Charisma is a projection, a sleight of personality that produces a hall-of-mirrors effect where the "real" person is lost in the feint of multiple reflections he or she has constructed (and has allowed to be constructed) around himself or herself, a wall that masks an almost manic insecurity at the same time that it betrays an excessive self-confidence.

In order to maintain that illusion, this individual must be "on" at all times. And this in itself is an art: the art of manipulation. It requires obsessive-compulsive tendencies to the point of being sociopathic, yet also gives the impression that doing so is completely effortless. But behind the reflection, behind the "star," is a person just like any other person, if a little bit colder and more controlled and subjugated by a machinelike efficiency to present himself in the best possible light in order to disguise the fact that beneath the glittering exterior is nothing but a soulless husk.

At one point in his article, Morley commented that when talking to Sting, he began to "look at him as if into a mirror (his will strangely imposes itself yet is quite selfless)." Another British journalist, *Daily Express* columnist Jean Rook—who was often referred to as "the dame of Fleet Street" and was as canny a judge of character as any—decided that meeting Sting was "like being locked in your car, with the windows shut, with a good-looking scorpion. Sting is polite, cold-eyed, intelligent, brilliant and ruthless."

Morley related an incident that suggests that for all their globe hopping to far-flung countries off the beaten track for rock 'n' roll, the Police might have also felt safer in the carefully controlled environs of a locked car. The journalist and the band and their manager were cruising in a huge white limousine from their luxury hotel toward Rang Bhavan, the five-thousand-person-capacity open-air auditorium where they were to perform. Miles Copeland sat with a tape recorder on his lap, recording casual conversation for posterity. But conversation was cut dead in its tracks when they stopped at some traffic lights and "an armless girl beggar" suddenly appeared at the window of the vehicle. Morley reported the reactions of the car's inhabitants to the sight of this child:

"Shit!" spits Stewart. "Can you imagine showing your deformities to everyone?" We all try to stare away. No one knows what to say. "Oh God," Miles repeats. The car moves off. "But if you give them money you're actually encouraging it, and I think it's not to be encouraged. "Where do you draw the line?" wonders a shaken Andy Summers." "Where do you stop? You can't give it to one and then leave seven million out."

Conspicuous by his absence here is Sting. Morley described him as sitting in the car "lost." Yet on his return from Bombay, Sting would wax lyrical about his experience on the Indian subcontinent and the nature of the poverty he had seen, rationalizing it into something that alleviated any guilt at the Western consumption that had caused it. He explained his observation that "although a lot of the people live in absolute squalor, absolute degradation and poverty, real poverty, they are generally happier than the average citizen of Moss Side, say, or Belfast. Or the poor areas of Birmingham. There's a spiritual side to their lives that rationalizes misery and there's no real despair."

Sting neglected to mention that during his stay, the Police were shuffled from party to party where they were patronized by the Indian nouveau riche. He also spoke of the concert in Bombay as if it was his missionary duty to deliver salvation through rock 'n' roll to people who had never heard Western rock music before and who didn't understand it. "One of the best moments of my life was in Bombay, playing for an audience that had never seen rock, that had no idea how to behave toward it," he told *Rolling Stone* magazine in 1981.

But Western rock music had been heard in India from the 1950s on, just as it had been heard all over the rest of the world, spawning its own indigenous variants especially in the sixties, when beat-influenced garage bands began to crop up in Bombay and Calcutta. The popular songs interpreted by playback singers for Bollywood movies were typically pitched at an emotional intensity similar to that of Western pop and rock music (and took the place of it within the culture), even if the instrumental arrangements were drawn from a more classical template. When Sting claimed that "those [Indian] kids just don't have a representative culture during that adolescent period," it was a comment made through blinkered Western eyes. And witnessing the crowd's reaction to the Police's music seemed to confirm that belief for him.

"There was an incredible range of social strata there—the intelligentsia, the media, the sophisticates, kids with no arms, beggars, hippies. Throughout the show I explained that this is dance music, please don't sit down—stand up in the seat or just dance. And by the end of the set, they did! They clapped in all the right places. It was quite emotional."

Unfortunately, the real police stationed in the venue didn't quite see it the same way. When elements of the crowd started to push to the front, uniformed authorities charged and beat them with batons, causing Sting to lash out again from the stage, just as he had done in Cairo. "Give a man a baton and he's got to hit someone," he said sarcastically.

Beneath the circus-tent showmanship, there was something rather crass about the idea of Western rock stars pitching up in the Third World for what was essentially a publicity stunt; a cheap holiday in other people's misery, as Johnny Rotten once put it. This aspect of the Police's world tour was keenly felt by Morley: "Even though you kind of knew that's what it was, a huge, almost grotesque publicity stunt—and the *Melody Maker* [was] out there and they were going on to Egypt—it was working."

"It worked with *NME*," Morley continued. "I mean, we gave them hundreds of pages with that Bombay piece, you know? I was writing the piece page by page and giving it, as I was writing it in my house, to the editor who had come around to collect it. It was chaos, you know? But it worked. We gave them all that space and all that coverage.

"I think some people would have thought it was absolutely appalling that the Police were getting this ridiculous cover with this sort of clattering air-brushed photograph of Sting. And that it might have been a break-down of some of the *NME* values. But, on the other hand, it was an interesting moment that the Police were obviously seen at that moment in time, not least because of Miles's machinations, as the biggest pop group in the world."

But most of Morley's story—which was so long, it ran over two consecutive issues of the paper—was taken up by a lengthy Q&A with Sting that was fawning and strangely critical at the same time. The other two members of the Police were not at all happy about this. Summers harboured a long-term grievance for this perceived slight against his importance to the group. Writing nearly thirty years later, Summers clearly still held a grudge, making a point to mention the journalist's "self-obsessed piece about Sting" in his memoir. It was as if Summers had completely misunderstood the tenor of the article. Although clearly lost in admiration of the singer, Morley also insisted on referring to him throughout as "the Sting"—object rather than subject, a pop star fashioned as the earthly manifestation of some god.

Morley "writes well enough," Summers decided, "although mostly with a morbid narcissism." Morley admitted to being perplexed as to why the guitarist would feel the need to settle the score for a perceived slight so late in the day. "He is so angry, so bitter," said Morley. "I could excuse my 'morbid narcissism' because I was twenty-two or twenty-three. But he's in his sixties now and he still seems to be clinging on to that kind of adolescent peevishness."

The Police seemed to have conquered the world and redrawn the map for touring rock groups, but that very peevishness was fast beginning to drive a wedge between members of the trio and would soon have catastrophic effects on relations within the band.

10

GIMME SHELTER

The money started pouring in around June 1980. So much of it that Sting and Andy Summers were advised to leave the country almost immediately by their accountant, Keith Moore, who was rapidly becoming the single most important person in the Police organization, other than their manager. Being a resident alien in the UK, Stewart Copeland was exempt from this instruction. Summers was none too pleased by this state of affairs, feeling that he had little option other than to comply. "It's a pain in the ass," he commented, "but the alternative is 80 per cent [tax] and anyone that did that would be stupid." He dropped £40,000 on a property in Kinsale, County Cork, on the southwest coast of Ireland, and moved in that summer with his family.

Writing about his new life in Ireland, Summers made it sound as if he had been exiled to another century. He complained about the "biting wind," "long grey hours," and visiting the local shop to "stare at the shrunken row of brown things that pass for vegetables in Ireland." He muttered darkly about being targeted as an outsider, with nails being placed under the wheels of his Audi and "taunts about the Police and being British" daubed on the walls of his house.

As the local rock star resident of a fashionable and picturesque port town, Summers was bound to attract attention, good and bad. He resided in a four-storey Georgian house beside a bowling green and high up on a hill with "chocolate box views of the harbour." Among his new acquaintances was a wine exporter and his family. Later, Summers also rather uncharitably blamed his time in Ireland for helping to hasten the breakdown of his marriage. "I can feel that my head is elsewhere, out there on the road; the unfamiliarity of Ireland, the cold, and the quietness of village life don't suit me. Kate and I begin a slow slide into estrangement."

It's more likely that it was domesticity, rather than Ireland, that didn't suit him. Summers was almost a stranger to his own family and especially to his two-year-old daughter, Layla. "As a result of the constant travelling, Layla hasn't seen much of her father and until recently was quite suspicious of him," noted the *Record Mirror* journalist who visited the family at their Kinsale residence toward the close of 1980.

By comparison, Sting seemed to take the isolation that came with country living in his stride. He had bought a large house overlooking Roundstone Bay on the west coast of Ireland. Located in a tiny village on the lake and surrounded by the foothills of the Twelve Pins mountains, it was a picture-postcard fantasy. In the two months he had off, Sting settled in to write songs for the next Police album, putting them down as demos with engineer Ken Kiernan in Keystone Studios in Dublin. He presented his self-imposed tax exile in a very different light to the press, claiming that he had moved out of the country in protest Margaret Thatcher's defence policy.

Stewart Copeland spent his time off from the Police promoting himself. Or, rather, promoting the career of his alter ego Klark Kent, who released an album and a single, neither of which managed to scale the heights of his debut. The single "Away from Home" was a slice of juvenilia about leaving the parental domicile for pastures new that was quite unnerving, sung, as it was, by a twenty-eight-year-old man. Copeland's singing was unconscionably bad; he sounded like a teenage girl serenading herself in the mirror. With Klark Kent's true identity well and truly out of the bag, the project served as little more than an in-joke for Police fans. Its tone suggested that Copeland was blithely unconcerned with the changes imposed on the lives of his Police colleagues.

Keith Moore had advised that for their tax arrangement to be effective, the Police would also have to record outside the UK; otherwise, all earnings that accrued from their trade would be counted as taxable income. From this point on in their career, the group would never record another album in their home country.

The band's financial situation allowed them to spend only forty days a year as residents in the UK. The long tours the Police had undertaken to establish their career would now be a requirement if they wanted to keep their finances out of the clutches of the tax man. But the constant workload had served to further stress the fissures that already existed within the band. "We were a bit fucked up emotionally," Summers later admitted. "On the point of possible breakup, in fact: for example, Sting was really chafing at the bit to do a movie and hadn't been able to."

Francis Ford Coppola and John Boorman were among the top-flight directors said to be interested in casting Sting—a huge improvement over Franc Roddam and his hacky teen drama *Quadrophenia*. No specific film titles were ever mentioned, but Boorman would probably have been considering *Excalibur*, his 1981 adaptation of Thomas Mallory's Arthurian legend. Sting's schedule wouldn't allow it, though. Instead, the sullen pop star would be relegated to acting out in the studio.

The stress was being applied externally, too. There was an awful lot riding on the commercial success of the next album before it had even been recorded. A&M wanted another Police album in stores before the year was out. The music business was tipping into an industrywide recession. The year 1979 marked the end of a period of unprecedented growth within the music industry. Retail sales, which had doubled from $2 to $4 billion between 1973 and 1978, suddenly slumped dramatically by 20 per cent.

Although A&M at that point was the largest independent record company in the world, it was not immune from the effects of this. In addition to widespread layoffs within the company, there was a cull in the artist roster, from a hundred acts down to forty-five. This, in turn, increased the pressure on the top echelon of the company's high earners. The income from a new Police album that was expected to sell in the millions could potentially make or break the company's finances for the year. And the band was made clearly aware of this state of affairs. Sting recalled an anxious phone call from his A&R at the label: "While I was writing [the album] I was getting messages from the record company saying retailers were waiting for it. I had this impression of thousands of people, cogs in a great system, waiting for this album and I was sitting there struggling. And I got caught up in it, frankly."

Although mindful that an inexorable pressure was beginning to bear down on the Police, Miles Copeland was reluctant to let the pace slacken and watch his boys slide back down the pop music league table. A new world tour was scheduled to start in Belgium at the beginning of August, leaving a window of exactly one month in which to record the entire album for an autumn 1980 release. Even this block of time was not considered sacrosanct. Copeland had planned for the tour to start earlier until he was browbeaten by his baby brother, Stewart, into pushing back the schedule. Despite A&M's continued reservations, the Police again requested that their affable engineer-producer, Nigel Gray, helm the sessions booked at Wisseloord Studio in Hilversum, Netherlands.

Built on a site once occupied by the grand villa housing the command centre of the Nazi Wehrmacht in Holland, Wisseloord had been completed just two years earlier, in 1978. At the time, it was one of the most state-of-the-art recording facilities in the world, and the Police were among the first international groups to record there. "It was a really posh, expensive, decked-out studio," said Gray. "It cost ten times more than what it cost me to build my studio."

The success of the first two Police albums, as well as work for the British duo Godley & Creme, had lent Gray (and Surrey Sound) a certain cachet. A month before heading to Holland, he had completed work on the third album by Siouxsie and the Banshees, *Kaleidoscope*, which he had coproduced with the band. The record would establish the Banshees as one of the premier post-punk groups in the UK. When the Police reconvened with the producer at Wisseloord, they noticed a change in Gray. "He has morphed from the local M.D. in Leatherhead to a rock star," sneered Summers. "His hair is now shoulder length; he wears cowboy boots and a long-fringed jacket." The extent to which Gray felt he was one with the band went even further than that. He had also dyed his hair blond. "Sting actually cut my hair for me," Gray recalled. "He used to cut his own hair so he cut my hair, too, while we were in Hilversum, in a sort of punky style."

With two multimillion-selling Police albums beneath his belt, Gray felt confident enough to try to renegotiate his position with the band ahead of working on the third album. He felt that he was owed a point on the new one and entered into casual discussion with the band about it prior to the start of the sessions. "They said, 'Yeah, we've been discussing that and we thought that was only fair,'" Gray said.

But dealing with the Police was not the same as dealing with their manager. Miles Copeland wasn't prepared to give the producer an inch. When it was suggested that Gray should have a point, Copeland blasted the trio. If they wanted to appease Gray, he suggested, they could give up a percentage of their own royalties, but he was going to do nothing of the sort himself. Gray reported the message Copeland sent back to him via the band as "Tell him to fuck off!"

Duly cowed, the trio offered Gray three-quarters of a point on the album, donating a quarter each, thereby making it clear that Miles Copeland (who had a quarter share of all of the Police's earnings) was the one holdout. Gray rejected the offer out of principle, thinking it derisory. There was talk of letters from the management arriving at Surrey Sound, reminding Gray that he would be a nobody if it wasn't for the Police. He settled for a £25,000 fee in lieu of further negotiations, but that was all he ever got.

When it came to recording a new album, the usual routine was for Stewart Copeland and Sting to bring in home-recorded demos of songs they had written. This time Sting came better prepared than the others. "He had recorded virtually the entire album on his own," said Gray. "He brought all the tapes in and said, 'I just want Stewart to do a bit of drumming on this,' and that was going to be the album." This was the point, Stewart later mused, where Sting's ego had landed: "He arrived with every aspect of his songs fully crystallized to the point of perfection in his mind."

Gray, for one, wasn't having any of it. "I did tell him to fuck off and we were not doing that. And I made him do them all again with the band. He's never spoken to me again." The very thing that had made Gray such an able and amiable collaborator in the studio—his chummy "all for one and one for all" approach to diplomacy and his straight-talking, no-nonsense attitude—had now proved to be his undoing.

"I came down on the side of the Police," he said. "It was fought three to one against Sting. Stewart and Andy were definitely on my side. They wanted it to sound like the Police." But by siding with Copeland and Summers, Gray unwittingly backed Sting into a corner, just as Sting was attempting to consolidate his position as the band's number-one songwriter. Gray had also given the singer an excuse to side with Miles Copeland, who now, like A&M, was looking for an excuse to ditch Gray. It was the last album Gray would produce for the Police.

Gray still holds that he was right to stand up to Sting in order to maintain the integrity of the band. "[The demos] sounded really jazzy and laid-back and had a sort of a sleazy nightclub vibe to them all. So *not* the Police." In fact, Gray maintains, they reminded him of Sting's old band, Last Exit. Summers went one step further. The demos, he said, "sounded like Sly and the Family Stone."

Some were songs that had previously been presented to the band and rejected. "They'd been around for a long time," Summers explained. Sting had merely dusted them off and re-jigged them in his home studio. As the band ground on, this situation would repeat itself several times. Sting had a store of old songs, some dating from his days with Last Exit, to which he still had an emotional attachment. They did nothing for the other two members of the band, yet he would continually re-present the songs at the start of recording for each subsequent album. Gray, however, was not entirely negative about the situation. Working in the studio, typically from noon to midnight, he encouraged the trio to band together and "Policify" the material. This was the term he used to denote the process of putting their stylistic stamp on whatever songs were brought in by the band.

This time, only two contributions from Copeland made the finished record, book-ending both sides of the album. The first, "Bombs Away," was recorded over an existing backing track by Siouxsie and the Banshees that the drummer had found at Surrey Sound studios and sped up to disguise its origin. The song, arch political statement disguised as satire, contained a rather naive assessment of the Soviet invasion and occupation of Afghanistan that had occurred eight months earlier, in December 1979. The lyrics seemed to speak more of Copeland's limited worldview, one shaped by growing up in a family steeped in conspiratorial Cold War politics. Chris Gray remembered going around to Copeland's house in the late seventies and being subjected to a "long stoned theory he'd devised about how the Russians really were coming."

Sting, too, had begun to write songs that attempted to step outside of a world barricaded by self-involvement. He told how "Driven to Tears," his first attempt at writing such a song, was inspired by watching footage of an African famine on TV while he was on tour in America. The song detailed his agonized and self-pitying personal response to this, posing questions but providing no answers. He was on much safer ground with two of the other cuts on the album, which proffered two examples of the showy songwriting style that had brought the Police fame.

One bore the title "De Do Do Do, De Da Da Da." The song was deliberately weighted toward the chorus, rather than toward the verse—during which the title was repeated endlessly to percussive effect until it rammed the melody home. It was an exercise in creating a song that was specifically dumbed down for mass appeal. And that was essentially how it was received. It became the first single by the band to make the top 10 on the Billboard chart, but it also reinforced the impression that the Police were musical stylists with lightweight intellectual pretensions. Sting took umbrage at that characterization, maintaining that the critics had deliberately ignored the content of the verses, which railed against meaningless proclamations and exhortations by poets, the clergy, and political classes and which, to his mind, justified the banality of the chorus. He also claimed that it was an homage to "Da Doo Ron Ron" and "Do Wah Diddy Diddy," the playful pop ditties penned by Barry and Greenwich. But, in this case, the critics were right. The song really was as glib as it seemed.

The other song, "Don't Stand So Close to Me," which would also become a huge hit for the band, stood on perilous ground. It was a narrative song like "Roxanne," also ostensibly about sexual obsession, but this time the forbidden love was between teacher and female pupil, a Lolita obsession. Again, Sting provided the song with a built-in literary reference in case anyone mistook his intention—inserting a clumsy lyric that compared the song's protagonist with the lecherous scholar in Nabokov's book. Many people assumed that the song was drawn from personal experience, from the period Sting had worked as a teacher. Given that he had been teaching five- to seven-year-olds, this seems highly unlikely.

Recording was briefly interrupted so that the Police could headline two massive outdoor shows—one just outside London at the newly opened Milton Keynes Bowl and the other at Leixlip Castle in Dublin, Ireland. The Milton Keynes show—which Miles Copeland christened Rockatta de Bowl—was advertised as a one-day festival with a headline performance by the Police. But it proved not to be the grand event that everyone expected. Although the venue was open for business, it was still under construction. A day and a night of rain had turned it into a mud bath, and the show was far from sold out. The crowd was "vast though scattered," reported one correspondent, with everyone's patience tested by five hours of support acts that included Tom Robinson's band Sector 27, Skafish, UB40, and Squeeze.

When Jim Skafish emerged with his Plantagenet haircut and nose, the crowd became enraged and the heavens opened again, this time with half-filled beer cans that rained down on the Skafish band. They gamely played on for seven numbers until a direct hit left a dent in the head of Jim Skafish that began to bleed profusely.

The Police used the show as an opportunity to road test material from their still-to-be-completed album, and Sting debuted the odd-looking stand-up electric bass with which he would later become synonymous. It was called the Z-bass, and he had acquired it in Holland from its designer, a retired racing-car driver named Henk van Zalinge. But the general feeling was that the band seemed to be only half-present at their own gig. "The Police aren't yet able to match the acclaim their two albums have brought them," concluded a review in *Record Mirror*. "Being there seemed to be enough; not quite delivering an exciting rock show seemingly a matter of no concern."

In short, Mudflatta de Bowl (the name for the event coined by *Sounds*) was a washout. It's likely that Miles Copeland inspired the negative press reception to the show by issuing demands that all of the photographers intending to shoot pictures sign a contract giving the rights to their work over to the Police. The majority refused to sign it. The blame for this breach in protocol was laid at the door of the band's Machiavellian manager. "Is this how the manager of a successful band should behave?" railed an editorial in *Sounds*. "We don't remember him trying to stop people photographing the Police before they were successful. When you consider the role photographers have played in making this band successful, it fair makes you puke, doesn't it?"

At Leixlip Castle, a section of the crowd turned on the band, raining bottles onto the stage. Stewart Copeland took a direct hit that gashed his leg during the show. Sting was clearly unnerved by the reaction. "After the first ten minutes—you saw all the bottles— it was quite a fleeting thing, but there was a bottle thrown at me almost every three minutes, and it's frightening," he told Irish music paper *Hot Press*. "And I had no interest in playing that day after that, or smiling or performing. I'm actually quite a violent person, and I'm not all that gentle, and being absolutely defenceless and being able to do nothing about it—having to stand there for an hour and a half whilst these missiles were thrown at me was the most frustrating thing that's happened to me since . . . since I was born. That day was a nightmare for me. I wanted to kill that day and the day after."

But there was no time for Sting to vent his frustrations. The band returned to the studio, demoralized further by the experience, with just over a week left to knock the album into shape. There was a lot of work to do—they were still several tracks short of a full album and had no hope of extending the deadline. A month-long European tour was scheduled to begin in the second week of August, leading up to the release of the album in October. With the clock ticking, the band was forced to sift through Sting's demos and make the best of what was there. Sometimes it was hard to see the woods for the trees. Gray recalled that the original demo of "Shadows in the Rain" was "a swinging little tune and really corny. I told Sting it was a pile of shit."

Copeland, too, had derided Sting's demo of "Canary in a Coalmine" as "almost candy pop." Even the completed version sounded half-finished. It whizzed along on a sped-up helium-pitch melody, not helped by inane lyrics that found Sting rhyming "Firenze" with "influenza." Even with the inclusion of these songs, the album still clocked in at only just over thirty minutes. What it needed was an instrumental.

Earlier in the sessions, Summers had enjoined Gray to help him work on a track of his own, apart from the others. "He said to me, 'Come on, give me a hand writing a song.' Andy doesn't really write songs, but he sat there, strumming some things. He likes old blues and stuff like that, so he just started singing lyrics that came to the top of his head. They were all just clichés from old blues songs. It was quite obvious that he wasn't going to write a lyric. But he had written this instrumental, so I recorded that for him in the studio."

The track was based around a Middle Eastern-sounding guitar riff that was distinctly out of character for a Police tune. When the song was presented to the rest of the band as a work in progress, Sting flatly refused to play on it. Summers was forced to play the bass parts himself. Copeland agreed with reluctance to put down some parts, "because there wasn't anyone else to play drums." Even then, he would only work on it after hours in a smaller studio at the Wisseloord complex, safely out of sight of the singer.

"Andy thought it was quite good," Gray continued, "but we didn't think for a minute it was going to be on the album. The song wasn't that good and it wasn't the Police; nothing to do with it. So we took the tape and put it into the rubbish pile with all the outtakes."

Many years later, Sting laid claim to sabotaging the track to prevent it from ever seeing the light of day. "I hated that song so much that one day when I was in the studio, I found the tape lying on the table. So I took it around the back of the studio and actually buried it in the garden."

Gray disputed this, claiming that the tape was simply "buried" among all of the outtakes in the monitor room of the studio. "In Hilversum, they didn't give you the tapes in the boxes or on wheels, they were just on the blank hubs, so when you get a little bit of tape, you don't know what was on it. So we had a great pile of outtakes on the floor, none of which were identifiable. They just became spare tape."

But now the band needed the track to complete the album. Gray dutifully dug out the tape, and Summers finished it off by giving it a suitably elliptical title, "Behind My Camel." Gray had an inkling as to what it meant. "[Andy] didn't tell me this himself but I'm ninety-eight per cent sure the reason is this: what would you find behind a camel? A monumental pile of shit."

A year later, to Sting's chagrin and Summers's delight, this "pile of shit" won the Police a Grammy for Best Rock Instrumental. Gray remembered attending the awards show and sitting at a table with the other nominees from the same category. "I was sitting with these ultra, ultra famous serious musicians who were really famous for their instrumentals, and they were shit-hot players who do the best instrumentals in the world," he said, unable to remember who exactly it was. It was most likely Rush, who were also nominated that year for a track on their *Moving Pictures* album. Gray, obviously delighted that the Police had won, regaled his fellow nominees with the story behind the song. "They were sort of amused but pissed off as well," he said.

After several gruelling weeks of nonstop work in the studio, Nigel Gray didn't relish driving his car all the way back to England. He took a flight instead and left the vehicle for a roadie to drive back. Unfortunately, the car contained the master tapes of the new Police album. When customs agents at the UK border spotted a Mercedes limo driven by a suspicious-looking longhair, they pulled the vehicle over to be searched. In the trunk, they found a selection of Amsterdam's finest pornographic magazines (explicit pornography was at that time banned in the UK), along with a canister of two-inch tape prominently marked "The Police." They promptly impounded everything.

"A&M blamed me for that," said Gray, pleading ignorance to any knowledge of customs regulations. "My job was to get the tapes back into England. I didn't know that I actually had to declare them or that they had any essential value. The tapes themselves were worth, what, 20 or 50 quid."

Customs and excise demanded that A&M pay the duty on the perceived value of the tapes containing the new Police album—a figure that Stewart Copeland put at "thirty grand". In an interview several months later, the drummer covered up this farcical incident by putting out the story that the tape seized by customs was actually just scrap tape, while the masters were, at that time, safely stashed at Wisseloord. Yet Gray confirmed that A&M duly paid the duty to retrieve its property. But this was not to be the end of Gray's travails with the tapes.

When he listened again to an acetate cut from the masters, "they sounded really weird. The bottom end was fuzzy and wobbly and there was no punch to anything." Listening to the playback in Wisseloord, he'd had no inkling that this would be the case. "They had these huge monitors there that were the size of a wardrobe," he recalled. "Two wardrobes! And these monitors sounded huge and big and fat. Everything we listened to on them just sounded wonderful. It was like being bathed in this wonderful sound."

"I can remember when we did the vocals on 'Don't Stand So Close to Me,' Sting does his harmonies in one take, and I was listening to all these harmonies and vocals. They were just soaring about the room."

While in thrall to the sound, Gray would pay the price of being out of the comfort zone of his own studio—the only studio he had ever worked in—and feeling his way around unfamiliar equipment in a large commercial studio. What he didn't take into account was that the sound might differ greatly from one studio to another. The damage was done, though. The cutting engineer told Gray that he couldn't rectify the sound imbalance. There was nothing left to do but remix the record. But because the album had been recorded using a European sound desk, which utilized different standards, it needed to be played back with the same equipment. Gray wasn't equipped to do this at Surrey Sound, so Godley & Creme's Strawberry Sound was hired out at great cost. And because A&M was screaming for a finished master that could be delivered to the pressing plant in time for an October release, Gray was compelled to remix the entire record in one night.

"I didn't have time to do a lot of things I would normally do to clean up the sound," he said. "Some of it was nowhere near as good as it should be. I could have done a lot better if there hadn't been the pressure of, 'We need this album tomorrow!' The biggest problem was that was the first album I recorded outside of my own studio. I'm used to my own studio and my own monitors. So when I hear something, I know what it sounds like, and I know it's going to sound the same on a record."

Summers was less discreet in his appraisal of the situation. The problem, he implied, was more chemical than technical. "Large piles of white stuff are placed in front of us," he said. But although he was coy about whether he himself actually indulged, he was not when it came to explaining how it influenced the sound of the production. Cocaine, Summers maintained, "affects your hearing, with the result that the more stoned you become, the more you turn up the high frequencies in the mix." The implication that it was the producer, not the band, who jeopardized the recording process was made clear when he revealed that "compounding this problem are Nigel's disappearances to the red-light district in Amsterdam, and he wants us to go with him."

Chris Gray suggested that his brother's indulgences were what really turned Miles Copeland against him. "He's a very straight, clean-living boy, Miles Copeland," Chris said. "He could almost be a Mormon. He even looks like a Mormon. He would buy three of the same items at a time: three pairs of trousers, three pairs of tops, little black polo necks and things. So, for a whole year, it would look as if he was wearing the same clothes. He'd have one in the wash, one waiting, and he'd be wearing the other one. He looked like John Denver. As clean as John Denver. Never touched any drugs. Would fire anybody in his organization that he found taking drugs—apart from his brother (Stewart), of course, who was smoking all the spliff. Whereas Nigel was the 'Rock Doc.'"

Simply "shooting the engineer" couldn't fix some of the album's other inherent failings. On its release, one critic noted that all but two songs on the record ended with DJ-friendly radio fade-outs. Stewart Copeland later admitted that this was because the band couldn't think of a way to finish them. "It's a kind of cop out, I s'pose," he shrugged. "But it's not serious. I think we can be forgiven for that."

Sting also had a ready answer when quizzed about what was felt to be a lack of coherence in the record. It was decidedly not as polished as the kind of record one expects from a multimillion-selling act. "I don't see albums as unified wholes. I think that's a pretentious idea, a sixties idea, where an album was a concept," he offered. "All I see in an album is a collection of songs, and a fairly random collection too. . . . I think of individual songs, separate from the other songs on the album and from the other albums. The output is just ordered in albums. There's no real plan."

The album would polarize critical opinion—and fan opinion, for that matter, too. There were those who thought the work was a revolutionary new approach to pop music, proof positive that the band's travels around the world had expanded their musical horizons in exciting new ways. *Rolling Stone* praised the use of "exotic modal progressions" and heard the influence of "Balinese monkey chant." Sting's vocal style was compared to the "Moslem call to prayer"—conjuring up the rather bizarre image of millions of Islamists throwing themselves to the ground in the direction of Mecca whenever "De Do Do Do, De Da Da Da" was heard blaring out of tinny transistor radios. Others were not so impressed and deemed the record half-baked. *Creem* magazine insisted that "once you skim off the hits, you're left with uninspired though well-crafted filler," noting that the album's worldwide success probably had more to do with the production than the songs. And sections of the British press took the opportunity to flay the band alive. Julie Burchill, the *NME*'s iron lady, had a field day: "[The album] sounds like something some shyster would dredge up from the vaults—out-takes and such to milk the nostalgia market should the Police meet their maker in an aeroplane disaster." Copeland and Summers, she opined, were obviously "born session-men, shot inappropriately to glory." Sting was similarly dispatched: "When the Police do non-instrumentals, you think maybe singing wasn't such a good idea." And her *coup de grâce*: "Where's Cherry Vanilla now the Police need her?"

A year later, during the press tour for their subsequent album, Sting would finally cop that the album was not all it was cracked up to be: "I think it's a reasonable pop album and I'll defend certain songs on it. It had some good moments—it had some really terrible moments!"

Nevertheless, once Miles Copeland christened the record, the Police had a brand-new product to sell. What was inside the box was irrelevant. The album would go on to be the band's best-selling record to date, racking up more than three million in sales in the States and the

UK alone. But even the naming of their newborn had caused queru-
lous debate among the trio. *Trimondo Blondomina* was Copeland's first
suggestion. But that was vetoed. *Caprido Von Renislam* was rejected
because it was nothing more than the name of the street the studio was
located on. Eventually, they agreed on the suitably inscrutable *Zenyatta
Mondatta*, a stroke of genius on their manager's part because delibera-
tion about what the album's title really meant would rage on all the
way through to the end of their 1981 US tour, becoming a stock question asked by almost every journalist they encountered. The answers
the Police came up with increasingly stretched credulity. *Zenyatta
Mondatta* was the capital city of an obscure African country. A combination of "zen" and the French word for "world" appended with the
name of Kenyan dictator Jomo Kenyatta. It was Sanskrit for "top of
the world"—the Police's position in the pop world pecking order. The
more ridiculous the explanation, the more likely it was to be believed.

"It's an empty bucket into which you can pour your own meaning and discover the meaning of nothingness for yourself," Summers
explained to a gullible female interviewer, during a Canadian TV
report on the band. "All our titles point to the room behind you which
is empty." At least, this was getting closer to the truth. Behind the door,
there was no mystery and no answer, just nothing. And in an April
1981 interview with *Creem* magazine, Summers finally admitted that
"it doesn't mean anything."

By contrast, the photograph that graced the cover of the album
spoke volumes, not only to the band's public image but also to their
private one. Three heads, as chiselled as Mount Rushmore, fantasti-
cally vain and self-important, were arranged in close proximity to
form a pyramid, each half in shadow, glaring out askance at oblique
angles. It said, We are a unit, we are implacable. But it also implied
three people all pulling in different directions.

11

THE NEW WAVE
CRUSADE

Miles Copeland was the P. T. Barnum of new wave: part professional huckster, part consummate showman. He had raised the Police to the giddy heights of rock success; now he would attempt to cast his net across an entire genre of music in one show-stopping stunt. Copeland's vision for new wave was punk rock for the *Porky's* generation, repackaged for college kids with all of the intimidating content taken out. The three-ring circus Copeland used to showcase his mastery of the genre took the form of a movie with a grunt for a title: *Urgh!*

The idea for the film was originally proposed by producer Michael White, who had made *The Rocky Horror Picture Show*. He suggested to Gil Friesen, the US head of A&M, filming a transatlantic battle of the bands between the States and the UK. Friesen in turn suggested that White talk to Miles and Ian Copeland. With their transatlantic business connections, the Copeland brothers were exactly the right people to put the project together. They were employed (and in fact credited) as creative consultants on the film. But their stamp is all over the film, from the selection of the bands—many of which were drawn from existing IRS and F.B.I rosters—to the presentation itself.

Ian Copeland set up eleven shows at ten different venues in the States and the UK over the course of August and September 1980. Two nights were booked at the three-thousand-person capacity Santa Monica Civic Auditorium, as well as one-off shows at iconic venues such as the Whisky A Go-Go and CBGB in the States and Hammersmith Odeon and the Rainbow Theatre in the UK. A large outdoor show at the Fréjus Amphitheatre in Provence, France, which the Police headlined, was also filmed. Their performances book-ended the film, giving the impression that the band was the leader of this new wave.

It was a huge undertaking: a film version of Miles Copeland's ill-fated Startruckin' 75 tour. Only this time, instead of flying bands and equipment around the world, Copeland sent the camera crew out on tour along with the film's director, Derek Burbidge, who was once again brought on board by Copeland. Other partners in the film included TV production companies Lorimar (the producers of *Dallas*) and Filmways (the company behind *The Beverly Hillbillies* and *The Addams Family*). The unorthodox nature of the film's funding was also reflected in its distribution. Rather than opening like a traditional movie, *Urgh!* was sent out on tour like a band, playing two or three consecutive nights at independent cinemas around the US. It was advertised with a poster featuring three punk rockers wearing Civil War uniforms and the lightning flash make-up synonymous with David Bowie's *Aladdin Sane* character. One held a pipe, the other a drum, and the last flew a flag. The poster was emblazoned with the command "Stand Up and Dance!"

The finished project was curiously flat, possibly the result of having to cram performances from thirty-five odd bands into a feature-length movie. Even the most dynamic of performers, like the Cramps, Devo, and Klaus Nomi, were rendered impotent by the workmanlike editing and odd choices of camera angles—wide-angle shots of the stage from way out in the audience were cut against extreme close-ups that created a disorientating sense of space. There was also an awful lot of filler from punk rock bands whose only claim to fame would prove to be their appearance in *Urgh!*

In at least three cases, Copeland used *Urgh!* as a pitch to make advances to bands he was interested in signing to IRS, promising an appearance in the film as a sweetener to negotiations. The ploy worked with Queens band the Fleshtones, as well as with the Dead Kennedys. In retrospect, front man Jello Biafra is convinced that the Dead Kennedys were put on the bill only for this reason.

Pointedly, the debut album by the Dead Kennedys, *Fresh Fruit for Rotting Vegetables*, would be the one and only release on IRS that Jerry Moss personally vetoed. He didn't want A&M to have any kind of association with the group. To get around the A&M ban, Copeland initiated an American wing of his Faulty Products label to release the album. (Initial pressings of the record gave the game away by listing the same Los Angeles address for Faulty Products as for A&M Records.)

Biafra claimed that Moss reached his decision because he was "a yachting buddy of the Kennedy family." But he also maintained that the intention behind the band's name was not meant to impugn the reputation of the Kennedys, "so much as to call attention to what happened after they were killed." In a British television interview with Jools Holland to promote the album, he explained that he wanted people to question "why people in this country [the States] turned more and more inward and became more and more self-centred and as a result set themselves up to be the corporate serving rodents that they are today. I think the Kennedy family killings are the source of what's called the 'Me generation' in this country."

Ironically, Biafra was just about to get into bed with his ideological enemy. With its exhortations to "Kill the Poor" and "Lynch the Landlord," the Dead Kennedys' debut seemed like an exceedingly odd record for Copeland to want to release. Until, that is, you take into account that Biafra was a fellow zealot and political animal, albeit of a different stripe, and that there was common ground between his and Copeland's anticorporate and libertarian beliefs. Despite Biafra's leftist leaning, Miles Copeland, freedom-loving advocate of

American democracy that he was, would no doubt have approved wholeheartedly of the sentiment behind a song like "California Uber Alles," which Biafra said "warns of fascism in disguise. It's not a pro-Nazi song in any way."

The alliance, though, did not last long. Biafra started up his own Alternative Tentacles label, the initial releases from which were also distributed through Faulty Products. The band soon fell out with Copeland over a seemingly trivial matter: a redesign of their album cover that they did not approve of.

Another group that was signed in the aftermath of their appearance in *Urgh!* were the Go-Go's, an all-girl rock band from L.A. that had been a fixture on the West Coast punk scene for several years. The Go-Go's weren't the first all-female rock band—that distinction goes to early-seventies group Fanny and, later, the Runaways—but the Go-Go's captured the imagination of the press, garnering enough buzz behind them to propel them to far greater heights than their forebears. Their official IRS bio sold them as "Sheer Unadulterated Fun." Copeland and Boberg were interviewed for a full-page article in the *Los Angeles Times* titled "IRS Records Gets Up for the Go-Go's," in which they offered details of the label's marketing strategy for the band.

"If we hype them, the Go-Go's could come across as Coca-Cola," Boberg explained. "Word on this band has to come up from the streets, so their tour will take them to Ann Arbor and Orlando and Kansas City as well as New York and Boston. They're going to play to four hundred people in tiny clubs and talk to out-of-the-way street newspapers and go into record stores because that supports the structure that IRS is built on."

Their debut album, *Beauty and the Beat*, was produced by Richard Gottehrer. As well as being the cofounder of Sire Records, Gottehrer had written the Crystals' classic sixties girl group cut "My Boyfriend's Back" and, more recently, had produced the debut album by Blondie. He lent the Go-Go's album, which was made up of songs that were all written by the band, a commercial pop sheen. When the second single, "We Got the Beat," climbed to the number-two spot on the Billboard charts in

January 1982, it took the album (which had debuted the previous July) with it. The Go-Go's became the first all-girl band to score a number-one album on the Billboard charts.

Within a year, they were selling out the same-size venues in the United States as the Police, whom they were also supporting on tour. An article by Robert Hilburn in the *Los Angeles Times* noted that the band had to drop off the Police tour before it got to L.A. to avoid cannibalizing their own headlining concert at the same venue—the eighteen-thousand-person-capacity Inglewood Forum—later the same month. Critically, the success of the group put IRS on the map and finally gave it some legitimacy in the American marketplace. From then on, IRS would be the most visible label associated with new wave music.

In London, Andy Czezowski of the Roxy had noted with withering sarcasm that Miles Copeland thought he could take over the UK punk scene. And similarly, when it became clear that "new wave" was the new game in town, Copeland grabbed the ball and ran with it. "IRS was visible because there were a lot of people in the room and we were the only ones waving the flag," he said. "There was nobody else. There were a couple of other Mickey Mouse labels jerking around, but nobody serious."

Some of the other labels he might have been referring to were SST (the label founded by Greg Ginn of L.A. hardcore band Black Flag) and Slash (which grew out of a fanzine of the same name), both based in Los Angeles. There was also Michael Zilkha's ZE Records in New York and 415 Records in San Francisco. All four might have been small-fry in business terms compared to Copeland's label, which had major label backing where the others did not, but they had both a musical aesthetic and a core audience. IRS had neither. What it did have was brand identity and a logo that made it extremely visible—a silhouette of a man in black who seemed more CIA than IRS.

On closer inspection, there didn't seem to be much of a consistent thread tying together the acts on IRS It was a grab bag of eccentrics and weirdos who would probably not have found a record deal anywhere else, thrown together with the most puritan of indie bands—like garage rock group the Fleshtones—and acts that Copeland picked up in the UK that he felt had a good chance of achieving cult success in the States. A few of the signings were inspired—namely, the Go-Go's and the Cramps—and some were inexplicable. Copeland even put out an album by Renaissance, the British prog-folk group he had managed in the seventies prior to the Police (singer Annie Haslam was a former girlfriend). He also scooped a few other old-timers left stranded without a record deal, including a reformed lineup of the original Animals. Some of the groups he signed would not bear fruit until their tenure at IRS was over. This occurred most notably with a band of college students from Athens, Georgia, who came to him by way of recommendation from Ian Copeland and who laboured under the oblique name of R.E.M.

On one level, IRS Records provided an outlet for Miles Copeland to play out all of his Colonel Tom Parker/P. T. Barnum fantasies of orchestrating a grand rock 'n' roll spectacle; on another, he felt that he was fostering a cultural revolution. British director Julien Temple (who had overseen the Sex Pistols film *The Great Rock 'n' Roll Swindle*) posited the idea that punk in the UK was concerned with shattering the illusion of (and sweeping away) the last vestiges of empire in British society. "By the end of the Second World War [the British empire] was no longer a reality," he said. "But kids were still taught in England to think that they were the chosen race, the sons of Empire. But the reality was, at the end of the seventies, there were a lot of kids being taught this stuff but when they left school, there was nothing for them."

The punk era would be hugely influential for many years to come—both as a musical and a motivational force. But what it chiefly inspired was more people to start bands. On an ideological level, it largely failed, and the genre that it morphed into, namely, new wave—which was no more than a commercialized version of punk—helped re-establish the primacy of rock 'n' roll in the marketplace. In keeping with Temple's analogy, new wave represented the resumption of the old order, the continuation of empire, but this time it was the American empire. When Miles Copeland talked with apparent earnestness about the transformative power of rock 'n' roll as a means to spread the gospel of American democracy around the world, critics (particularly, British critics) thought he was joking. But that wasn't the case at all.

The Games Player, one of several memoirs by Miles Copeland II (the father of the Police manager and his brothers) that detailed his experiences in the spy world, is instructive in helping to define the mind-set of the Copeland brothers. The spy chief recalled how his number-one son, Miles Axe Copeland III, once created an "intellectual exercise" for the two of them to work on together. They would produce a policy paper with the working title "A Dozen Ways to Destroy America," game-playing the ways that Soviet spies would seek to infiltrate and undermine the US political system, based on exactly the same techniques that the CIA had used while attempting to do the self-same thing to the Russians. "He said he wanted an idea of how solid, right-thinking Americans such as himself would see the dangers," Copeland the elder said of his son's motivation.

For some time, Miles paid his father a stipend to keep "a diary of political markets" while working from his suite in the Wardman Park Towers on Connecticut Avenue in Washington, D.C., in order to see whether they could infer "patterns of cause and effect" that would enable them to make sound financial investments in the currency markets to further increase the family fortune. Without any apparent levity on his part, the elder Copeland relayed his son's hope that "he might one day put Hollywood behind him to become Secretary of State"—suggesting that behind the curtain of entertainment lay political ambitions. There was no separation of the two. The Police manager was a political animal who worked toward fulfilling the agenda that was required to sustain his belief system. His approach to business was as bellicose and militaristic as his politics.

Waving the flag of "new wave" was synonymous with waving the flag for American democracy. In this respect, the actual content of the records Copeland was releasing through his International Record Syndicate was irrelevant. The medium was the message. The genre would transmit the gene that stimulated new outgrowths in stagnant cultures. And once this took hold in America, the idea was to propa-

gate it in other countries and other cultures that might be antithetical to the idea buried within its form: Western freedom. If punk was
a musical revolution, then new wave was a crusade in the form of a
meme. In the words of eighties British synth pop one-hit wonder
Re-Flex (which Copeland also managed), the music was driven by
"the politics of dancing, the politics of feeling good."

In "Soviet Crusade against Pop," a 1985 essay for an edition of the
academic journal *Popular Music*, Terry Bright outlined the critical
mass of resistance building up within a new wave of youth-driven,
frivolous rock music that had swept the Soviet Union and the dangers
that posed to the hegemony of Soviet order:

> It was the New Wave groups that occupied the centre stage
> of Soviet Pop in the eighties, and they proved to be the big-
> gest shock so far for the authorities. Although they shunned
> the bad language of the punks and were more conventionally
> dressed (business suits, dark glasses and short hair, in the style
> of Madness), they were more of a threat because of their music,
> which was of excellent quality, fun and danceable, and because
> of the sharp irony and accurate realism of everything they sang,
> said or did.

This new musical movement seemed so persuasive and urgent to
this generation of Soviet youth that within a year, new groups were
forming at the eastern extent of the Soviet Union. Even something
as seemingly innocuous as songs about love, another popular theme
of the Soviet New Wave, caused the authorities anxiety. Prevailing
Soviet propaganda called for harmonious and lifelong male-female
relationships, but the love songs performed by the new wave groups
were characterized by a hard-nosed cynicism about affairs of the heart.
They were also distinctly macho. Bright cited a song by a popular
band from Leningrad called Zoo about "a girl whose only virtues are
a love of sensual pleasure" and another by a group from Riga called
"Train Has Left" that defined the "ideal girl" as "one who eats so little
that a guy on a state salary can afford her."

Stewart Copeland
and future wife,
Sonja Kristina, with
Curved Air, 1974.
Getty Images

Andy Summers
(left) with the Kevin
Coyne Band, 1975.
Getty Images

The original line-up of the Police: Stewart Copeland (centre), Sting and French guitarist Henry Padovani, London, 1977. *Peter Baylis/Rex Features*

The Police sign their US deal with A&M in New York, November 1978. *Getty Images*

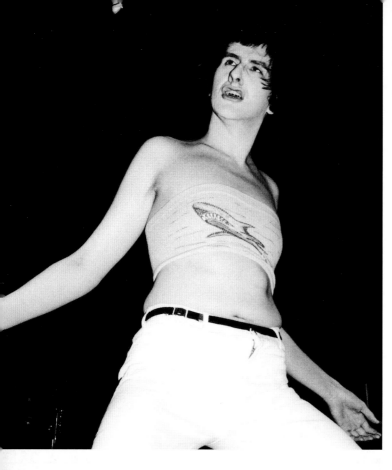

Jim Skafish, the 'Tiny Tim of new wave', onstage at the Whiskey-A-Go-Go, Los Angeles, February 1978.
© David Arnoff

The Cramps and producer Alex Chilton recording *Songs the Lord Taught Us*, A&M Studios, Los Angeles, 1979.
© David Arnoff

A rarely seen image from one of Sting's early pre-Police modelling jobs for girls' magazine *Patches*.   *Reprinted with permission from DC Thomson publishing.*

A 1979 comic strip about the rise of Sting and the Police from British boys' weekly *Buddy. Reprinted with permission from DC Thomson publishing.*

Sting onstage at the Whiskey-A-Go-Go, Los Angeles, January 1979.
© David Arnoff

Andy Summers onstage at the Whiskey-A-Go-Go, Los Angeles, January 1979. *© David Arnoff*

The Police with Jerry Moss (centre) and Herb Alpert (right) backstage at the Whiskey-A-Go-Go, January 1979. *© David Arnoff*

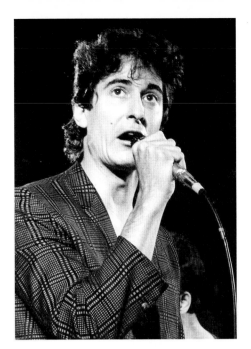

Stan Ridegway of Wall of Voodoo (above) and
Stiv Bators (right) at the Urgh! A Music War
concert, Santa Monica Civic, Los Angeles,
August 1980. © *David Arnoff*

Miles Copeland checks out the acts at the Urgh! A Music War concert, August 1980.
© *David Arnoff*

Stewart Copeland arrives at Narita airport,
Tokyo, February 1980. © *Akihiro Takayama*

The Police jamming in the studio at Alfa
Records, their Japanese label, Tokyo,
February 1980. © *Akihiro Takayama*

The Police in concert at Nakano Sun Plaza,
Tokyo, February 1980. © *Akihiro Takayama*

Sting meets female admirers after the
show at the Nakano Sun Plaza, Tokyo,
February 1980. © *Akihiro Takayama*

Happily married? Sting and wife Frances Tomelty pose outside the High Court in London during the court action against Virgin Publishing, July 1982. *Getty Images*

Four days after denying the existence of his 'mystery blonde girlfriend' onstage in Gateshead, Sting and Trudie Styler are photographed together at Stringfellows in London, August 1982. *Getty Images*

Is this the moment Sting decided to bid adieu to his bandmates? The Police play Shea Stadium, New York, in August 1983 as part of their *Synchronicity* tour. *Getty Images*

The Police play in Atlanta, Georgia, after reforming for Amnesty International's Conspiracy of Hope tour in June 1986. *Getty Images*

The Copeland brothers (Miles, Stewart and Ian) at an IRS Records-sponsored benefit for the American Cancer Society in New York, December 1985. *Getty Images*

Sting in Paris, April 1989, with Kayapo indian chief, Raoni, whom he took on tour with him to promote his newly-formed 'Rainforest Foundation'. *Sipa Press/Rex Features*

The Police play the final show of their reunion tour at Madison Square Gardens in New York, August 7 2008. *Debra L. Rothenberg/Rex Features*

The phenomenon of a "new wave" of homegrown rock music challenging the *diktat* of authoritarian regimes was not only limited to the Soviet Union. China saw the rise of *yaogun yinyue* in the mid-eighties, a genre based on Western rock music whose chief features were "its 'oppositional lyrics' (thinly veiled criticisms of life in modern China) and 'aggressive sound.'" In Argentina, then under the rule of a military junta, the music produced by the *rock nacional* movement began to exhibit the influence of US and UK new wave rock. It was transformed, Argentine sociologist Pablo Vila contended, into the idea of "rock as a form of life, as a daily concern, as ideology, as the sphere of the self, as a valid interlocutor, as a practice of freedom," and it utilized "the concert as the principal channel of participation." The live show was the forum by which the artist could communicate directly with members of the audience, exhort them to dance and scream and express the freedom of thought and action that would ordinarily not be permitted in daily life. It's no coincidence, then, that when the Police undertook their offroad world tour in early 1980, Sting continually exhorted audiences to get up and dance in the face of an intimidating police presence at the shows.

The extent to which conservative thought and politics guided Copeland's ambitions in the music industry probably owes more to his adherence to the principle of "moral self-interest" rather than any kind of grand neo-con conspiracy. A lynchpin of conservative thinking (according to cognitive linguist George Lakoff), "moral self-interest" holds that if everyone was free to pursue his or her own self-interest, then this would also serve the self-interest of the body politic. It's unlikely that Copeland's concept of the new wave had any direct influence on the emergence of these extraneous musical movements, but he was certainly in sympathy with its aims. Copeland had spied a trend—the corporate cooptation of punk rock—and seized an opportunity.

In 1982, the Canadian Broadcasting Company ran a radio report on punk rock in Canada, which featured an interview with Brad Weir, an executive at Columbia Records Canada about the marketing of punk in America. "You wait for it to get to a point where it has some effect on the masses," Weir explained, revealing the depths of the cynicism that pervaded the record industry in the service of capital. "You wait till it looks as if it's something that can be marketed to the masses."

The politics of a social phenomenon such as the British punk movement, born of economic and class frustrations in the early seventies, had no commercial value, Weir explained. He cited the Sex Pistols' poor record sales in the US market as proof. "Suburbanites don't understand it," he continued. "What do you want them to do, go out and blow up their lawn-boys? They can't identify. They might buy the thing once just to check it out, but their lifestyle isn't going to change just because of it."

The show's reporter noted that while "punk" was clearly a no-go for consumers, "the new music trends that followed punk, while still innovative, were largely de-politicized and could be effectively packaged and sold."

New wave was that trend. It wasn't just depoliticized but also homogenized and declawed so that it could be absorbed within the hegemonic culture, which by the early eighties had taken on a marked swing to the right. Just as the Police found their footing in the free enterprise culture of Thatcher's Britain, new wave established its foothold during the Reagan era, with its bellicose politics and its brash promotion of America and American values, both at home and abroad.

The corporate pasteurization of punk rock into new wave also coincided with the drive to find a new format for rock music that would challenge the dominance of disco. In 1978, A&M, which prior to its association with Miles Copeland had little or no legitimacy in the youth music market, issued a sampler album to raise awareness of its younger and hipper acts: the Police, the Stranglers, Squeeze, Joe Jackson, and the Dickies. The album bore the title *No Wave: A Musical Dip into the Ocean of Contemporary Sounds*. The cover featured an androgynous punker girl with spiky orange hair, dressed in a black shirt and trousers with a skinny tie and leopard-print socks. She is surfing on an ironing board. The promotional material for the album bore the slogan: "No Wave. Nothing clever to say, just some place to say it."

The record was also released in a picture disc edition. On one side was printed the album cover art; on the other, a slice of pizza. It was rock music as junk food: mass-produced and easy to swallow, it tasted good but was probably bad for you. Even the use of the picture disc format itself, which became increasingly popular as a marketing gimmick in the early eighties, gives an indication of a shift in the priorities of the music industry from music to product. Everything had to be packaged as "new": new wave, new pop, new romantic— the latter two genres both emerged from Britain and were essentially subsets of new wave. They included groups such as Culture Club, Duran Duran, Tears for Fears, and the Eurythmics, who enjoyed phenomenal chart success on both sides of the Atlantic and formed what became known as the "second British invasion" of America. This advance was trumpeted on a January 1984 cover of *Newsweek*, which featured a photograph of Boy George and Annie Lennox under the headline "Britain Rocks America—Again."

Dave Rimmer, a former journalist for eighties pop magazine *Smash Hits*, attempted a definition of new pop in his book *Like Punk Never Happened*, a contemporaneous account of the rise of Culture Club and associated acts. He decided that it was the product of a "generation that had come of age during punk, absorbed its methods, learnt its lessons, but ditched its ideals." New pop and new romanticism were both heavy on style and light on substance, taking the garish, riotous colours of punk rock fashion and recasting it as carefree, day-glo pop.

The thematic differences between punk and new wave (and post-punk and new pop) could be clearly discerned, claimed cultural studies academic Lawrence Grossberg, by comparing the lyrics of two specific songs, one from each genre—respectively, Gang of Four's "Anthrax" and the Human League's "Love Action." Both presented very different takes on the subject of love. The Gang of Four song offered a straightforward proposition—that a dose of love could kill like anthrax—negating the consensus view and dispelling any trace of sentimentality. By comparison, the Human League song set up a series of contradictions within its lyrics that remained unresolved and offered no firm commitment. A belief in truth and the temptation to lie. A belief in love but not in God. Love without lust and sex without physical contact. "In the universe of the Human League," Grossberg explained, "it doesn't matter whether one believes in the truth and lies, or doesn't believe in the truth and lies, or doesn't believe in the truth and never lies. It is all inscribed on the slippery surface because any content or depth puts one at risk of being coopted."

The nonchallenging nature of this slickly produced, attractively packaged pop enabled it to slip into the mainstream without resistance or confrontation. The phenomenal success of acts like Culture Club, Human League, ABC, and the Eurythmics gave rise to another wave of British groups (like Flock of Seagulls) who followed in their wake, diluting the new pop formula even further. The songs moved from coy and ambiguous to inane and banal. The apogee of new pop was the rise of Kajagoogoo, a British group whose name derived from baby talk.

At this point, American critic Robert Christgau was moved to decry all the talk of a second British invasion as "basically bullshit," an Anglophile delusion wherein "every pale-faced new youth on MTV is taken for a conquering hero." It was—to paraphrase the title of the *Village Voice* column in which Christgau made his assertions—"the music biz on a joyride" to re-establish the dominance of pop music, a "reactive return to normalcy." What it was reacting to was another strain of music that was far more difficult to contain.

Not all new wave music was without merit or without teeth, and not all of it had the desire to conform. In truth, the same tendencies within the culture that sought to smother anything that gave off a whiff of radicalism had also given rise to one of the strangest periods in popular music, during which it seemed as if the floodgates had been opened for all manner of freaks to invade the airwaves—precisely the kind of acts Andy Summers would have probably described as "no-chance weirdness." Yet this was also music that was acutely self-aware and self-conscious.

The vanguard of new wave not only set out to re-establish the primacy of rock 'n' roll's primitive energy—which had also been the aim of both the UK and American punk scenes—but cast itself as a leap so far into the future that it was almost unrecognizable. Crucially, the new wave acts who seemed to be on the cutting edge were formed pre-punk, not post-punk. At its most challenging, this was art rock that took complex ideas and stretched them over primitive forms. Possibly the most radical of them all was Devo, a sextet formed at Kent State University, Ohio, in 1973, who were inspired in equal parts by the post-modernist theories of Foucault, Derrida, and Lacan and a bizarre 1924 illustrated pamphlet titled "Jocko-Homo Heavenbound" that railed against creationism—one of several such religious tracts written by a Methodist minister called Bertram Henry Shadduck.

Devo began life as an arch commentary on the war between modernism and fundamentalism (whether in religion, science, or art) that assumed the form it aimed to critique. Devo was more than just a rock group; it was performance art, a satire on corporate identity and commercial branding. In interviews, they expounded on their theory that the human species was engaged in a process of de-evolution (hence Devo) and de-individualization, heading toward a bright new future as a formless, thoughtless mass. To this end, the group even adopted identical, utilitarian uniforms of lab coats and radiation suits and donned plastic pompadours and red flowerpot hats.

Musically, Devo ploughed a similar off-kilter groove to two other early seventies bands also from Ohio: Rocket from the Tombs and the Electric Eels, both of whom are often cited as "proto-punk." The Electric Eels, in particular, sounded positively unhinged and possibly even dangerous. By 1975, the group had already imploded. They never saw the inside of a recording studio and played only a handful of gigs in their three-year existence, most of which (legend has it) were poorly attended and often ended in violence, either through altercations between band members or with their audience. Their prime motivation as a group was to provoke, and one of the most effective tools at their disposal was their music, which they claimed was an attempt to recreate the sounds of Sun Ra, Albert Ayler, and John Cage but, to the uninitiated, sounded like a disordered and discordant noise re-constructed from the broken shards of rock 'n' roll. Among their repertoire was a deranged version of the Jan and Dean surf classic "Dead Man's Curve," in which the tragic aspects of the song were amplified by Eels front man Dave E's whiny, crybaby vocals.

Devo also took to reworking the classics, including a version of the Rolling Stones song "(I Can't Get No) Satisfaction" on their 1978 debut album, *Q: Are We Not Men? A: We Are Devo!* In his 2004 essay "Performing the Avant-Garde Groove," Syracuse University music history professor Theo Cateforis describes how the group reduced the song to "an absurd procession of minimalist, stunted riffs and nervous vocals." As if to confirm their intentions to turn the song inside out, the band even retitled the track as "Satisfaction (I Can't Get No)." Devo often used time signatures (like 7/8) that sought to defy the established conventions of pop music while also attempting to recode them. "Those kind of timings actually make you feel rigid right away," said Gerard Casale, Devo's guitarist and founding member. "They give you that stiff, non-gut feeling to make you get into it on a whole different level than you would on a normal 4/4 beat that people just take for granted." As long as the beat remained steady, Casale explained, the disharmonious elements of the music—the bits that sounded "off"—would be reincorporated into the rhythm no matter what the time signature.

That jerkiness and rigidity would come to be one of the defining characteristics of new wave music, along with a mechanized vocal style that was consciously clipped of emotion and drew attention to its lack of soul. It played instead on its artificiality and a sense of dis-engagement that seemed to embody the anxiety of the modern age.

The most extreme form of this appeared in the persona and performance style of New York artist Klaus Nomi, who, like Devo, had emerged from an art background and crossed over into music. Born Klaus Sperger in Germany, Nomi arrived in the States in 1972 and found employment as a pastry chef in the World Trade Center. He also involved himself in the downtown art scene, appearing in productions by Charles Ludlam's Ridiculous Theater Company and a 1978 performance art event called "New Wave Vaudeville" that took place over four nights at Max's Kansas City and marked the first appearance of his Klaus Nomi persona.

Nomi drew attention away from his rapidly receding heart-shaped hairline by styling his remaining hair into a three-point crown. He shaved off half of his eyebrows until they looked like two accents shooting away from the bridge of his nose. His face was painted white and his lips were painted black and drawn into an angular pout, like Otto Dix's celebrated portrait of Weimar Republic dancer Anita Berber. Nomi's body was usually encased in exaggerated costumes that looked like geometrical forms. Although he appeared asexual and androgynous, he sang in a piercing mezzo-soprano voice. The total effect was quite alienating. Nomi did not look human and he did not act like a human. "Some people think I'm not human," he bemoaned. "That's why I can't eat, can't have sex, I can't burp, I can't do anything really."

Despite its peculiarities, new wave spread rapidly from coast to coast and all points in between with the help of music television, the speed at which it established itself accelerated by its conscious attachment to eighties consumer culture. In Grossberg's view this was because new wave rock seemed to "reaffirm pleasure as resistance but cannot escape its own desire for commercial success." In other words, new wave (and the oft-times superficial radicalism it affected) was compromised by its need for validation in the marketplace.

Compared to all this activity, Miles Copeland's stable of acts at IRS seemed incredibly staid and conventional. Its only concession to art rock was a cult group from Atlanta, Georgia, called R.E.M., whose musical output seemed as vague and ill-defined as their name. The title of a 1989 retrospective IRS compilation aptly summed up the label's conception of "new wave": *These People Are Nuts!* The label's public image was largely defined by a painfully self-conscious frat boy humour.

Although Copeland seemed genuinely excited by acts like the Cramps and Lords of the New Church, he didn't really "get" them. His conservative worldview provided only a limited perspective on what they were really about. Lords' guitarist Brian James explained that while Copeland "wanted a wild and crazy band, he didn't want all the problems that came with a wild and crazy band." In short, he wanted to shoehorn them into his conception of wild and crazy. In Copeland's eyes, rock 'n' roll was nothing more than entertainment, and he was focused entirely on the business of entertainment. The idea that for people like Bators and the Cramps, musical expression also went hand in hand with a lifestyle was antithetical to the puritanical aspect of Copeland's character.

In 1985, Copeland thought it would be a gas if Stiv Bators recorded a version of Madonna's "Like a Virgin." Not too long after the song had become a huge worldwide hit, Copeland corralled Bators and James to attend a late-night studio session to record their parts over a prerecorded backing track. The Lords of the New Church broke away from Copeland shortly afterward. "Miles has got a lot of good ideas and he's got a lot of crap ideas," said Brian James, "but unfortunately the people that work around him are basically yes-men, so he never knows his good ideas from his bad ideas, because nobody has the bollocks to tell him."

These kinds of problems did not present themselves to Copeland when he worked with the Police, whose ambitions mirrored his own. But those with a clear musical vision, as well as a vision of how they wanted to present themselves, inevitably clashed with Copeland's autocratic style. Stewart Copeland described his brother-manager as "good on overall strategy but bad on important details—like the time I needed my drum kit for a TV show and found he'd lent it to Gene October for a Chelsea gig."

One of the "important details" that Miles Copeland was consistently bad at was the prompt and accurate payment of royalties. IRS, like Faulty and BTM before it, seemed to be plagued by cash-flow problems when it came to settling up with its artists. Copeland's relationship with the Fall, whose first two albums were released by Step Forward in the UK, broke down for exactly that reason. Following the release of their second album, *Dragnet*, in October 1979, the group jumped onto Rough Trade. "Miles is basically honest," maintained Nick Jones, his second in command at BTM and Faulty. But there was a caveat to that statement. "He's gonna take your money, but he tells you—it's dead honest, that," said the Fall's manager Kim Carroll.

In early 1980, the Fall's Mark E. Smith was still sanguine about the faults of the label. Copeland had, after all, given them the opportunity to release their music when no one else was interested. "Step Forward aren't too bad," he said. "They continuously owe us money, but that's the price you pay for freedom. We have final say in everything—art, ads (if any!!), tracks, studio producer."

By 1985, Smith's patience had run out. In an interview with a British fanzine, Smith described Copeland as a "glorified con man." "He's never paid us any royalties in five years from *Dragnet,*" Smith railed. "He just paid us two weeks ago." But not before the singer had already seen fit to vent his frustrations in song, inserting a sly swipe into a track called "What You Need Is" (on the Fall's 1985 album, *This Nation's Saving Grace*). To get on in the music industry, Smith determined, what one needed was a book written by the brothers Copeland called *Theft Is Vision*. He later described this as a "private joke."

Mark E. Smith wasn't the only musician who felt moved to decry his experience with Copeland. Stan Ridgway of Wall of Voodoo put down his feelings about his association with IRS in song. Copeland had signed Wall of Voodoo in 1980 after seeing them support the Cramps in Los Angeles. Ridgway, in his song "Talking about Wall of Voodoo Blues," described Copeland as a shark (referring to him only as a "big manager" of Sting rather than by name) and told of being enticed to sign a voluminous contract on the promise of future fame and riches but receiving just a dollar per song.

Ridgway's main gripe, though, was said to be with comanager Mike Gormley, who also appeared in the song in reference to the group's slot at the 1983 US Festival, an ill-fated Labor Day music event that Apple Computer cofounder Steve Wozniak sank up to $8 million of his own money into. In the song, Ridgway claimed the band was paid a forty-thousand-dollar fee for their appearance but that they didn't see a penny of it. After this show, Ridgway and three other members walked out of the band. Ridgway released one solo album on IRS in

1986 before moving to Geffen (IRS continued to release Ridgway's albums in the UK until several years later).

While it's clear that Copeland was extremely pro-artist in his own way, he also did himself no favours by seeking to wield executive control over large swathes of the careers of some of the musicians he worked with. To complement his record companies. Copeland expanded his activities, setting up a raft of other companies in both the UK and the United States that included no less than six different music publishing companies (all later consolidated under the umbrella Bugle Publishing Group). Another company with a waggish acronym, L.A.P.D. (Los Angeles Personal Direction), was established in 1982 to handle his management concerns. He wooed Gormley, who had been president of marketing and promotion at A&M (as well as assistant to Jerry Moss), to head that company. They started out representing the Police and Oingo Boingo.

Drawn in by Copeland's passion, groups were often persuaded to sign some combination of recording, publishing, and management deal. The Lords of the New Church were one such band. Although front man Stiv Bators famously held a conspiratorial view of the world, he apparently thought nothing of putting his career in the hands of a man whose family was synonymous with the CIA. But Bators learned the hard way. In 1986, a full year after the Lords had split from Copeland, one of their songs ended up on the IRS-released soundtrack for *Texas Chainsaw Massacre 2*. Bators had a simple explanation for this: "Well, Miles (Copeland) is our manager, publisher, and ex-record company. So our manager approached our publisher, who approached his record company."

In at least one case, Copeland seemed to be up to his old tricks again. When Jim Skafish overran the minuscule budget assigned to record his debut album for IRS, he was persuaded to relinquish 50 per cent of his publishing on the album to Copeland in return for the funds he needed to complete it. When the Cramps challenged their royalty statements by filing suit against IRS in 1981, they were left in the lurch for two years while they battled Copeland in court to get out of their contract with IRS.

"Miles loved the Cramps," said guitarist Kid Congo Powers, who admitted to taking little interest in the band's business affairs while he played with them. "I could tell he really loved the Cramps. But I guess they didn't love him back! He was also a very staunch businessman so I think there was a bit of a war going on. I figured that he couldn't work out why they were mad at him. That's what I gathered from my seat far away in the back row of Cramps land. And so Miles played hardball with them."

It was a war of attrition. Locked into their contract while the suit remained unresolved, the Cramps were unable to record any new material. Their only means of support during this period was playing live. But even then, they were hampered. "The Cramps were so heavily bootlegged at the time that anything they did was immediately on vinyl a week later and then widely distributed," said Powers. "So we didn't play any more new original material, just a lot of cover songs. It was actually very stressful."

At the same time, Copeland sought to continue profiting from the band during the period of their contract, releasing *Off the Bone*, a compilation of deleted singles, without their participation or approval. In November 1983, close to two years after the Cramps had originally filed suit, the group reached an out-of-court settlement with Copeland that freed them from their contract.

What the situation with the Cramps revealed was that Copeland, like his father, could either be the staunchest of allies or the most incorrigible enemy. There was no in-between. The "syndicate" in International Record Syndicate started to take on a very different connotation. Loyalty was rewarded with largesse, betrayal with an intransigence that amounted to a blockade. Copeland, given his tireless enthusiasm for the Cramps, had almost certainly taken the lawsuit they filed against IRS as a personal affront and used his considerable muscle to crush them into submission.

After scoring a second gold album for the label with *Vacation*, the Go-Go's also filed suit against IRS in 1982 over a royalty dispute. The Go-Go's meant more to IRS than any other group on the label. Copeland apparently often told his staff, "As go the Go-Go's, so goes

IRS" They were the only act on the label to have scored a gold record. He couldn't afford to lose them. "There were a lot of ins and outs in terms of acts that he was involved with," said Bob Garcia. "Isn't it funny that with all these relationships it always comes down to percentages, and sometimes money, and all the rest of that stuff?"

The Go-Go's eventually settled out of court with Copeland and resumed dealings with IRS Their third album, *Talk Show*, was released in 1984 after a two-year hiatus. By then, the buzz had dissipated and the album failed to crack the top 10. Riven by drug problems and infighting, the group split in 1985. By that time, Copeland had already signed up their replacements, the Bangles, a prettier and even less-challenging version of the Go-Go's. Copeland became their manager, but the Bangles would not sign to IRS, because they did not want to be seen as the poor man's Go-Go's. Instead, Copeland released an EP through Faulty Products and used the buzz to negotiate an album deal with Columbia, which signed the group in 1983. But he was now starting to repeat himself.

The success of the Go-Go's had given IRS a modicum of independence. It moved into its own building across from the A&M lot. In 1984, its relationship with A&M ended, and the label was born anew with a fresh production-and-distribution deal at MCA, the company that would later poach Jay Boberg to be first vice president, then head of the label. By this time, Stiv Bators, for one, had noted a change. "The original IRS was great—they had people who really liked rock 'n' roll! You go into their offices now and it's like any other big corporation."

Miles Copeland might have relinquished control over his empire building because he was distracted by a battle being raged on another front. The integrity of the Police, the band at the vanguard of his new wave crusade, was beginning to disintegrate under pressure.

12

DYSTOPIA IN
UTOPIA

I n only three years, the whole world had opened up for the Police. But they were so locked into their own private world, gazes cast inward, that they failed to notice. The pressure of churning out an album a year for the previous three years, followed by six months or more of near constant touring, had begun to take its toll—and there was no letup in sight.

In an attempt to alleviate some of the pressure on the band, Miles Copeland arranged for the group to record at Beatles producer George Martin's Air Studios on the Caribbean island of Montserrat, a sparsely populated, teardrop-shaped volcanic island in the southern arm of the Antilles. Unlike the tight deadline imposed on them for *Zenyatta Mondatta*, they were booked for a leisurely six weeks of recording during June and July 1981. Time was now on their side and, as Stewart Copeland noted, because it was a "twelve-hour flight to the nearest record company," executives were unable to drop in to check on their progress. But the facilities at Air were so expansive that the band could afford the luxury of flying their families out to the island to stay with them.

Martin had first visited Montserrat on holiday in 1977 and immediately fell in love with the place. He decided that its verdant hills and coastal view would make an idyllic location for a residential studio. He acquired some land, and construction was completed in 1979. There were other, more practical, considerations that made it an ideal place to locate a studio. While being a British overseas territory, Montserrat was also a tax haven, meaning that the top echelon of performers could record albums that were expected to be high earners, safe in the knowledge that the profits would remain out of reach of the tax man.

During their stay on Montserrat, the Police lived like colonial masters. Each man had his own villa close to the beach, equipped with its own garden and swimming pool and a coterie of personal staff drawn from natives of the island. The studio was a brisk thirty-minute walk uphill. It occupied two buildings: one housed the studio itself, the other a recreation area, a kitchen, and a dining room. Outside was a swimming pool constructed on a platform that provided magnificent views of the island. But all of this apparent comfort was wasted on the Police. Internal pressures had begun to splinter the group apart. The studio became a territorial battleground where it was every man for himself. Marooned on this idyllic Caribbean island, the Police could not escape one another, and not even a message in a bottle could save them.

Crucially, this time they did not have the temperate hand of Nigel Gray to guide the sessions. This meant there was no one to step in and mediate when arguments flared up, no one to encourage the group to work as a team, and no one to challenge the excesses and demands of ego and ambition that had begun to take root within the group.

Gray's replacement was a twenty-six-year-old engineer named Hugh Padgham, who had been recommended to the group by XTC.

Just before flying out to Montserrat, Padgham had completed work on Phil Collins's debut solo album *Face Value*, on which he had pioneered the use of a gated drum sound that would become not only his hallmark as a producer but the bane of artificial-sounding eighties productions. Unlike Gray, who had been with the group from the start, the quieter and more reserved Padgham was thrown in at the deep end and quickly had to establish his place within the Police fraternity. Also in attendance at the sessions were the band's regular tech crew—Danny Quatrochi, Jeff Seitz, and Tam Fairgrieves—and former road manager Kim Turner, who had now assumed the role of their day-to-day manager.

Padgham's first decision as an engineer might not have been the smartest in terms of fostering group morale, but it made sound technical sense: Stewart Copeland and his kit were set up outside the studio, in the dining room of the main house, where the gabled ceiling and wooden floors provided a natural reverb. There were a few drawbacks to this arrangement, though. "We couldn't really record at night," said Padgham, "because the room didn't have windows, it had shutters, and the tree frogs would get a little loud." During the day, it got so hot that Copeland was slick with sweat and resorted to taping the sticks to his hands to prevent them from flying off.

Recording in the dining room had one other disadvantage. The drummer's only link to everyone else was via a television monitor and an intercom, through which communication could be initiated only from the studio. This had the effect of making him extremely paranoid, a trait that was no doubt exacerbated by the large amounts of marijuana he was known to smoke. Copeland explained that "instead of finishing playing and going, 'Hey, that was good there,' there is silence. I can't hear what they are saying unless one of them presses the talk-back button. They aren't pressing the talk-back button, but I can see that they are talking and I assume it's bad."

While achieving separation in the sound, they also managed to isolate themselves from one another even further. Andy Summers played guitar in the studio itself, while, tellingly, Sting recorded in the control room alongside Padgham. When Squeeze keyboard player turned TV presenter Jools Holland arrived with a BBC camera crew to shoot a piece on the making of the album, the Police made nice and performed together in the studio. Lights placed on the floor arced up over the walls, casting half of the studio into shadow. Copeland and Sting played wearing sunglasses. It certainly looked dramatic, but it was all for show. For the first time in their history together, the Police were recording an album without being physically present in the same room with one another.

To ease themselves into the sessions, they started out with a cover version. Oddly, it was the cover of a song that Sting had written himself—"Demolition Man"—but it had been recorded by Grace Jones previously that year and released several months earlier as the first single off her *Nightclubbing* album. "We all listened to the Grace Jones version and thought, 'Shit, we can do it much better than that,'" said Summers. "It was a one-take job. To me, our version is much more ballsy, which is what you'd expect from Grace Jones." What they ended up with was a song that was stripped of all the pulsing menace and feral charm of Jones's original.

Once this had been dispensed with, the group returned to their usual working method, listening to the demos each had brought with him and then working out their parts separately. Here, Copeland freely admitted that he was at a distinct disadvantage to the other two: "Whoever wrote the song will show the others the chords. In my case, I don't know the names of 'em so I just play 'em. Andy looks at my fingers and says, 'You moron, that can't be done,' or 'Why have you done that?' and everybody figures out whatever they can."

Yet a much more fundamental problem impeded their work flow. Prior to arriving at Montserrat, Sting had again recorded a series of finished-sounding 24-track demos to present to the band. Although ostensibly on a family holiday in Canada, he had booked some time at Le Studio (Morin Heights), a state-of-the-art residential recording facility in the Laurentian Mountains in Quebec. The studio's owner, André Perry, had first attracted notice as the man who recorded "Give Peace a Chance" during John Lennon and Yoko Ono's 1969 "bed-in."

A keyboard player named Jean-Alain Roussel, who lived close to the studio, was drafted in to help Sting flesh out some songs.

Roussel remembered a casual phone call from Perry one day asking whether he wanted to come by the studio to play some music and have dinner with a visiting English musician. When Roussel arrived, he was introduced to Sting and Frances Tomelty and their now four-year-old son, Joe. After a friendly chat, Sting played Roussel some songs he had been working on. "As far as I can recall, he was thinking of doing a solo album, or wanting to do a solo album," said Roussel. "I don't know if he was intending to leave the group, but I felt that he wasn't very happy with the group situation."

This seems to tally with the song Sting picked out for Roussel to work on. "Every Little Thing She Does Is Magic" predated the Police. It was written in early 1977, around the time Sting first moved to London, and demoed shortly afterward with Mike Howlett. But try as he might, Sting could not get Copeland and Summers to agree to cut it with him; as an out-and-out love song, it was deemed too soft for the Police.

After listening to the song, Roussel laid down some keyboard parts, while Sting played the melody on guitar to a digital click track provided by a Roland Compurhythm beat-box. "I went crazy and overdubbed multiple pianos on it," said Roussel. "I also had a mini-Moog, which I kept in the studio because I was working there quite a lot, so I put some of that on there, did the 'sweep,' and programmed a marimba sound on it, which gave it a Caribbean feeling. Sting put the bass on it, did a vocal. I also did some Clavinet-type fun things on it. I basically conceived an arrangement for the song." It was all done in a couple of hours, and then they went to dinner.

Sting recorded some further demos at the Pathe Marconi studio in Paris at the end of May before travelling on to Montserrat in mid-June. When he presented his work to the group, they were less than happy. "Sting doesn't bring in half-finished songs any more," Copeland griped. "He's doing so much homework that there's not much room for new ideas." It had long been band policy to throw out the arrangements of the demos each member of the band brought in so that the trio could remake them in their own collective style. But now, Copeland revealed, Sting was "liking it less and less when we mess with them."

The demo for "Every Little Thing She Does Is Magic" completely confounded them. They gamely attempted to record the song over, tearing it apart and reconstituting it. They sped it up and played it more aggressively, then slowed it down and rearranged the chords. But nothing they did sounded as complete as the demo, which everyone agreed sounded like a hit single. "That was the most castrating effect," said Copeland. "Every time we recorded a take, somebody'd say, 'That doesn't sound like a number-one hit song, but the demo does.'"

After chasing their tails trying to make it work, they agreed to fly Roussel down to Montserrat to recut his keyboard parts. Summers, for one, did not take kindly to Roussel's arrival. "He must have played twelve piano parts on that song alone," Summers recalled. "And as the guitar player I was saying, 'What the fuck is this? This is not the Police sound.'"

But even with Roussel's keyboard parts in the mix, they still could not come to an agreement on an arrangement for the song. "By the fifth day we'd given up on everything," Copeland said. "I was feeling stiff and pissed off: 'Not another day on this—what the hell are we gonna do?'"

Roussel concurred: "It wasn't going far at one stage, so I very humbly suggested that it might be a better idea to fly over the 24-track demo that I did and add drums to it." Copeland would claim it was his idea to play over the demo and that he had instructed Padgham to punch in the track one morning so that he could play over it and prove "how crummy it was." Yet rather than prove his point, the opposite occurred. The track started to sound "right."

"We overdubbed everything on top of his demo," Copeland said, "gradually replacing everything on his tape with us. That was what worked." Copeland's and Summers's input into the song would be minimal at best. On the final track, Summers's guitar is almost lost in the mix and is reduced to parroting the piano. Copeland was relegated to playing a phoned-in back beat that replicated the rhythm of the digital click track. "The drum box played half of it and I played the other half," he later admitted. "I thought I was being very clever, a lot of work went into what I did play. But I just didn't play very much at the end of the day."

The experience was a slap in the face for Summers, who prided himself on being able to add the crucial ingredient that would transform and toughen up Sting's mawkish demos. He refused to even mention Roussel by name in his account of the session, describing him instead as a "Canadian keyboard player . . . a heavily-built guy with an oversize ego to match his bulk," who has "bamboozled Sting into flying him down from Canada." But this was not the case at all, and Roussel was not just some keyboard player. He wasn't even Canadian.

Born in Mauritius but raised in England, Roussel was a prodigious musician who had carved out a career as a noted session player in the 1970s, while still in his early twenties, playing with Cat Stevens and Bob Marley. He contributed the Hammond organ riff to the studio version of "No Woman, No Cry." Oddly, he also had several connections to Summers. Roussel had played on "Marjorie Razorblade," the most celebrated song by Summers's ex-employer Kevin Coyne, and in a blues rock group called Juicy Lucy fronted by ex–Zoot Money singer Paul Williams. In this light, Summers's repudiation of Roussel seems very strange. Speaking later about the band's decision not to bring a keyboard player on tour with them, Summers might have revealed the real reason Roussel's presence proved such a threat: "A keyboard player and myself would be in the same harmonic area. Figuring out who'd do what would just not work."

Summers could not bear to be upstaged by a more seasoned and professional musician than he. "Nobody was ever nasty to me," said Roussel. "I have nothing bad to say about any of them." But he did sense that there was "some tension" between members of the group, noting that "Andy seemed to be not talking to many people at the time."

The finished song was a turning point in relations for the band and a victory of sorts for Sting, who had managed to keep the spirit of his demo in the material world. It also established his primacy over the other members of the group, once and for all. But in doing so, he had violated the spirit of the agreement between them, breaking the bond that enabled them to maintain the tenuous balance required to "Policify" the material. Summers later decided that the album was the turning point when he and Copeland were reduced to "backing a singer doing his pop songs." In retrospect, Summers seems to have displaced the animus he felt toward Sting onto Roussel. It must have rankled him even further when "Every Little Thing She Does Is Magic" not only became a huge worldwide hit but the band's biggest-selling single to date.

Before Roussel left the island, he also laid down parts on two other tracks, including "Spirits in the Material World" and "Invisible Sun." Once they had finished laying down the basic tracks, individual responsibilities among the group members broke down even further for the remainder of the sessions. Copeland explained to *Trouser Press* magazine that the usual scenario was to find "one of us overdubbing in the studio, one of us off by the pool, and the third sitting by the mixing desk being abusive, insulting and inflammatory. Which, as it turns out, gets the job done." He pointedly did not reveal who did what or whether they took turns.

The same article noted soberly that "the Police's system of checks and balances keeps egomania under control," but this clearly wasn't the case. Taking advantage of Padgham's compliant personality, Sting now had carte blanche over the direction of the sessions. He laid down swathes of saxophone over several other songs, further diluting what Summers considered to be the Police "sound."

"Sting's demos had provided a fair idea as to what he wanted, and so my production work really amounted to getting a cohesive sound," said Padgham, adding that "there weren't any particularly deep conversations about the direction the record should take"—the reason being that the majority of the songs they worked on were all written by Sting.

Out of the eleven tracks selected for the final cut of the album, Copeland and Summers would have only three writing credits between them. In a desperate grubbing for power and control, the singer increasingly used his veto to bar any written contributions by the other two. Summers described the studio at this point as "a canvas for dirty fighting." On occasion, they would all hang over the faders in the control room to ensure that their respective instruments weren't wiped out in the mix. At the same time, Sting's ego was beginning to take on tyrannical dimensions. Summers remembered one episode in which "Sting goes berserk on me, calling me every name under the sun with considerable vehemence, leaving everyone in the room white-faced and in shock."

The day after this incident, Summers received a call from his wife, Kate, who was in Ireland, informing him that she wanted a divorce. Unable to talk her out of it, he was left shell-shocked for the rest of the sessions, stuck on an island several thousand miles away from his estranged family. He implied in his memoir that he suffered in silence and kept the situation to himself, rather than confide in his bandmates. "I know I will have to say something eventually," he said. Although this clearly wasn't a time for personal crises to impinge on the recording process, it also suggested how little camaraderie there now was in the trio. Summers's distracted state of mind might explain his performance on the record. On some tracks, his guitar can barely be heard at all; on others, he is reduced to battling it out with Sting's saxophone. The Police were no longer "the sound of tight compromise," as Summers had been wont to describe the product of their creative friction, but simply the sound of compromise.

Another tradition was broken when it came to naming the record. Every previous Police album had borne one of Miles Copeland's mock Esperanto titles. Summers said that prospective titles for this record were pinned up in the studio during the sessions. One, he claims, was "Blanco de Bunker." It's difficult to believe that this was given any serious consideration, but it does speak volumes about the band's embattled state of mind. Just as Sting had dictated the direction of the album, he also took the initiative to name it: *Ghost in the Machine*. The title—which did not at all reflect its fizzy ska-inflected sound but did seem as joyless and forbidding as the band's experience recording it—was lifted directly from the title of a book by writer Arthur Koestler.

Sting had cited an interest in Koestler prior to the recording of *Ghost in the Machine*, revealing in a 1980 interview that he was reading Koestler's book *The Act of Creation*—a treatise on the psychological mechanisms underpinning the creation of art—in order to gain greater understanding of the working of his own unconscious mind. Yet increasingly, consciousness of matters external was finding its way into his songs. A case in point was "Invisible Sun," which referenced the Troubles in Northern Ireland. It would seem to have been natural subject matter for Sting during a period when he was still partly residing at his house in western Ireland. He was, of course, also married to Frances Tomelty, an Irish Catholic who hailed from Belfast.

"The stance of 'Invisible Sun' is a normal kid in Belfast torn between systems of violence, between the army, the IRA, the UVF, different flags," Sting explained. "We're all after some sort of fairness in society. And if there isn't another way between blowing people up, starving them to death, torturing them, imprisoning them, then we're finished. I'm just saying there has to be another way, let's look for it. Because the real victims are those kids that you see on the film, and they're real kids, they're not actors. I know a bit about Belfast, and I've lived in Ireland for about a year. My wife knows people in the Maze [prison], and we talk long and hard about politics in that area."

He claimed that the song was written from personal experience—his and Tomelty's—rather than from simply watching television reports of the Troubles. "It's something I feel deeply, and I think something has to be said," he claimed. Years later, Sting would undermine this statement by making the bizarre assertion to a journalist that during the trips he made to Andersonstown with Tomelty (the Republican stronghold neighbourhood she hailed from in Belfast), he would adopt a Belfast accent, presumably so that he could fit into the crowd.

For all of Sting's talk, the song was ultimately noncommittal, kowtowing to what academic Bill Rolston described as the "political subservience of pop" (in his essay "This Is Not a Rebel Music") and the "pale mimicry" of protest. "Invisible Sun" skirted around the politics of the situation and offered only a "spiritual" understanding of the problem. Sting's "message in the bottle" was replaced by an "invisible sun" that provided hope where there was none. Essentially, he set the Troubles in Northern Ireland firmly within the songwriting idiom he had already established for himself.

When the song was released in September 1981, as the first single from *Ghost in the Machine,* it was to a background of widely publicized hunger strikes by IRA prisoners that had been going on for more than a year. Derek and Kate Burbidge were commissioned to make a film clip to accompany the release. It utilized emotionally charged footage of children in the desolate militarized zone of Northern Ireland. Tomelty was drafted into the editing room to check that the resulting film was nonsectarian and was tasked with "balancing every Catholic and Protestant image," which suggests there was considerable anxiety that the clip might inflame tensions, rather than tame them. The film succeeded in toughening up the song, but to such a degree that it was banned by the BBC, which (not surprisingly) balked at showing a relentless barrage of images of Belfast ghettos patrolled by British armoured personnel carriers on primetime TV.

"Invisible Sun" was not released as a single in the United States. The subject matter may well have been considered too region specific and alienating for an American audience. Sting began to pull back from the controversial aspects of the single even before its release, introducing "Invisible Sun" to an August 1981 concert audience in Philadelphia as a song that "applies to any British city now." In later years, he would reduce the song's message further by claiming that the title was a play on the words *invisible son,* a reference to the distanced relationship he felt he had with his own father.

On the song's release, it was certainly the most high-profile song to reference the Troubles, but it was by no means the first. In 1972, Paul McCartney and Wings had released a plain-speaking protest song called "Give Ireland Back to the Irish" that was also banned by the BBC. In 1980, Gang of Four had recorded "Armalite Rifle," a song that Sting would almost certainly have been aware of. He even admitted as much in his interview with Paul Morley a year earlier: "Gang of Four, yeah. Well, you see, I am into that school of bands. That's the sort of knife edge if you like where pop and rock is going." While making it clear that he felt the Police had more common ground with out-and-out pop acts like the Boomtown Rats and Blondie, he maintained that he was still "very aware of where the actual musical barriers are being broken. I'm not saying we rip people off. I'm just interested in what other musicians are doing."

Sting's commitment to any clear political credo was inconsistent at best. Although in 1973 he was a committed Marxist, protesting the plight of IRA hunger strikers the Price sisters, outside Durham Prison, he later decried punk bands with leftist leanings as posers. By 1981, Sting was a tax exile. When challenged on whether his financial status contradicted his avowed socialism, Sting gave the kind of answer one would expect from a politician, claiming that he was a tax exile because he didn't want to pay tax to a Thatcher government that was "building sites for American nuclear warheads and sending working-class kids to get killed in Belfast." The newly rich pop star took strenuous efforts to convince the record-buying public that he was worth the money he was being paid and that, unlike a regular pop star, he actually had something of import to say. "My concerns at this moment aren't whether I have a number-one record this week, or whether we sell ten or seven million, or whether we're the biggest group in the world," Sting maintained. "My concern really is whether there's going to be a world left for us to be successful in. Michael Foot [then leader of the Labour Party] was right, everything else is trivial and childish. The real issue is whether we're going to survive as a race."

In short, Sting seemed to be engaged in exactly the kind of questing for meaning you'd expect from a rock star with too much money and time on his hands. He was also perhaps subconsciously drawn to find a substitute for the Catholic faith he was raised in. The songs he contributed to the Police at this stage increasingly explored quasi-spiritual themes. Another song on the album, "Secret Journey," was said to be inspired by G. I. Gurdjieff's book *Meetings with Remarkable*

Men. But Koestler was Sting's real literary passion. "Through the book [*Ghost in the Machine*], I became more spiritual in a very scientific way," he claimed. "It spoke to me, and in a logical way it ended my lazy grip on logic. Prior to that, I was very much a robot."

Sting's interest in Koestler is significant and noteworthy because not only did he cite it as inspiration for the title of this album, as well as for three songs on the record—namely, "Spirits in the Material World," "Rehumanize Yourself," and "Demolition Man"—but it also informed the album that followed it, *Synchronicity*. That record was inspired by a book by Koestler titled *The Roots of Coincidence*, an exploration of Jung's work not in the field of psychology but in the murkier world of parascience—namely, the purported psychic phenomena of telekinesis and ESP.

Sting presented the ideas he gleaned from Koestler's book in the most sober and rational fashion, almost as if he had learned them by rote. This might even be borne out by the findings of a rock writer who interviewed Sting in the early nineties and snuck a look at his then current reading matter, a biography of Rimbaud, and noted that the book was "heavily-thumbed and much underlined." Sting attempted to explain the idea behind *Ghost in the Machine* to *NME* writer Lynn Hanna: "According to Koestler there are two brains. Well, there are three, but for our purposes there are two. There's the old brain that the lizards have which involves fear, hunger, aggression, sex, the beast in us. The other brain is quite a recent addition and involves abstractions, things that transcend the body. Unfortunately the two brains are entirely separate and there's no communication between them. Therefore there's a kind of schizophrenia. One side is looking at the stars and wanting to transcend the human condition, and the other side is grovelling round looking for the next person to rape or beat up. I think he's right, that is what's wrong with us. He does offer a solution which is a bit extreme, but I think he does have a point. I won't tell you what it is or I'll spoil the book."

The reason he didn't reveal it was because Koestler's solution was in the realm of the unreal: he advocated a chemical castration of the mind to exterminate the bestial brain of man. Koestler's philosophical tracts were often written off as the musings of an enthusiastic but misguided amateur, the implication being that his brilliance was as a writer, rather than as a scientist or a thinker. The more wayward his fields of enquiry—he was particularly obsessed in later years with telekinesis and clairvoyance—the more his credibility was called into question. Toward the end of his life, Koestler was said to be conducting experiments into levitation in the basement of his house. He had first come to prominence through an entirely different type of subject matter. Koestler's landmark book *Darkness at Noon* was a 1956 novel that purported to reveal the true horrors of Stalinism during an account of a Moscow show trial in 1938. It was to political writing what Truman Capote's *In Cold Blood* was to true crime.

In the sixties, Koestler moved away from this form of narrative journalism and into the field of parascience and parapsychology. But the connecting thread was the same: a desire to challenge totalitarianism in all of its forms, whether it be political ideas, scientific theory, or philosophical thought. (As such, the promotion of Koestler's theories by the Police seemed wholly in tune with the Copeland family philosophy, too.) Koestler seemed to be permanently embattled. He was sometimes described as a "malcontent." French philosopher Simone de Beauvoir said that he was "touchy, tormented, greedy for human warmth, but cut off from others by his personal obsessions"—making him sound more like a cosseted rock star than a philosopher.

A longtime advocate of voluntary euthanasia, Koestler died by his own hand in 1983, aged seventy-seven, overdosing on Tuinol washed down with whisky, in an apparent double suicide with his third wife, Cynthia. In recent years, his private life has overshadowed his writing. A controversial, widely publicized and criticized biography of Koestler—David Cesarani's *Arthur Koestler: The Homeless Mind*, published in 2000—made the allegation that he was a serial rapist and an abuser of women. It was supported by interviews with women who had encounters with Koestler, as well as by numerous anecdotes. Armed with this knowledge, one critic slavishly reexamined Koestler's early novels and pinpointed passages that suggested that his sexual appetite was reflected in his protagonists' encounters with women. The study of Koestler was increasingly split into friends and devotees versus those who advocated the flawed image of the man. The latter poses the question as to whether the drastic solution Koestler proposed within the elaborate pseudoscientific treatise of *Ghost in the Machine* was on some level a method of killing the self-destructive urges within himself.

There exists the possibility that on a subconscious level, Sting, too, was drawn to the book less out of philosophical inquiry into an altruistic solution for the betterment of his fellow man and more as a form of denial to excuse his own behaviour. Within a year, the choices that he would make in his personal life would overshadow the Police. As he rose to prominence in the group, the contradictions in his personality threatened to torpedo everything they had worked to achieve.

13

DESTABILIZE, DESYNCHRONIZE

The Police were living double lives. In public, they maintained their image as happily married family men, albeit dropping hints that this was not the full story. Walking clichés for rock 'n' roll excess they clearly were not. They practised excess in moderation, but temptation was dangled in front of them wherever they went. When Stewart Copeland boasted about his exploits, they sounded rather hollow. "As far as sex, drugs and rock 'n' roll goes," he said, "let it be noted that we were pop stars after the Pill and before AIDS. And I'm down on my knees at this moment praising Allah for his magnificence in giving me this life."

Copeland hinted that he enjoyed a relaxed relationship with girl-friend Sonja Kristina, intimating that she turned a blind eye to his indiscretions on the road, knowing that he would always return home to her. What was not common knowledge at the time was that Copeland had fathered a child by Marina Guinness, the daughter of

Desmond Guinness, a scion of the Guinness clan. The boy, Patrick, was born in July 1981. The Police had played Leixlip Castle, the Guinness family home, in July 1980 and stayed there overnight at the behest of the owners. Copeland would marry Kristina in July 1982. Their first child together, son Jordan, was born a year later.

Andy Summers's indulgences included a friendship with John Belushi that began just as the comedian embarked on his accelerated descent into the drug addiction that would kill him in March 1982. "Substances were imbibed, and the opposite sex was dealt with in huge numbers," Summers said. "How many? Gentlemen stop counting after three hundred. I'm giving it to you vaguely, but I'm not going to deny anything."

If anything, though, the indulgences of the band merely served to hone the more obnoxious aspects of their personalities, fuelling egomania and interpersonal conflict. "I am a rock 'n' roll arsehole, an emaciated millionaire prick, and fuck everything," Summers reflected within the pages of his memoir. Drugs had also exacerbated the obsessive need for control that had caused Sting to transform the recording sessions for *Ghost in the Machine* into such a nightmare. "Sting was never really into drugs until being around coke," observed Kristina, who had visited Montserrat. "It had a bad effect on his personality. It made him less considerate, therefore more prima donna-ish and tiresome."

Sting was increasingly becoming a Janus-faced pop idol. His public image presented a cool, calm, and collected, serious-minded individual. But behind the scenes, he seemed set on sabotaging the stability that had enabled his rise. His private life was falling to pieces. The singer had succumbed to the seven-year itch and embarked on an affair with a young actress named Trudie Styler. Sting seemed convinced that their meeting and eventual partnership was fated to occur. In Styler, he would find his female half. She, too, had ruthlessly reinvented herself, papering over her roots as a working-class girl from Birmingham, England. She was also extraordinarily vain and ambitious and, like Sting, driven by upward mobility.

The affair with Styler, who was six years younger than Frances Tomelty, was perhaps inevitable. They had all lived in close proximity for years. Sting dates their first meeting to April 1977, shortly after he and Tomelty had just moved into their Bayswater flat and several days after he had returned from the Police's jaunt around Europe with Wayne County. Styler lived in a basement flat two doors down with her then boyfriend, a fellow actor. Sting recalled going around there for a meeting of housing association tenants. Styler, though, believed that her first sighting of Sting came a year later. She remembered seeing him sitting with his two-year-old son on the steps of his house, having locked himself out, and she invited them to wait in her flat. This recollection only seems to confirm Sting's account, suggesting that they were on familiar enough terms for her to invite him into her flat. Styler did note, curiously, that Sting had green hair at the time. This could be either a previously undocumented flirtation with a punk image on his part or a blond dye job gone wrong.

As the years passed, Sting, Tomelty, and Styler progressed from being friendly neighbours to firm friends, the two women sharing the camaraderie that came from working in the same profession. In 1980, they appeared together in a production of *Macbeth* at London's Old Vic. Legendary Irish actor Peter O'Toole, then the director of the theatre, put Tomelty up for the part of Lady Macbeth. Styler was cast as "First Witch." At some point, Styler and O'Toole embarked on a short-lived relationship. Certainly, by the time the ill-fated production opened in September—garnering some of the most scathing reviews ever received for a production on the London stage—it was already being reported that Sting was sharing the First Witch's bed, rather than that of his lady wife.

Sting wrote "Demolition Man" while staying at O'Toole's cottage in Clifden, Ireland, earlier that summer. (Sting and Tomelty's house was located in a neighbouring village, Roundstone.) "O'Toole said he liked the lyrics," Sting recalled, giving the impression that the hell-raising actor had given his blessing to Sting's hell-raising song, which was ostensibly inspired by Arthur Koestler's idea that man's dualistic mind was the cause of mankind's self-destructive nature. On closer inspection, though, the lyrics seemed more concerned with a personal, rather than a philosophical, fatalism. The verses were crammed with imagery about someone facing imminent destruction—tied to ticking bombs, facing oncoming trains, strapped to crashing planes— hurtled along by circumstances that the song's narrator claimed was not of their choosing.

Between the lines, the lyrics to the song offered the possibility that the fuse was about to be (or had already been) lit on the combustible sexual chemistry between Sting and Styler. The "Demolition Man" was almost certainly Sting himself, faced with the prospect that he was about to lay waste to his family life. When, in August 1981, Tomelty became pregnant with their second child, he really would be faced with an impossible situation, albeit one that had been within his responsibility to avoid.

When quizzed about his infidelity several years later, he suggested that nature had created this course of events: "I can't say I've sinned because I failed to be monogamous. It's a matter of chemicals in a relationship—as the chemicals become acclimated to one another, the chemical reaction between people lessens. There's a less violent coming together. It's as if you become addicted to orgasm, addicted to a violent, strong sensation, and when it ceases to be powerful, you must shake your situation up to get it again."

Sting's domestic situation was shaken up again in March 1982, when he was forced to beat a hasty retreat from his home in Ireland. He never publicly revealed the reasons for the move at the time, but Summers hinted that the singer had received death threats in the local area. The controversy surrounding the release of his song "Invisible Sun" five months earlier had increased awareness of Sting's presence in Ireland. The defining moment may have been when Sting foiled a break-in at his house. After catching the burglars in the act, he announced that he was going to call the police. Apparently unfazed, the intruders replied, "We thought you were the Police." The house was quickly sold, and Sting moved back to London, where there was yet more upheaval in store for him.

A battle had been brewing for years over Sting's publishing contract with Virgin. Miles Copeland could never reconcile with the idea that Sting had signed away his publishing rights to Virgin just prior to joining the Police, and as the group became more and more successful, this continued to eat away at Copeland. Had Sting not signed to Virgin, Copeland would in all likelihood have administered the publishing himself—as he had done with Squeeze and other acts he managed— thereby cutting himself in for an additional slice of revenue.

Carol Wilson, who had signed Sting to his publishing deal at Virgin and maintained a friendly relationship with the singer, claimed that for a period of three years after the Police first became successful, Copeland repeatedly enjoined his client to sue Virgin. "Sting used to come to me and say, 'I don't know what to do, he's my manager, what shall I do?'" Wilson said. "I felt that it wasn't an unfair deal for that time. We also took legal advice when he told us that Miles was telling him to sue. I felt that he didn't have a case and I said to him, 'Take independent legal advice, completely separate to Miles, and then do whatever you need to do'—because we'd always got on very well personally. He went to a lawyer that Miles gave him and was told to sue."

When Virgin licensed "Don't Stand So Close to Me" for use in a TV commercial for Body Mist deodorant, Copeland finally had the pretext he needed to push Sting into taking the company to court. In mid-July 1982, Sting presented himself at the high court in London for the trial, with his wife standing dutifully by his side. They dressed in coordinated outfits and wore forced smiles. He wore a white shirt and sweater under a brightly coloured striped sports jacket and tie that made him look more like a rake from an Evelyn Waugh novel than a rock star. She wore a white jacket and a striped dress.

During the trial proceedings, much was made of the couple's perilous financial affairs in London, during the period after Sting had signed with Virgin but prior to the Police's success. Several heavy-handed extracts from the singer's diary were read out during the first day of trial to illustrate Sting's apparent state of mind at the time. "Depression— responsibility weighs heavily. Went to social security for the first time— depressing and demeaning," read one entry from January 1977.

"The Despair of Sting When He Was on the Dole," read a tabloid headline that accompanied a report on the proceedings. The diary entry suggests that his pride was hurting more than his pocket was. Certainly, Sting and his wife were not well-off, but they lived in a housing association flat that afforded them cheap rent in Bayswater, which even in the mid-seventies was a fairly well-to-do area of West London.

Another day, another story; this one headlined "My Trust in a Woman Cost Me Millions," concerned Sting's testimony that his friendship with Wilson had blinded him to the realities of the contract. In contrast to his testimony, Wilson maintained that she sat beside Sting through the proceedings and they giggled like naughty children. Wilson, who had by this time left Virgin's employ and was in a pay dispute with the company, was considered a hostile witness by Virgin's barristers. "There was a feeling that this was done to both of us by Miles and Virgin," Wilson confirmed.

The picture Sting painted outside of court was not entirely honest, either. Although, technically, Sting and Tomelty were still husband and wife, they no longer lived together. Tomelty had given birth to their second child (daughter Fuschia) in mid-April. Their divorce would be granted on March 10, 1984, on the grounds that they hadn't lived together for two years, which suggested that the split had occurred when Tomelty was at least eight months pregnant, if not before. In order to preserve Sting's good-guy image, this sequence of events was fudged over to imply that he had left Tomelty soon after she had given birth. But in a 2006 interview, Fuschia Sumner plainly stated that her parents "broke up before I was born." When quizzed by reporters outside the court in July about rumours of a breakup, Sting categorically denied it. "These stories just aren't true," he said. "I don't read the newspapers that spread them."

At the end of the first week of the case, the judge adjourned the case for the weekend. Tomelty was due to testify on Sting's behalf the following Monday and then immediately fly to America to start two months' work on a film. The judge granted the couple compassionate leave so that husband and wife could spend their last weekend together before Tomelty's trip, without the restrictions imposed from being under oath in court. But the following weekend, with Tomelty now safely out of the country, Sting himself jetted off to Monte Carlo with mistress Styler to attend a lavish birthday party for Saudi arms dealer Adnan Khashoggi.

Time magazine once described Khashoggi as "an international symbol of sybaritic self-indulgence," who was said to spend up to $250,000 a day to maintain his lifestyle. His parties were legendary. The day after the party, Sting and Styler returned to London in Khashoggi's private jet to enable the singer to attend court again on Monday. The paparazzi were lying in wait for them when they arrived at Heathrow airport. Sting's bodyguards scuffled with photographers who tried to get a shot of the couple.

The painstaking façade Sting had presented with Tomelty for the benefit of the hearing had been shattered even before the verdict was in. But his behaviour also called into question his sincerity as a songwriter. Not ten months earlier, he had decried the military occupation of Northern Ireland in a plaintive voice, through the lyrics to "Invisible Sun," which featured a line about not wanting to spend a life staring down the barrel of an Armalite rifle. Now he was partying with an arms dealer. That stain on his credibility would remain in place for a long time. Many years later, when quizzed as to whether attending the party was a smart thing to do, Sting pleaded ignorance and presented himself as a harmless observer. "Frankly, I didn't know who he was," he said of Khashoggi. "Somebody invited me to a party. Do you think I'm his best mate? It was great to go to his party and see all these chronically wealthy people having a good time."

But the only reason Sting was there in the first place was due to his own wealth and fame. The person who "invited" him was in all probability Styler, who in the late seventies had supplemented her meagre income as an actress by working as a compère and hostess in Xenon, an exclusive nightclub in London's Piccadilly frequented by oil-rich Arabs and Saudi royalty. Khashoggi had a weakness for pretty blondes and prostitutes and was linked (in a 2006 British newspaper exposé) to another rock star muse, Heather Mills McCartney.

Sting did not officially acknowledge the breakup of his marriage for close to a year. He finally went on record about it in an October 1983 interview for (of all publications) *Playgirl*. By that time, Styler was already six months pregnant with their first child. "We're separated," he said of his marriage to Tomelty, offering the blandest of reasons for the split. "It's impossible to sustain a marriage, or any sort of commitment like that, when you're on the road most of the year or locked up in some recording studio."

As the court case drew on, Wilson said it became clear that a central plank of Sting's defence was that he'd signed the Virgin contract without adequate legal representation. Unfortunately for him, Wilson had a draft contract in her possession that proved exactly the opposite. After presenting Last Exit with a contract, Wilson had suggested that the band get a lawyer to look over it and, she claimed, also gave them a list of music industry lawyers they could consult.

In his memoir, *Broken Music*, Sting remembered the band joking and arguing all the way back to Newcastle about the merits of spending money they didn't have on legal advice. Eventually, band drummer Ronnie Pearson offered to take the contract to the lawyer who had drawn up the deeds when he bought his house. The rest of the band agreed. "When Ronnie brings the aforesaid contract to the attention of his legal genius," Sting reported, "the latter looks at it curiously, shrugs, and claims that it looks okay to him."

Wilson claimed otherwise. She said that the lawyer's inexperience in entertainment law led him to be overzealous in his questioning of the document, and she recalled that when the contract was returned to her, it was awash with red ink. "This man tore the contract apart and questioned every clause," she said. Curiously, the one thing that had not been subject to dispute was the percentage Virgin had offered Sting. It was only in retrospect, and under Miles Copeland's urging, that Sting decided he was locked into a deal that was grossly unfair.

The draft contract remained on file at Virgin. Toward the end of the third week of the trial, Virgin's lawyer challenged Sting's contention that he had not had adequate legal representation, citing the existence of the contract amended by Pearson's lawyer. "Sting just hung his head and said nothing," said Wilson. She remembered the barrister asking him why he had made that claim. "Sting said, 'I don't know,'" reported Wilson.

At that point the case collapsed, and an out-of-court settlement was quickly reached. "I don't believe that Sting put himself through that," said Wilson. "He was definitely manipulated, and I think it was really appalling that Miles pushed him into doing that." But equally, was Sting really that naive? During his account (in *Broken Music*) of the casual discussion Last Exit had among themselves as to whether they should get a lawyer to look over the contract, Sting mischievously attributed an entirely fictional quote to himself: "Well, I was just imagining that in six years' time, say, after we've sold millions of records all over the known world, that fifty-fifty deal will translate into millions and millions of pounds for Virgin Publishing, unearned, mind you, apart from a few donated hours in Pathway Studios. And we'll have to sue Richard Branson in the high court, at great personal expense, in order to regain our most valuable copyrights."

Written after the fact, this idealized future for Last Exit doubled as a self-serving justification for Sting's court action. Wilson maintained that Sting had signed what was a standard deal for the time. "As it was, Sting's deal was not just a fifty-fifty deal. I had actually knitted into the deal that [Virgin's percentage] would go down year by year, so he got a bigger percentage each year. That was already showing the signs of how publishing was moving." The renegotiated terms extended Sting's contractual period with Virgin beyond the next Police album but at a reduced percentage in favour of the singer. Virgin also agreed to return the copyrights of his songs once the contract had ended. Despite the two parties reaching agreement, hostilities between them continued in the press.

Incensed that reporting of the case implied that Sting had lost, Miles Copeland went on the attack. Virgin, he claimed, had reaped a £5 million reward on Sting's songs, having invested no more than £200 to promote them. The singer also found himself in the position of earning less in publishing royalties than the other two members of the Police, despite writing three-quarters of the material—although, to be fair, this was due to the fact that it was Copeland who had convinced Sting to split his royalties with his bandmates in the first place.

Virgin head Richard Branson disputed the numbers. He said that £2,000 was spent on Last Exit; and Virgin collected £1.5 million.

In a report on the aftermath of the case that ran in the *NME*, Copeland and Branson went head to head. The Virgin boss went public with his belief that Copeland had provided the impetus for Sting to sue. Branson described the Police manager as a "despicable character" and "hypocritical," given that Copeland's own contract with Squeeze, which had recently broken up and whose ex-members were themselves involved in litigation with Copeland over unpaid royalties, was signed without legal advice and offered worse terms than the one Virgin had entered into with Sting. Squeeze's publishing deal included a clause that extended the agreement indefinitely if the group did not write a specified number of songs and allowed Copeland to retain 50 per cent of publishing for that period, a percentage he retains to this day.

"The allegations are horseshit," Copeland responded. The Squeeze contract was looked over by their manager, photographer Laurence Impey, he told the *NME*, implying that they did have adequate representation; he neglected to reveal that Impey was largely inexperienced as a manager. Copeland also maintained that he had, as yet, not recouped the money he had spent to break the group, having outlaid money to pay their rent for two years.

Branson wasn't finished, though. He presented similar allegations that were dredged up about Copeland's business arrangements with his BTM clients: Wishbone Ash, Caravan, and Renaissance. "I've never stolen off a group," Copeland maintained. "I don't care much about the money. It's the excitement of making things happen. But it is a risky business, and if you are creating value for the group, it is rightful that you get a fair return."

Despite the animosity between them, which was promoted as a battle between two music biz moguls, both Copeland and Branson magnanimously kept Sting clear of the hostilities. He was, after all, a breadwinner for both, and it would do neither party any good to tarnish his reputation. Branson maintained that Sting's role in the affair was as "an innocent victim." But it certainly didn't seem that way when Sting was wheeled out to speak his piece to the tabloid newspapers.

"My songs are like my children. You want to protect them when they're being abused," he told the *Daily Mirror*, choosing a rather inopportune analogy. "I won the case because I will get my songs back," he continued, spinning the outcome in his favour. "Any kid with a contract should go to a music industry lawyer. I didn't spend the necessary £600. It's cost me millions and far more heartbreak."

If Sting was laying it on thick, it was because he was safe in the knowledge that whatever happened in court would remain unreported. Three days after the trial had ended, he sounded more like a sore loser than someone who had won a court case. "Body Mist Stinks! The legal process stinks!" he railed from the stage just prior to playing "Don't Stand So Close to Me," during an outdoor show the Police headlined at Gateshead Athletic Stadium.

The show had been trumpeted as the triumphant homecoming of a Newcastle boy done good. Support came from U2, Gang of Four, and the Beat, but the show drew only around six thousand people, who seemed dwarfed by the twenty-five-thousand-capacity stadium. The combination of a costly ticket price, industrial layoffs in the area, and poor weather was blamed for the low turnout. But it was undoubtedly a humiliation to a band of the Police's status.

From the stage, Sting also poured scorn on the tabloid interest in his private life, ridiculing reports that had broken in the press about his "mystery blonde girlfriend." But his duplicity had finally caught up with him. The pressure was bearing down on him. Sting suddenly found his every move under intense scrutiny. "They harassed me at home and they harassed my wife and my mistress and they harassed my children," he said in a July 1985 interview with *Playboy* magazine. "They had photographers out behind the house one day—fuck knows what for."

He did not like the image he saw of himself reflected back through the media. "I became the Devil for a few months—always a philandering, drug-taking Devil, totally evil. I just had to sit through all that bullshit. But now I'm glad of it, glad I've been through that mill, frankly. Luckily, my son was just a little too young to be bothered with it. I'll never forgive the press, and I know the people directly responsible for it. Anyway, anyone who reads that stuff and believes it is a moron. None of my friends who read it believe it. It's written by morons."

In order to evade the inexorable press attention and extricate himself from what he described as "a horrific, endless nightmare," Sting fled to Jamaica, spending several weeks holed up at Goldeneye, the secluded coastal estate where Ian Fleming wrote his James Bond novels, then owned by Island Records founder Chris Blackwell. But he didn't leave straight away. Although his "nightmare" began in July, he didn't get to Jamaica until September. He had also visited the island in June, just prior to the court case and his affair with Styler being exposed.

In Jamaica, Sting set to work writing songs for a new album that was scheduled to be recorded at the end of the year, again in Montserrat. His world had collapsed. His sanity was frayed. When faced with a blank page, his writing took on a paranoid, apocalyptic edge. The quest for a spiritual solution to man's psychological ills that had so dominated the writing on *Ghost in the Machine* again gave way to morbid self-obsession and solipsism. The latter was as plain as day on a song called "King of Pain," in which he imagined his soul as a "black spot" on the sun. The "invisible sun" that gave hope to everyone was now infected by a sore that represented his mendacious personality. In song, he wallowed in pain, while recolouring his life to cast himself as the victim.

"Every Little Thing She Does Is Magic" found its opposite number in "Every Breath You Take." The former, written in the first throes of Sting's marriage to Tomelty, concerns an infatuation that enchants and enthralls, a love that can do no wrong. The new song bookended that relationship, recasting it as an infatuation that has tipped into obsession, characterized by a protective instinct that feels like control. The song suggests that a partnership that is out of balance, in which all the love is one-sided, can suddenly feel like a trap. And the song provided a means by which Sting could rationalize his exit from the relationship.

"I think love has something to do with allowing a person you claim to love to enter a larger arena than the one you create for them," he told

Playboy magazine in 1985. "We fall into the trap of finding someone we think we love and then locking it up, or being locked up ourselves by that. And I think we have to be bigger than that. I think our souls have to be larger. Of course, I'm as jealous and small-minded as anybody else. [Laughs] On the other hand, I can't really change my life to accommodate people who are jealous. I don't see why I should."

This didn't seem particularly fair to the wife he had just abandoned for a younger lover. Now, again, he was trying to retroactively justify his actions in the press. Another song, "Wrapped around Your Finger," seems to be about the fallout from all of those events, casting his relationship with the press in quasi-mystical terms that trace his own rise and fall. In it, a young initiate, bamboozled by dreams and riches, makes a Mephistophelean pact with a sinister and more powerful figure than he. Then, having been bound up by his greed, he resolves to escape by adopting a new disguise and turning the tables on his captor. The servant becomes the master, Sting sings, before turning the chorus inside out to indicate that he now had the upper hand.

Sting liked to maintain that his public image as presented by the media bore little relation to his private self. "It's generally a perception of a perception of a perception," he said, "which I don't mind. If anything, I can hide behind the polarity." Just as he once admitted to a journalist that he was "Machiavellian," he revelled in throwing out these kinds of double-bluffs during interviews. "I'm very devious, in most every way," he had told an *NME* writer in 1981. "No apologies. I'm just very devious." Here he suggested that his true nature was hidden behind distortions thrown up by the media like a hall of mirrors. But his attempts to conjure up hidden depths to his personality were not so much mirrored as made of glass: transparent. The songs were shot through with vanity, self-pity and duplicity. Many years later, he would still maintain that his character could not be discerned through his songs: "I've suffered a lot from amateur psychoanalysis over the years, people investigating my lyrics."

Yet in another song written that month at Goldeneye, it seemed as if Sting was performing psychoanalysis on himself—but in reverse—constructing a nightmare to paper over the cracks in reality.

"Synchronicity II" would be the most ambitious and central song on the album that bore its name. It took the form of a multipart narrative that drew from the work of Swiss psychiatrist Carl Gustav Jung, specifically his theory that apparently coincidental events were linked by some underlying connectedness (Jung described it as an "acausal connecting principle"). Sting had traced a path to Jung through his continuing interest in Arthur Koestler, whose book *The Roots of Coincidence* explored the parascience of coincidental events.

The lyrics to "Synchronicity II" seemed to contain a patriarchal hostility toward women, something that had lurked beneath the surface of his songwriting since "Roxanne." In "Synchronicity II," the male protagonist of the song (Daddy) is tormented to insanity by a harridan, a hysteric, and a gaggle of harlots. The symptoms of this descent into psychosis are juxtaposed with the image of a hidden horror rising from the depths of a "dark Scottish lake," clearly the monster of Loch Ness. The family home becomes the locus of all this foreboding. The thing crawling out of the "slime" clearly represented Sting, or at least the beast he imagined lurking within him. The song was also wrapped up in heavy-handed dystopian imagery that alluded to an industrial behemoth strangling individual freedom and sanity. It seemed that Sting was attempting to communicate the intense pressures he felt bearing down on him as the lead singer of the world's biggest rock band.

Ascribing actions and emotions to some nebulous force that was unseen and irrevocable (namely, Jung's "synchronicity") provided Sting with another means to evade personal responsibility. He presented himself as a puppet on a string, yanked around by a collective, connective thread and driven by fate. Not only was he in denial, he was in denial about his denial. The songs were simply too entangled in his personal affairs for him to acknowledge their true import. Sting had, in effect, replayed the adulterous affair that had wrecked his parents' marriage. He was now forced to identify with his mother, a figure for whom he had previously reserved all of his hatred and scorn. Within the songs, she in turn is merged with the other strong female figure in his life: ex-wife Tomelty, the woman who had helped nurture his career from the start. Collapsing all of the women in his life into himself caused a fissure to open up inside him, and the tremendous sense of guilt and self-loathing Sting felt had erupted into these songs.

Jungian theory could provide an understanding of what was happening to him—not synchronicity, though, but archetypes. Sting's personality was a hand-in-glove fit for the Apollonian archetype: emotionally distant, narcissistic, and arrogant. His public image epitomized the cool blond Adonis. Jung, borrowing from Nietzsche and Schopenhauer, utilized the image of Apollo as the lonely man on a boat cast onto the sea of the world, with only himself to rely on, in order to navigate the choppy, chaotic waters of life. It's an image that dovetails neatly with Sting's "Message in a Bottle." Apollo, of course, was also the name given to NASA's programme of manned missions to the moon. And Sting had been drawn to the image of man isolated from his emotions, walking on the moon. But now he had isolated himself within a hostile environment of his own making. The Apollonian state, said Jung, again citing Nietzsche, "is a withdrawal into oneself, or introversion." At that time, Sting would have no truck with any kind of psychoanalysis of his work.

"The theory that the *Synchronicity* album is entirely a function of Sting getting divorced is a gross oversimplification, and naive," he maintained, curiously referring to himself in the third person. "Pain wasn't a new idea to me last year. But to have a creative outlet for feelings that would normally be ground up and internalized and reformed—you feel cauterized. Some of the things on that record are quite sinister and angry and twisted."

When the band reconvened in December at Air Studios in Montserrat to begin recording the album, that anger would make its presence keenly felt. The sessions for *Synchronicity* made *Ghost in the Machine* seem like a walk in the park. Again, the Police recorded in separate parts of the house. But this time it wasn't enough to prevent increasingly volatile arguments from breaking out between the band members. Hugh Padgham did his best to maintain order but was quickly reminded of his place in the Police pecking order.

"There were both verbal and physical fights in the studio," he recalled. "Often, when these would take place, I'd try to be Mr. Producer and get in the way, saying, 'Come on, do you have to kick the shit out of one another?' but they'd just turn around and shout, 'Get out of it! What do you know? You don't know anything about us!'"

Now they were out of control, and there was no reining them back in. The tension between Copeland and Sting came to a head while they were working on "Every Breath You Take"—demonstrating the acausal connecting principle that linked it with "Every Little Thing She Does Is Magic," the song that had caused them so many problems on the previous album.

"Sting wanted Stewart to just play a very straight rhythm with no fills or anything," Padgham said, "and that was the complete antithesis of what Stewart was about. Stewart would say, 'I want to fucking put my drum part on it!' and Sting would say, 'I don't want you to put your fucking drum part on it! I want you to put what I want you to put on it!' and it would go on like that. It was really difficult."

To make sure he got his own way, Sting resorted to wiping Copeland's drum parts after the band had called it a day and recording new ones on his own at night. The singer later admitted that he went out of his way to cause friction. "I don't have to suffer and be miserable to create. I thought I did. I thought the only way to operate was by creating conflict, tension, putting pressure on myself and other people." Copeland appeared more understanding of the situation. "[Sting] was going through a phase in his life where he temporarily thought he was the devil."

After ten consecutive days of this behaviour, Padgham realized that they had nothing useable on tape. He called his own manager for help. An emergency meeting was convened to debate the future of the project. "That album was actually one meeting away from not happening," Padgham revealed.

Miles Copeland flew into Montserrat and read the band the riot act. There was too much riding on the album to let it all fall apart through petty arguments. Somehow this tactic worked. The group knuckled under to complete the sessions. But there was still the matter of which songs would appear on the final album. Sting, who had lost all sense of fairness and equality, had decided of his own volition that *Synchronicity* was to be a solo album by proxy. He had too much of a personal stake in the songs for the album to be diluted by what he saw as Summers's and Copeland's inferior attempts at songwriting. In fact, Sting didn't want any songs by the others on the record, but this was not going to wash with the other two. They reached a compromise in a manner similar to settling a dispute in a school playground: they flipped a coin. Summers and Copeland were given one song each on the record to appease them.

Summers's contribution to the album, "Mother," was a companion piece to "Be My Girl," the song he wrote on the first Police album about a blow-up doll. This one was about screwing his own mother. Summers described it as a "psycho rendition in seven/four" and "more Captain Beefheart than the Police." It is generally considered to be one of the worst songs in the Police's canon, even by the band's diehard fans. Stewart Copeland turned in a song exploiting his continued obsession with Cold War politics. "Miss Gradenko" was a song about a female apparatchik itching for freedom in a totalitarian state. The drummer now clearly embraced a worldview that was in almost direct opposition to Sting's, who sought a philosophical and spiritual solution to the world's ills.

The last order of the day was to determine the running order of the album, a process usually fraught with indecision and tension. Summers managed to sidestep the inevitable arguments by coming up with an elegant, if expedient, solution. They would put all of the fast songs on one side and the slow songs on the other. The album was now complete but at the expense of draining every last remaining reserve of tolerance the men held for one another.

The photographic portrait of the band that took up one side of the album's inner sleeve didn't require Jungian analysis to expound on relations among the Police. It was as plain as day. While Copeland and Summers looked directly into the camera, Sting wore mirrored shades, his gaze not only hidden but turned away from the others to suggest that he was looking somewhere out of the frame: out into the middle distance and into the future, toward a path as a solo artist that now seemed inevitable.

The Police had enjoyed an enviable career trajectory for a pop act, with every album release garnering increased sales over the one before it. *Synchronicity* skyrocketed past the band's previous four albums, eventually racking up more than eight million in sales. There were two reasons for this: CDs and MTV. The record business had harnessed investment in new technologies to pull itself out of a recession that, just three years earlier, had led to industrywide layoffs. Although album sales as a whole were still dropping, sales of albums by the top acts in the industry had gone stratospheric.

Synchronicity was the first Police album to be released on the new compact disc format that was being heavily pushed by the music industry as the medium of the future. The compact disc promised superior sound that was advertised as above and beyond what consumers could expect to hear on any other sound format. But it was introduced partly as a means to forestall the threat to music industry revenues that had been introduced by the previous format, cassette tapes, which had created the spectre of teenage music consumers being able to make their own home copies of albums owned by friends or taping songs from the radio, for only the cost of a blank tape. The music industry, in a foreshadowing of a phenomenon that would reoccur in the 2000s with the introduction of digital music formats, produced exaggerated forecasts predicting that the vast financial losses incurred through music piracy would cripple the record companies.

That would change in 1983, when just three albums would dominate the top of the Billboard chart for the entire year and achieve combined sales beyond anything imaginable. One was the soundtrack to the movie *Flashdance*; another was *Synchronicity*, which sat at the top spot from the third week of July to the third week of November with a break of only one week, when it was knocked from its peak position by the top-selling album of the year: Michael Jackson's *Thriller*. Worldwide sales of these three albums alone would approach close to a hundred million copies. All three benefited hugely from the extra promotional push that came from the advent of music videos.

Since MTV first aired in America on August 1, 1981, it had steadily grown in influence. Despite music videos being relatively expensive to produce, compared with radio promo releases, the industry marshalled its efforts behind them; certainly, it was gladdened by polling data that suggested up to 68 per cent of MTV viewers had purchased albums after seeing their music videos. Miles Copeland actually coordinated the release of *Synchronicity* and the extensive nine-month world tour that would begin a month later with a barrage of heavy promotion through MTV. The band was prominently featured in MTV's own ad campaign, imploring viewers to tell the US cable operators, "I Want My MTV." There were Police specials on the channel and news segments devoted to announcing the tour dates.

The Burbidges, who had provided the band and Miles Copeland with years of service but whose understated film-making style was out of step with the demands of the new medium, were summarily replaced by Godley & Creme. The British duo had reinvented themselves from pop stylists to visual stylists, becoming prestigious directors of visually arresting pop promos. Godley & Creme had been responsible for directing a notorious clip for Duran Duran's "Girls on Film," a piece of synth pop soft-core erotica featuring naked mud-wrestling girls that had helped break the band, which aired in a heavily censored version on MTV. The videos that they worked on for the Police were far more tasteful.

A specially commissioned and slickly designed four-minute promo for the album was filmed and screened exclusively on MTV. Shot in arty black-and-white, it featured the same imagery that would also appear on the album cover itself. During a slow pan around a sparse set, the video showed props that included the skeleton of a dinosaur, the skeleton of a man, a metronome, a Doric column with a flaming telephone sitting on top of it, and a stuffed goat. For the keen-eyed, there was also a quick shot of a book: Carl Jung's *Synchronicity*. All of this played out against a soundtrack that was collaged from tracks off *Synchronicity* and segued into a clip from the stark black-and-white promo that had already debuted to accompany the release of "Every Breath You Take," the first single from the album. The single hit the number-one spot on the Billboard chart in the second week of July and stayed there until the end of August. The clip for "Every Breath You Take" ran on heavy rotation for almost fourteen months.

Godley & Creme filmed two other video clips for the album, one for "Wrapped around Your Finger" and another for "Synchronicity II." The former used a simple piece of technical trickery to make an eye-catching video. Sting, his hair dyed almost ginger blond, cut short and spiked up, wears mirrored shades and bounces around in a baggy white suit within a maze of candles. It was shot at double speed, with Sting miming to the sped-up music track, and then was slowed down afterward to give a dreamlike effect to all of the movement.

For "Synchronicity II," they employed a vast dystopian set that looked like a junkyard strung up on cranes. Sting, Summers, and Copeland each performed in his own separate turret on the construction. They were heavily made up and styled in primary-coloured costumes that looked like cast-offs from some apocalyptic science-fiction film. Sting appeared wild-haired, wild-eyed, and gaunt, his physical condition betraying the pressure he had wrought on himself during the recording of the album.

Having scored their biggest album to date, the Police now attempted to make it a double by playing their biggest concert to date, a show at New York's Shea Stadium. Not surprisingly, given their profile on the Billboard chart, tickets for the show sold out within hours of being issued. All seventy thousand of them. Summers made great play of the run-up to the Shea Stadium show in his memoir. Various chapters are interspersed with sunny flashbacks of Summers noodling on the guitar in his room before the show. The group was staying at a mansion in the Hamptons that had been loaned to them. They were due to be picked up there by helicopter and whisked off to Shea Stadium. To Summers, the Shea Stadium gig was to be the towering achievement of his musical career.

"Shea Stadium has been forever associated with the Beatles since their first historic US tour of '65," Summers wrote in his memoir. "We are the first band since then to play there." The implication being that eighteen years later, the peroxide three had ascended to the same heights as the Fab Four and that the Police had swiped the crown previously held by the Beatles. And they had sold more tickets than the Beatles to boot, Summers preened, filling up the playing field as well as the stands. Only the reality of the situation didn't quite square up to Summers's take on it. The Police were not the first band to play there since the Beatles. Simon and Garfunkel had played Shea Stadium just twelve days before the Police. The Police couldn't even lay claim to being the first British band to play there since the Beatles. Jethro Tull had scored that honour in 1976. The Who and the Clash had played there in 1982, also selling out the venue within hours.

The comparison to the Beatles was one that had cropped up throughout the band's career, no doubt encouraged as a healthy part of the group's myth making. A year earlier, during an extremely uncomfortable interview for Chilean TV when Summers was asked how he felt about the Police being talked up as the successors to the Beatles, he had gritted his teeth to reply: "It's a very honourable comparison, but comparisons are odious. And we would rather just think of ourselves as the Police with no comparisons."

In a sense, though, the Police had already had their Shea Stadium moment several years earlier, when Miles Copeland managed to pull off the band's audacious world tour of Asia. That was the tipping point in their career. Shea Stadium was the tombstone. The subtext of Summers's book—which uses the build-up to the Shea Stadium show as a framing device for the recollections of his life—is that he also felt dwarfed by this achievement, given that it would mark the end of the road for the Police. The Beatles were only just hitting their peak when they played Shea; the Police had already reached theirs and then threw in the towel. John Lennon was said to have told promoter Sid Bernstein that he saw the "top of the mountain" while playing at Shea. And there was also an element of this in Sting's recollection that while onstage, he, too, came to the realization that "This is it, you can't do any better than this," and there and then he "decided to stop." In his mind, Sting left the stage as the conquering hero. In doing so, however, he left Summers and Copeland in the lurch. But whatever decisions the band made internally were never revealed to the public.

The Police continued to tour the world for seven more months—ending in Melbourne, Australia, on March 4, 1984—but they were clearly on a road to nowhere, heading for the point of no return and just going through the motions. There was no going forward and no going back. Sting had bent the group to his will and then wrapped them around his finger to such an extent that it was unlikely they would ever be able to work together again.

The three men could barely even bring themselves to be civil to one another in public. During an interview for MTV with VJ Martha Quinn, backstage at one of their shows. Sting and Copeland got into a verbal scuffle, causing Copeland to throw a glass of water over Sting, who promptly got up and chased the drummer. A bemused Quinn was left sitting with an exasperated Summers.

When Stewart Copeland was interviewed for Australian TV prior to the final show on the tour, he seemed distinctly uncomfortable when quizzed about the band's future plans. "The last concert for two years, they say," prompted his interrogator.

"Well, two years, three years, six months," Copeland said and shrugged.

"Was it a joint decision by the three of you?"

At that question, Copeland visibly clenched his jaw and lied. "Yeah," he said, seemingly unconvinced himself. "It was . . . we're in a good mood now. We're feeling very positive and optimistic. We're getting along well and band morale is very high. So we're ready to take on stuff. But then we pulled back. So we have no studio time booked, no concerts booked. Nothing booked."

It was a bizarre state of affairs. The biggest band on the planet was about to fall off the face of the earth.

14

ROCK OF CHARITY

Sting hit the ground running and never stopped. All he could think of was escape, running from the Police. And he wasted no time in doing so. By the close of summer 1984, Sting had already recorded demos for his debut album as a solo artist and had approached both Quincy Jones and Gil Evans to produce the album. But then, in December, he decided instead to ask *Musician* magazine journalist Vic Garbarini to put some feelers out for jazz musicians he could record with.

Garbarini realized that he couldn't very well audition musicians of the calibre Sting wanted to play with, so he organized a series of "workshops" in New York and invited select players to participate, cherry-picking the best jazz musicians in the city. There was young New Orleans saxophonist Branford Marsalis and keyboard player Kenny Kirkland (both of whom played in Branford's brother Wynton

Marsalis's quartet); Omar Hakim, a drummer for a latter-day incarnation of jazz fusion group Weather Report; and Darryl Jones, a twenty-two-year-old bass player who was playing with Miles Davis.

Sting arrived in New York in mid-January 1985 to conduct some informal rehearsals with the musicians whom Garbarini had picked out for him. When Sting was satisfied that he had a group whose members would work well together, he set up three shows at the Ritz in New York for the end of February, which would be his first shows as a solo performer with a new band. The Ritz (now called Webster Hall) was a disco and rock venue with Old World charm, located in an 1880s Latin ballroom with Art Deco fixtures. At the time, it was one of the hippest venues in the city.

"He is clearly eager to move outside the Police's light, international groove," wrote *New York Times* critic Jon Pareles, on hearing Sting's new material at the Ritz. What Sting replaced it with was light jazz and light funk. Two weeks later, he was recording with the band in Barbados at Eddy Grant's Blue Wave Studios. For the first time, Sting was able to direct the musicians and the music the way he wanted. The endless battles that characterized the Police were no more. He got the band to lay down a new version of "Shadows in the Rain" in the style he had originally intended, an "up-tempo R&B romp." Sting commented to Garbarini that "often I felt the demos [recorded for the Police] were better than what we used on the record." Now he had the chance to prove he was right.

Sting even reached all the way back to the beginning of his career, turning one song that had been a staple in the repertoire of Last Exit into a wholly new creation. The subject matter for "We Work the Black Seam" also dug into the past. The industrial tradition of the Tyne & Wear heartland was inspiration for a work song about the daily grind of the coal miners. The album traded back and forth between songs that again dealt with his split with Tomelty—"If You Love Somebody Set Them Free" and "Fortress around Your Heart"—and out-and-out message songs.

One of these, "Russians," seemed to be a rejoinder to Stewart Copeland's obsessive paranoia about communism and the Soviet

Union. The song, which featured a melody lifted directly from Prokofiev's "Suite from Lieutenant Kije," marked a departure for Sting, in that it was written in very spare and direct verse, without the use of allegorical imagery. He posited the idea that the Cold War was unwinnable, given the moral equivalence between Soviet and US leadership. The payoff in the song was a line that asked listeners to consider whether the Russians loved their children like everybody else in the world—a sentiment that was particularly fatuous and irksome.

The album was done by April and was set for a June 1 release, preceded by a week of shows in Paris at Théâtre Mogador. As intimate a venue as a pop star like Sting could reasonably play, this thousand-seat theatre in the 9th arrondissement was designed like an old-fashioned English music hall. The run-up to the shows was to be filmed for a feature film project funded by A&M and helmed by British director Michael Apted.

Apted was best known as the director of *7-Up*, a ground-breaking documentary television series that dropped in on the real lives of several Britons at seven-year intervals in their lives, beginning in the 1960s. He had also directed mainstream entertainment such as *Coal Miner's Daughter*, the Oscar-winning biopic about country singer Loretta Lynn, and *Stardust*, a vehicle for David Essex. Apted brought all of these sensibilities to bear on *Bring On the Night*, which was part concert movie and part documentary. What seemed to be a naturalistic portrait of the artist at work was also ruthlessly manipulative in its attempt to reinvent Sting as an entity outside of the Police.

The film gives the impression that the viewer has been let into the process surrounding the launch of a new record by the Police front man and the preparations for a new live show. It opens with a press conference at the top of the Centre Pompidou in Paris, where Sting introduces himself and his band. They had been installed since May in the eighteenth-century Château de Courson, once home to Napoleon's cousin the Duke of Padoue and still stocked with many of the emperor's personal possessions. A large drawing room was converted into a rehearsal space, the period furniture pushed to the edges of the room to make way for amps and cables and stands. Apted used multiple cameras to capture all of the action. His crew roamed around the room, tracking the interplay and capturing reactions between Sting and the band as they rehearsed. Sting seemed relaxed and at ease, a different person entirely from the intense and strained-looking character who had led the Police on their final tour.

To try to untangle the self-destructive urges that had stretched his sanity to the point of madness during the last days of his marriage to Frances Tomelty and the final days of the Police, Sting had embarked on a course of Jungian analysis. He claimed that for the first time in his life, he was remembering his dreams. And that through analysis of those dreams, he became aware of his "shadow side" and the impact it had on his life. This, he said, had given him a new outlook and had forced him to come to the realization that he did not need to manufacture conflict and tension in order to create, something he had done all through his tenure with the Police. At least, this was the story he told while carrying out promotional duties for the album. In a 1993 profile for *Esquire* magazine, he admitted that he'd made up most of the dreams he'd told his Jungian analyst.

Dream of the Blue Turtles was the album title he decided on. This, he said, also came from a dream—whether one that was real or imagined, he never did reveal. In his telling of the dream, he recalled "four enormous, prehistoric blue turtles" that were "drunk on their own virility, very athletic and macho" and that completely destroyed a beautiful garden behind his house in a display of their athletic prowess. The turtles, he concluded somewhat improbably, represented the members of his new band; the garden, his creative work. And the dream told him that he was right to destroy everything that represented the past—that is, the Police—in order to begin again.

When Sting was asked, in a July 1985 interview for *Playboy* magazine, why he felt the need to move on from his former group, he said, "The Police played Shea Stadium. Where do you go next? You fall into the rut of doing the same things or you shake things up and try something new and start all over—and play a little theatre in Paris. You go back to start again. You take new risks—sort of like Sisyphus."

It's not clear here whether Sting is referring to the Greek myth, about the wicked man condemned to rolling a stone up a hill for eternity, or Albert Camus' interpretation of it as a parable for the absurdity of life. Both fall short as summations of the position he found himself in. The idea that his career was founded on taking risks was a theme Sting returned to time and again. But in this regard, he flattered himself. If he fell flat on his face, he still had the Police, which had not officially announced their dissolution, as a safety net. Sting consistently sought to present himself as a risk taker, while nevertheless playing it safe as an artist. Even during his tenure with the Police, he had never written a song that stepped far from the parameters of what people expected from him or recorded anything in a style that might alienate or frighten off either his fan base or radio programmers.

Sting's comanager Kim Turner and A&M boss Gil Friesen both testify to Apted's camera that Sting was taking a tremendous risk by embarking on a solo career that traded on a different style of music from that of the Police. Vic Garbarini appears on camera, too. He recalls asking an A&M executive what Sting's debut album means for the company. "Salvation," comes the reply.

"So what's riding on opening night?" Apted himself quizzes Friesen. "Sting's career?" Friesen answers rhetorically, before letting out a laugh and then denying that was the case at all. All this, of course, was carefully stage-managed to create drama for the film. The copy that graced the film poster again hammered home the idea that Sting was in some kind of precarious position in regard to his career: "The story is, he risks it all on a dream. The problem is, he's not acting."

But the risk was apparently not great enough to dissuade A&M from investing $3 million in *Bring On the Night*. In the film, Sting himself maintains that the real risk is in performing material his audience will be unfamiliar with. But even then, the cinematic reality presented in *Bring On the Night* doesn't quite concur with what was really going on. The Paris shows took place in the last week of May, with the final date occurring just two days before the worldwide release of the album. The film was, in effect, one big marketing ploy to extend the life of the album, another example of Miles Copeland's obsession with presentation and publicity.

What was not at all readily apparent, partly because Apted traded on a dubious chronology to disguise the true order of events, was that the shows had been staged specifically to enable production of the film. The stage set was designed by Apted's production designer. The band's costumes were created by his costume designer Colleen Atwood, whom Miles Copeland is seen engaging in a heated debate while the band limbers up for a dress rehearsal in the theatre. In the scene, Copeland expresses his intense dislike of the grey suits that Atwood has dressed the band in, mainly because they blend into the stage set, which is also grey. "Why don't we film in black-and-white," he snipes.

"Our original concept and meetings with Sting were all for a very minimal kind of thing," Atwood counters, getting more and more flustered. "He wanted it to be *Brechtian*."

Apted also filmed Sting miming without an audience in order to get enough footage to use as coverage. What he specifically didn't include was a jape perpetrated on the singer by the road crew during the first night of the residency. As the band ploughed into his song "Fortress around Your Heart," a miniature fortress was lowered onto the stage in tribute to the film *Spinal Tap*, released a year earlier in 1984.

The press conference was at least partly real, but Apted had drafted in actors to pose as journalists, fearing that the invited members of the press didn't look colourful enough. One extremely attractive young Frenchwoman asks Sting an awkwardly phrased question in broken English: "I would just like to know if you like France . . . and if you would like to play with a French director."

Apted's camera captures Sting's reaction. He flirts outrageously with her. She becomes a little flustered and embarrassed, flirting back at him. She, too, was one of the plants. The question was staged. Sting looks wired and rugged, and that's because he has just been spirited across town from the hospital where earlier that morning Trudie Styler gave birth to their second child, a son, Jake. That was filmed by Apted, too.

At the press conference, the singer introduces the band and the concept of the film, thereby solidifying it in the minds of audience members during the opening scene. "It's about musicians from different areas forming a common language," he explains, making great play of his band's provenance in his introductions—here is Omar Hakim, the drummer in Weather Report, and there Darryl Jones, Miles Davis's bassist.

Jones had previously taken Sting to a New York studio to meet Davis, of whom he was fan. Davis was in the middle of recording his album *You're Under Arrest*. Sting would dine out on the story of their meeting for years. Immediately on being introduced, Davis set him a task. Sting was to play a policeman (of course) on the title track of the album, reading out the Miranda rights (recited to suspects by US police) in French, which he was given to translate on the spot. Sting accepted this challenge but had to sneak off to call Styler in England to help him brush up on his schoolboy French. Once he had recorded his part, Sting was promptly ejected from the studio. He later said that he felt like he'd been mugged.

Davis had a different take on their encounter: "He is a nice guy, although I didn't know at the time that he was trying to hire Darryl as a bass player for his band." Although Jones would play with Davis from time to time over the next three years, he was eventually sacked for copping an attitude. "He was a dramatic motherfucker," Davis said, "especially after he came out of Sting's band, that rock and roll big arena thing, which is all show business." Jones's pop reputation and jazz chops would later secure him a gig as the replacement bassist for the Rolling Stones (following Bill Wyman's retirement). The hiring of Branford Marsalis and Kenny Kirkland also effectively ended the acclaimed quintet that Wynton Marsalis fronted. The trumpet player, whose views on maintaining the purity of jazz were controversial even in jazz circles, was openly scornful of pop's malign influence on the genre.

Davis was more sanguine about having his musician poached, recalling that he had done the same thing himself to other musicians. But the fact that it was a white musician who had lured him away with money—and certainly more than Davis could afford to pay—was a bitter pill to swallow. Not content to simply poach Jones from Davis's band, Sting also made overtures to percussionist Mino Cenelu, who would play on some of Sting's later solo albums. Yet in a piece that went straight to camera for Apted's film, Sting presented himself as a fervent champion of black music and black musicians.

"One of my philosophies about music," he said slowly, picking at his fingers as if preparing to impart something exceedingly profound, "popular music anyway, is that it is dead. And one of the reasons it is dead is that it has become very reactionary and, uh, racist—where black musicians are not really given the opportunity to be heard on white radio or in white publications. And it's just as bad the other way. This band, being made up racially as it is, is an open challenge to that system."

Miles Davis, for one, didn't buy it. He was a smarter operator than Sting would ever be and could see the singer for what he was: a pop star making a bid for credibility. When the band on Sting's second solo album, . . . *Nothing Like the Sun*, was voted Best Jazz Group in *Playboy* magazine's annual Jazz Poll, Davis decided to say his piece. "Now ain't that something!" he exclaimed in his autobiography. "A black group couldn't get that kind of recognition if they were, say, crossing over from fusion-jazz to rock."

"Sting's last album was a motherfucker," he continued, "but you don't hear nobody's personality but his and he ain't no jazz musician." Davis was essentially charging that Sting had bolstered his own limited experience with the form by surrounding himself with better players than he. Sting did, in fact, admit to Garbarini that he was in awe of Kirkland's instinct and spontaneity, whereas his own approach to composition was far more studied. "I have to gather bits and pieces and vector them together on a machine like this [a Synclavier synthesizer that he is seen composing on in the film] till the different pieces fit." He could well have been talking about the racial makeup of his band. At least one critic called Sting out on his apparent tokenism; the review of *Bring On the Night* in *Creem* magazine ran with the headline "Black Like Me."

The camaraderie among the musicians certainly seemed to be forced at times. In one scene, Marsalis theatrically reads out a tabloid newspaper story headlined "Sting: From Milkman's Son to Millionaire Pop Star" in the rehearsal room, while the band members fall about laughing. A pained smirk spreads across Sting's face as he chews gum with gritted teeth. "Have we had our fun now?" he asks in a school-masterly tone, attempting to bring Marsalis's teasing to an end. In a piece filmed straight to camera, bassist Jones also expresses his reservations concerning the democratic nature of the enterprise. "I'm not so totally sure that this is a band in that everyone has a totally equal say in what happens," he says. "I'm curious to know whether it will eventually become that."

Miles Copeland is later seen in a Paris café discussing the contract negotiations undertaken with the individual managers of the band. "They're saying, 'How much money's on the table, man?'" Copeland says. "I said, Yeah, but that's Sting's table. That's not your table." The implication is that Copeland has played tough to bargain down the musicians' fees, based on the increased exposure they would all get from playing with Sting. But the manager's tactics also contradict Sting's assertion that his band is an "open challenge" to the racist music industry. Instead, it seemed like a continuation of the same old story: a white musician abusing his power and influence. Sting's continued pillaging of black idioms to lend some heft to his songwriting efforts— initially with the reggae and ska that formed the backbone of the Police sound, now jazz and funk—merely sounded like pale imitations.

In the strangest scene in the film, Sting is seen accompanying his heavily pregnant girlfriend Styler to a maternity ward in a Paris hospital immediately after he comes offstage from the first live show. As they wait for the birth of their second child together in the hospital room, Styler reclines on a bed reading a newspaper, while Sting tenderly strokes her hair. Both are dressed in green surgical smocks. The camera pans around to show Styler reading a review of last night's performance in the morning newspaper. Later, she is filmed giving birth to their son, Jake. As Sting looks on, he brushes a tear from his cheek.

"The fact that he allowed the camera into the delivery room is very much within the character of Sting," said *Sunday Times* critic Iain Johnstone in his review of the finished film. "Some rock stars are inaccessible and remote; he's accessible and remote."

In another (even more remote) part of the world, Stewart Copeland was also indulging in his own bit of reinvention. No longer simply the founding member and drummer of the Police, Copeland had restyled himself as "the Rhythmatist"—an intrepid explorer of world rhythms. The drummer had become friendly with a Belgian filmmaker and explorer named J. P. Dutilleux. Together, they hatched a ploy to make a movie that would portray Copeland as gonzo ethnomusicologist collecting rhythms as he travels around Africa.

Like Sting's film, *The Rhythmatist* also combined documentary footage with staged sequences, only Copeland's film didn't attempt to hide it. *The Rhythmatist* boasted an Indiana Jones-style plot that found the drummer touring the Serengeti in search of undiscovered rhythms and then getting sidetracked to rescue his blonde American love interest from a tribe of pygmy cannibals. Copeland's voiceover laboriously explains the narrative as the film proceeds, like a wildlife documentary, offering up his own nonsensical pearls of wisdom. "It occurs to me that in life, as in rhythm, if you know where the beat is going to land you can jump on it," he offers at one point.

The value of the ethnographic portions of the film are largely squandered by the slapstick of the fictionalized sections. During the opening sequence, Copeland walks into a village where a ritual dance is taking place. He is dressed in a black suit and a black wide-brimmed hat, like a South American gaucho cowboy cum computer geek— Henry Morton Stanley with drumsticks and a Casiotone keyboard. He sits down and watches for a while, then opens up the large square case that he has been carrying to reveal a portable recording device. Soon he seems to tire of this, tears off his hat, and cartwheels into the centre of the tribal performance to begin breakdancing.

In another scene, Copeland plays a full drum kit inside a chain mesh cage while lions charge at him, attempting to rip off pieces of meat that dangle tantalizingly on the cage. He was David Blaine before his time. The Crocodile Hunter on the drums. Rather than exploring African music, it seemed as if Copeland was indulging in his own schoolboy fantasies. An interview he gave on the *Today* show to promote the film seemed to bear this out. When asked why he wanted to go to Africa, Copeland replied, "Everyone wants to go to the Dark Continent, don't they?"

Part of the "Dark Continent" was at that point in the throes of a famine causing human devastation on a massive scale. While Copeland was larking around in the Congo, nearby, in Ethiopia, people were dying.

In England, on October 24, 1984, Boomtown Rats singer Bob Geldof watched a report on the BBC evening news about a famine in Ethiopia that, it was announced, had already claimed the lives of thousands and threatened seven million more with starvation. In spare but affecting prose, reporter Michael Buerk described the situation as he saw it at a refugee camp in Korem, northern Ethiopia, where thousands upon thousands of people had gathered, camping out in desert conditions, sustained only by meagre food rations. Buerk characterised it as a "biblical famine" and "the closest thing to hell on earth". The gruelling footage that accompanied the report seemed to provide stark confirmation of this.

Moved by what he had seen and determined to assist the relief effort in any way he could, Geldof teamed up with Midge Ure of Ultravox and together they decided to write and produce a song to raise funds for the starving of Ethiopia. Within a month, the duo had browbeaten and bullied a gaggle of high-profile pop stars (including Sting) to participate in the recording of their charity single, "Do They Know It's Christmas?". On its release, four days after that recording session on November 29, 1984, the song became an immediate smash hit. It sold a million copies in its first week of release and millions more in the weeks that followed, becoming both the fastest and the biggest selling single in UK pop history.

Buoyed by the unprecedented response to this venture, Geldof set about organizing a far more ambitious event: a transatlantic charity concert called Live Aid that was staged the following July at stadiums in London and Philadelphia and broadcast to billions worldwide through simultaneous television coverage. The concerts raised more than £50 million for the Band Aid Charitable Trust. As the instigator of the whole affair, Geldof received the lion's share of attention and credit, earning the sobriquet "Saint Bob". No longer just a mere singer with a middling power pop band, Geldof was now the belligerent and scruffy Mother Theresa of pop, a figure who could do no wrong.

Compassion politics of this type would assume an unprecedented role in the pop music culture of the 1980s. Live Aid initiated a fad for "charity rock"—grandiose musical events predicated upon the idea that pop stars, with their vast and loyal, worldwide fan bases, were the perfect advocates for causes and charities of a global concern; able to communicate and engage with their audience on an emotional level about issues that world governments were either unwilling or unable to legislate solutions for. A rash of copycat concerts and records came in the wake of Live Aid—among them Farm Aid, Hear 'n' Aid (the heavy metal version of Band Aid) and Artists United against Apartheid. Hastily-assembled supergroups of musicians would busk and shill for any conceivable cause that seemed worthy of public attention, bleeding pop consumers of cash seemingly without concern at the possibility of inducing compassion fatigue.

Writing about the USA For Africa single "We Are The World" (the American response to Band Aid), rock critic Greil Marcus identified one troubling aspect to pop music's new passion for humanitarian deeds. While advocating the collective identification and engagement, the lyrics to the song also seemed to be solipsistic and self-indulgent. The song and its performance, Marcus said, represented a "voracious aggrandizement in the face of starvation" on the part of the pop stars involved; a desire to take centre stage and, above all else, be *seen* to be doing good. And this was a criticism that could also be levelled against Live Aid itself.

The most cynical view of charity rock is that it generated massive worldwide exposure and sales for all of the artists involved—something that was borne out by the subsequent "bounce" in the careers of those who performed at Live Aid. It was, in effect, an extremely effective advertising campaign for the commercial music industry. The then-chairman of the Conservative Party, Norman Tebbit, confirmed as much when he described Live Aid as a "triumph of international marketing" during a speech at the British Phonographic Industry awards ceremony in 1986.

Charity rock was built upon the idea (first propagated in the 1960s) that, collectively, pop stars represented a community of philosophically-aligned individuals of one mind and one voice. That idea was fostered largely through the Monterey Pop Festival in 1967, the world's first rock festival, which was conceived as a grand event, curated by musicians themselves, that would unite the counterculture and send a message to the world that music was a force unto itself, a force for good and a force for change. To allay suspicion that the concert was really just a commercial venture intended to line the pockets of musicians and their record companies, organizers Lou Adler and John Phillips (of the Mamas and the Papas) decided to take money out of the equation entirely and make the event a non-profit. The musicians' expenses were covered and they performed for free, with any monies earned earmarked for donation to a modest cause—a free clinic in Los Angeles.

Artist-curated events became common-place after Monterey. In 1971, George Harrison put together an all-star group of musicians (including Bob Dylan and Eric Clapton) to play at his Concert for Bangladesh in Madison Square Garden. This was the first high-profile benefit concert. Unlike Monterey though, where music was the cause, altruism now took centre stage.

Paul McCartney also got in on the act by organizing Concerts for the People of Kampuchea, a series of shows at the end of December 1979 to send aid to the famine-stricken population of that country. UN Security Council Chief, Kurt Waldheim, also lent his name to the event, which featured Queen, the Clash, the Who and Wings.

Live Aid, then, was not an original idea, but it was the first event of its kind to rally the global media (particularly television) to promote its cause. Geldof ruthlessly exploited this to his advantage, even naming the BBC controller Michael Grade as one of the trustees of his

Band Aid trust. The BBC television broadcast of the event did little to hide its propagandistic intent, mercilessly cutting back and forth between live transmission of the concert and blunt appeals for cash from Geldof that turned the airwaves blue and sounded more like sheer thuggery than a plea for compassionate contributions. "There's people dying now," Geldof famously barked, "so just send us the fockin' money."

The entire tone of the broadcast was summed up in a music video screened at continuous intervals through the live transmission. Crowds of desperate and forlorn Africans clothed in rags sat in the dust, naked African women breast-fed their emaciated infant spawn while swatting flies away from their faces and dead-eyed children expired on sheets of sackcloth, their mummified skin hanging off skeletal bodies. These images were cut to a soundtrack that seemed deeply inappropriate—an agonising ballad by US new wave group, the Cars, entitled "Drive".

The emotive nature of these images stimulated a knee-jerk response that could be measured in hard currency yet, removed as they were from any context, completely failed to take into consideration the incredible complexity of the situation on the ground. The famine was caused not by a natural disaster, as reported by the BBC and reiterated by Geldof et al, but a political expediency that was remorseless in the extreme.

Ethiopia was then under the rule of a Marxist-Leninst military junta lead by Mengistu Haile-Mariam, who had gained power in 1974 after engineering a coup against Emperor Haile Selassie. Three years later, after initiating a ruthless purge of "enemies" of the state (known as the "Red Terror"), Mengistu began a program of collectivization, expropriating farmland from wealthy landowners and redistributing among the Ethiopia's peasant population. So, in 1984, while there had been a drought its effects had been exacerbated by a dramatic fall in crop yields in the transition from private to state ownership. Propped up by billions of dollars in military aid from the Soviets (that had swelled the Ethiopian army to quarter of a million, making it one of the biggest in Africa), Mengistu's regime was also fighting secessionist movements on two fronts in Eritrea and Tigray. The drought was then used as a pretext to institute a resettlement policy intended to drain the rebel movements of support amongst the peasant population there.

Resettlement took place at gunpoint. Armed militias would lay siege to a village during the night and round up the inhabitants at daybreak. Villagers were taken to camps—like the one featured in the initial BBC report watched by Geldof—patrolled by guards armed with whips and guns. There, the villagers were put on a starvation diet and given limited access to water to weaken their resistance. Western aid agencies working at the camps were forbidden to provide food, shelter or clothing, only medical aid. They could do little more than watch as military vehicles pulled out to the camps, picking out hundreds of people at a time for resettlement and herd them into trucks and military planes. It was estimated that hundreds of thousands of these people died en route during gruelling journeys that lasted an average of five or six days.

Mengistu would steadfastly maintain that population movement was an effective solution to the famine in order to encourage further Western aid. "What we are doing is really praiseworthy," he told Canadian television channel, CBC. "We have two courses of action open to us. Either we take these people and provide them all with the opportunity to produce, or simply leave them there to their fate and perhaps to annihilate themselves."

Geldof apparently had no qualms about dealing with a man who had been described as the "black Stalin", the "African Pol Pot", and the "butcher of Addis Ababa"; a man who, according to an Amnesty International report, had directed the slaughter of up to 10,000 students and intellectuals during his Red Terror campaign of 1977-8, and tortured and imprisoned many thousands more. Some estimates put the number of victims of the Mengistu regime as high as half a million.

"I will shake hands with the devil on my left and the devil on my right, as long as it gets us what we want," Geldof told Rolling Stone in December 1986, describing this approach as "pragmatism".

Others would describe it as "collaboration" with a deadly regime. French aid organization, Médecins Sans Frontières (MSF) were expelled from Ethiopia for speaking out against Mengistu's forced resettlement program, which was compared to "night and fog" operations in Nazi Germany. MSF President Claude Malhuret maintained that "the situation is so bad, that no one should collaborate. We must denounce it."

Geldof would maintain his moral high ground, believing that the political problems could be overcome if people were kept focused on efforts to provide a humanitarian solution to human suffering in Ethiopia. "I feel it incumbent upon me to keep as many people alive as I can," he said. "But I find it burdensome."

Save The Children described Band Aid as naïve—a charge that infuriated Geldof. Criticism of any kind directed at either his motives or his suitability for running a charity only caused Geldof to become even more indignant. In response he began to lash out at perceived critics. When *Spin* magazine published a highly-critical report on the activities of the Band Aid Charitable Trust (in July 1986, entitled "Live Aid: The Terrible Truth"), Geldof directed his considerable ire at MSF, who had supported findings in the article.

Geldof also invoked the spectre of the Jewish Holocaust, but as a motivation for action. "If we had been in existence during the Second World War and we heard that people were dying in concentration camps, would we refuse to give them food and aid in those camps? Of course not. The same principle applies here."

An anecdote related by Miles Copeland II (the Copeland family patriarch) in his 1989 memoir, *The Game Player*, seemed to confirm that Geldof's efforts were seen as more of an irritation than a help by Mengistu's government. Copeland reveals that his sons made a contribution to Geldof's Band Aid appeal that amounted to a "planeload of medicines and food" and asked him to accompany the delivery to Ethiopia in order to make sure that it reached its final destination.

"After visiting a refugee camp where thousands of people were lying on the ground starving," the Copeland elder writes, "I had talks with a top government official who: (1) referred to those of his fellow countrymen who were lying on the ground as 'horizontals', and those [who] could stand on their two feet and shoot guns as 'verticals'; (2) remarked that six million fewer Africans was not such a bad idea; (3) implied by other remarks that his government owed more in appreciation to the Soviets than to the Americans and Western Europeans because they supplied arms with which the 'verticals' could support a government operating 'for the good of all the people' while we Westerners only supplied goodies which would prolong, but in no way cure, the misery of the useless 'horizontals'."

The arch conservative Copeland would have been keenly aware that a previous famine (in 1973) had hastened the downfall of Haile Selassie, a US ally. It stood to reason that the current famine, if left unchecked, might spur another popular revolution that would remove the Soviet-backed Mengistu from power and allow the Americans to regain control of the region.

Copeland also revealed that his sons "and other tycoons of the film and recording industry pooled their resources and made tax-exempt contributions to a variety of philanthropic institutions." One of these was a US neoconservative think-tank called the Ethics and Public Policy Center, which was founded by Ernest W. Lefever, a former lay preacher, a fervent supporter of the CIA, and an old buddy of Copeland's. Lefever was of the opinion that human rights legislation should not be able to interfere in any way with the advancement of American foreign policy interests.

The Copeland family ideology always seemed distinctly at odds with their peers in the entertainment industry. The war of words that erupted in 1985 between Sting's manager, Miles Copeland, and a rival British pop idol provided a clear indication of how wide that chasm was.

That year, Paul Weller (the former front man of the Jam) and several other politically oriented British pop musicians—including singer-songwriter Billy Bragg and Communards singer Jimi Somerville—formed a collective called Red Wedge, largely in response to the heavy-handed tactics used by the authorities to break up the year-long miners strike (beginning in March 1984), who were facing widespread unemployment through pit closures. The stated aim of Red Wedge was slightly more modest than that of Geldof's Live Aid. It sought to oust the increasingly unpopular Conservative government of Margaret Thatcher at the next general election by increasing youth awareness of (and support for) the opposition. In this regard, Red Wedge was a precursor to Rock the Vote—the organization founded in 1990 to promote voter registration amongst American youth—albeit more explicitly partisan. The collective took its name from a lithograph by Russian constructivist artist El Lissitzky titled "Beat the Whites with the Red Wedge" and allied itself with (and was in fact funded by) the Labour Party—which up until its leadership by Tony Blair in the mid-1990s remained staunchly socialist. There was nothing that irked Miles Copeland more than a pop musician spouting socialist ideology. When he was invited to give a speech at the 1985 Conservative Party conference, he went on the attack. "I believe I have never met a socialist in the music business," he said, describing pop music as an example of the "free-enterprise system at its best." He went on to lambast Weller, in particular, for the hypocrisy of talking about class struggle in his lyrics but behaving, so Copeland claimed, like a small businessman when it came to negotiating his deal and managing his money. Weller responded by denying that he was a hypocrite and firing off a tart rejoinder in Copeland's direction. "People think pop music should be about frivolity," he said. In 1986, Copeland was given an even broader platform to expound on his views about the benefits of free-market capitalism as a model for the music industry, during an hour-long television documentary that he hosted called *My Britain*.

Both the spat with Weller and Copeland's television appearance proved deeply embarrassing to Sting. The singer's long-term PR man, Keith Altham, maintained that the situation almost caused a split from Copeland. It could be that Copeland's remark about never having met a socialist in the music business struck too close to home. On the surface, at least, Sting was still avowedly socialist. In his 1985 song "We Work the Black Seam" (written in response to the British miners' strike), Sting seemed to cast his lot alongside the working man. But when challenged directly as to where his political sympathies lay, he was less willing to be pinned down. "I'm not in the political arena," he claimed. "I'm making personal statements." The behind-the-scenes manoeuvring that accompanied Sting's involvement in another charity rock event would illustrate just what uneasy bedfellows pop and politics could be.

In 1985, Jack Healey, the head of Amnesty International, came up with an audacious (if not entirely original) idea to help raise awareness of the charity: a touring version of Live Aid. Healey pitched the idea to rock promoter Bill Graham. His response, Healey reported, was all business: "You get the talent, I'll do the show." At subsequent meetings, Healey would harangue the promoter about his "emotional commitment" to the issue of human rights—perhaps unaware of the fact that Graham was not only a German Jew by birth but that his mother and five sisters had all been interned at Auschwitz (where his mother had died). Graham had previously handled the US segment of Live Aid, which is clearly why Healey had come to him in the first place.

Undeterred by Graham's terse response, Healey set out to bag some prime rock talent for his show, extracting a letter from U2 that promised commitment for a full week of their time. (The group had previously shown interest in Amnesty, playing a benefit show for the organization in late 1984.) This letter Healey used as bait to lure other high-profile acts onto the tour, among them Bruce Springsteen, Peter Gabriel, and Lou Reed.

Second on his hit list, though, was Sting, who had performed at one of Amnesty International's benefit concerts several years earlier. Sting invited Healey for lunch at his apartment. "It was really neat," the veteran human rights campaigner recalled, coming over like a boyish fan. Healey inquired whether Sting would reunite the Police for the event. The bassist was typically coy. "If you keep it a secret, Jack," Healey reported Sting saying, "I'll try and do that and I think I'll be able to. I'm not positive, but I think I'll be able to."

It was exactly the kind of PR opportunity Miles Copeland needed to relaunch the Police onto the world stage. They would be reuniting for a solid cause, along with the great and the good of the rock world. But he also had to tread carefully in order not to antagonize Sting. The solution was that Sting would play the first three dates of the tour as a solo act, and the Police would perform for the final three. In that way, the integrity of Sting's solo career would not be seen to be compromised. It was as if the Police were being brought on as his backing group.

Although there was agreement that none of the acts would be paid to perform, this came with a tacit understanding, at least by those who handled their business interests, that the attendant publicity that the tour was likely to attract would be worth millions. The jewel in the crown, publicity-wise, was the final date in front of a 55,000-strong crowd at Giants Stadium in New Jersey. That show was due to be telecast in full on MTV and syndicated nationally as a live broadcast across TV stations in the United States (through MTV's owner Viacom) for the last three hours of the show. This meant that the closing acts would potentially play to an estimated 43 million people in America.

Copeland, for one, was not about to let that opportunity slip. "[He] wanted the Police reunion to be foremost in everyone's mind. He wanted them to close the show," said Robert Greenfield, the coauthor of Graham's autobiography. Healey, though, felt that the slot should rightfully be given to U2, because the tour would probably never have happened without them. The jockeying for top position among the lineup (and the fringe benefits it offered) made negotiations so tricky that they went on until the eleventh hour.

Miles Copeland's strategy was to object to the national TV syndication by Viacom and a proposed broadcast on radio in Japan on the grounds, Graham claimed, that it would interfere with his own business plans. He threatened to pull the Police entirely from the tour. "This man was just inhuman," Graham bristled. "He didn't give a flying fuck about his fellow man. The only reason Miles Copeland was tolerating it at all was because Sting was *really* involved."

It's possible that the righteous anger Graham displayed here was also a smokescreen that veiled his own competitive nature. In the world of tour promotion, Graham believed that he had a right to primacy above all of the other players. There was no way he was going to be beaten down by a rock manager. His account of the tour singles out the Police and, more specifically, Miles Copeland, as the only act to cause "major problems." But Copeland wasn't the only one who wanted to veto the TV broadcast. The managers of both Peter Gabriel and Bryan Adams also had reservations.

Sting had signalled to Jack Healey and Mary Daly, Amnesty's communications director, that he would do anything possible to resolve the situation. He also offered to pull out if no agreement could be reached through his manager. Despite these assurances, Copeland had been wheeling and dealing behind the scenes to ensure that the Police headlined their first show on the tour. "When the Police closed in Atlanta without my knowledge . . . I was upset about that," Healey said, "deeply upset about that."

U2 manager Paul McGuiness magnanimously agreed that the Police could close the last three dates on the tour, including Giants Stadium. But the politicking between the managers had put the tour organizers at a distinct disadvantage when it came time to crunch negotiations over the televised broadcast at Giants Stadium, the revenue from which was needed for the tour to break even following disastrous ticket sales in Denver.

A meeting was called to resolve the issue in a boardroom at Omni Stadium in Atlanta immediately after the show there. The atmosphere in the room was extraordinarily tense. After people had laid out their positions, Sting made a small speech balancing his own personal commitment to Amnesty alongside the need to safeguard his career. "I'm very torn about this," he is reported to have said. "My point of view is that we're all geese who can only lay so many golden eggs."

"Miles had all of Sting's insecurities working," commented Mary Daly, who believed that Copeland had been playing on Sting's fears that everything he had achieved so far as a solo artist would be subsumed by all of the attention given to the return of the Police. This line of thinking throws up the scenario that a dog-eat-dog mentality existed within the Police camp. Although Sting clearly had the upper hand over the other members of the Police, Miles Copeland obviously held sway over all of them.

In the service of effecting the most advantageous business decisions for Sting, Copeland would attempt to manipulate his client around to his way of thinking, just as he would manipulate every other situation to his advantage, whether by wile, reason, or bombast. There was clearly a modicum of truth in this, given the mess that Sting had gotten into over his Virgin Music publishing deal. But in this instance, it is also possible that Sting and Copeland were merely engaging in a classic "good cop, bad cop" routine.

Michael Ahearn, the production coordinator for the tour, reasoned that Sting was more concerned with preserving his nice-guy reputation: "The artist will say yes to everything, go behind the door, and say, 'Miles, listen. I'm a nice guy. I'm doing this because I love peace, light, freedom and all that kind of stuff. Would you please go and tell these people that the answer is no? It can't be me saying it because how can I be an arsehole?'"

Daly felt that she needed to make people focus on the reason they were all there. She addressed Copeland in an impassioned speech: "We need awareness because the publicity from this can make it easier for us to pressure governments to free prisoners, stop torture, stop executions. This same awareness affects your bottom line. We're dealing with the bottom line of people's lives."

Having said her piece, she burst into tears. Copeland's response to being backed into a corner by a guilt trip was to attack. He let everybody know that he had the measure of what drumming up "awareness" really meant for an organization like Amnesty.

"I think Jack Healey is an opportunist just like Willie Nelson," Copeland snapped. Nelson had piggy-backed the success of Live Aid to initiate his own charity concert, Farm Aid. The comment reveals both the depth of Copeland's cynicism and his own self-righteous belief. He did not go in for the kind of woolly-headed idealism practised by his client Sting. Copeland was, as he saw it, a truth talker. Self-interest was the goal in every negotiation. Everything else was a manipulation to those ends. His comment about Healey—whose relentless glad-handing of celebrities would not only help make charitable causes fashionable but turn them into a billion-dollar industry—was actually quite an astute observation. Years later, Healey would adopt the nickname "Mr. Human Rights."

After much heated debate, an accord was finally reached that night, with the other managers giving their assent for the Viacom deal to go ahead. Copeland's one condition of agreement was a veto on the Japanese radio broadcast. It later turned out that he was in the middle of negotiating a separate deal for Sting in Japan.

In any event, the group that benefited most from all of the publicity was not the Police but U2. The Irish band was already building steam in the United States, but the Amnesty tour would send its profile soaring. The members of U2 were not averse to opportunistic gestures that would advance their careers. An EP of live tracks (and B-sides) released just prior to the Amnesty tour bore the title *Wide Awake in America*, but it was recorded at various dates in the UK.

On the release of their next album, *The Joshua Tree* in 1987, U2 would seize the mantle of "biggest band in the world" from the Police, and, arguably, they have never let it go since. The reasons for this were manifold but were chiefly because, along with hubris and ambition, U2 added another ingredient into the mix. Where Miles Copeland's conviction was bolstered by ideology, U2 and Bono had God on their side, too. Their presentation of fundamentalist religion and capitalist ideology as a radical gesture was enthusiastically embraced by the deeply conservative heartland of America. The inherent contradictions of being multimillionaire rock stars while presenting themselves as a mouthpiece for the poor and the downtrodden seemed inconsequential when God served as your guide and your conscience.

Emboldened by the reunited Police appearing on the Amnesty tour, Miles Copeland's next goal was to get them working together again in the studio. Sensitive about how to broach the subject so as not to alienate Sting, Copeland proposed a greatest hits LP with a couple of new tracks tacked on to the end as a sweetener for the fans. Sting proposed a compromise. He wanted to re-record some Police standards to give them a new spin. Copeland immediately put in the calls to his brother, Stewart, and Andy Summers, broad agreement was reached, and studio time was booked in London. What no one had foreseen was how far the three musicians had grown apart in the three years since they had last recorded together.

The chaos that those sessions descended into were only revealed in a 2003 article by journalist Garbarini, whose association with the Police stretched back many years. He was essentially their officially sanctioned writer, the only journalist given untrammelled access to the band and virtually on the payroll. This allowed him to write largely within the heads of the protagonists, suggesting that either the journalist was actually present during the sessions (although he does not let on that he was) or he pieced everything together from extensive interviews with all parties, which may be more likely, given that the article was not published until nineteen years after the fact.

It was synthesizers at dawn in the studio. Sting's Synclavier was set up at one end, Stewart Copeland's Fairlight at the other. A keyboard duel was in the offing between the two planks of the rhythm section. It didn't bode well for the band's first studio session in three years and was a crucial test to see whether the Police were even capable of working together again.

Sting came in with some ideas already sketched out about how they could rework "Don't Stand So Close to Me," transforming it into the MOR stylings of his own solo recordings. Copeland turned up with a fractured collarbone and his arm in a sling, having had a rather nasty fall while riding his polo ponies the day before the sessions. He obviously couldn't play the drums in his condition but gamely suggested that he could knock out drum patterns on his synthesizer instead. Summers was caught in the middle, his mood soured now that their opportunity to cut loose on their instruments had been squandered by Copeland. He believed that if they had only been able to jam together, the ice would have been broken and the bond between them reformed. Now, he wondered why he'd even agreed to participate.

As it was, Copeland's arm broke before the tension did, splintering to the bone when he awkwardly reached over his synthesizer to grab something. He howled in agony and was wheeled off to the nearest hospital to undergo emergency surgery. It was not a good start to the reunion.

The sessions carried on without him. The next day, Sting took the first opportunity to wipe all of Copeland's drum patterns and replace them with his own, claiming that they weren't suitable for him to sing over. When Copeland returned on the third day, he took the sabotage with stoicism but then replaced Sting's work with his own again later that night. The rivalry between them continued almost as if it had never ended, and Summers realized that nothing was ever going to change.

But they still had another track to complete, a version of "De Do Do Do." As one of their biggest hits, it was an odd choice of song to re-record, but it was also the song at which some of the harshest criticisms of the Police had been levelled. Sting had found himself endlessly defending the banality of the chorus, and, evidently pained by the censure, he wanted to re-record the song with more emphasis on the verses. Yet it wasn't long before they hit on problems again.

Ironically, according to Garbarini, it wasn't musical differences that proved to be the final straw. It was something as innocuous as a magazine that Summers had brought into the studio. It happened to contain a scathing review of a film that Sting had appeared in: a schlocky remake of *The Bride Of Frankenstein* that took itself far too seriously. Called *The Bride*, it was helmed by *Quadrophenia* director Franc Roddam, and Sting had the starring role, playing Dr. Frankenstein himself. The film had been given a poor critical reception on its release, and Sting's acting in particular was singled out for scathing reviews. The *New York Times* described him in the role as "a glowering supercilious fiend spouting philosophical gibberish." Without even glancing through to survey the content, Copeland began to read the review out loud to the rest of the studio. He got halfway through before he realized that this was not such a great idea and threw the magazine aside, highly embarrassed.

That night Copeland watched a video of *The Bride*, determined to come to the studio the next day armed with his own opinion on the film. But he was not impressed and, rather than mollifying the situation, he exacerbated it by blurting out an asinine comment about Sting's acting that so infuriated the singer, he slipped away from the studio while the others were working and failed to reappear for two whole days.

On the eighth day of the sessions, Copeland worked alone in the studio. He fielded a call from Miles, who was in America: "What the fuck is the matter with you, Stewart? . . . Why did you have to insult him?" Garbarini reported Miles screaming at his younger brother, apoplectic with rage. Later that day, a motorcycle courier walked into the studio with a delivery for Copeland. It was a letter from Sting. "Stewart, you have always been jealous of me," the letter read in part. "I've had to put up with your petty cutting me off at the knees, your total disregard for my feelings and lack of respect."

Copeland wrote a letter back. He apologized profusely, while at the same time denying any responsibility for intentionally setting out to hurt Sting's feelings. Neither side was now willing to communicate or compromise. The situation had reached a deadlock. With no other recourse, Miles decided to plough ahead as if nothing was happening. He set a date to mix the tracks, in the hope that Sting would realize it made sense for him to attend. The way Miles saw it, Sting could either argue his position and leave his mark on the songs or throw the entire project into jeopardy by refusing to approve them if they were finished without him. The ball was in his court. The manager's hunch was correct. On the appointed day, Sting appeared at the studio and, without saying a word, walked straight up to Stewart.

"He comes to me with a rose, a hug, and then—flick! a twelve-inch switchblade!" the drummer recalled. "He said, 'This is for you, Copeland.'" It was an extreme method of diffusing the tension, but it evidently worked. "We got along famously for the rest of the day," Copeland added, "and the snare on that single is a mix of the two samples."

Garbarini managed to graft a happy ending of sorts onto his tale. "In truth," he wrote of those final sessions, "nothing has been resolved. But Sting, Stewart and Andy realize their business has been concluded. The Police, and the animosity that marred much of their existence, are finished."

The promo video made for the new version of "Don't Stand So Close to Me" was a stark illustration of how clearly the song's title had come home to roost. Floating in a *Tron*-like digital world, each member of the band rotates on his own separate axis. They give the impression of being robotized rock stars, cloned from the originals but devoid of emotional response. In the background, old concert and video footage of the Police in lighter, happier days reminds the viewer of the band that was. The finished version of the song is a travesty of the original. The chorus has been slowed right down so that the track stays at the same leaden pace throughout. Sting delivers the vocal in the most solemn of tones. He might as well be reciting the band's own requiem.

As if to compound the sense that the Police were now going out with a whimper rather than a bang, the last song they ever recorded together—the re-recorded version of "De Do Do Do"—was considered so lacking that it was never released, only surfacing years later as an extra track on a collector's edition CD of their greatest hits that was remixed in Dolby Surround Sound. It was all too evident to anyone who heard the song that the Police, as a group, were now a spent force.

15

CLASSICAL GAS

The Police were no more. The challenge was this: could each man make it on his own outside the protective cocoon of the industry that had built up around them? Could they reclaim and reassert their own individuality and survive beyond the entity known as the Police? Was there air enough to breath outside the bubble?

All three members of the Police now found themselves possessed of the kind of wealth and privilege that allowed them to indulge their every creative whim. But they all sought the one thing that commercial success had not provided: credibility. Determined to not only be taken seriously but give the impression that they were serious-minded, each pursued loftier goals, tackling the kind of highbrow projects that would eventually accord a semblance of virtuosity to their respective CVs.

Sting had already powered ahead, successfully establishing himself as a solo artist in his own right. He was now able to concentrate all

of his energies on his own career, without having to consult with or
be held back by anyone else. He set about working on his second solo
album in 1987, the recording of which would turn into a tortuous
experience. Again, Sting's personal life conspired to yank him back
down to earth, but this time he was faced with circumstances that
were not of his making, a situation beyond his control.

His mother, Audrey, was in the final throes of a terminal illness, a
cancer that had first been diagnosed two years earlier. Conflicted by
the unresolved hostility he still felt toward her for the infidelity that
had destroyed his parents' marriage, weighed down by the guilt that
sat like a stone in his gut for repeating her behaviour and splitting up
his own family, Sting found it hard to focus.

The two months of planned recording sessions at George Martin's
Air Studios in Montserrat stretched into almost four. Nothing was
coming together, nothing was getting finished. "Until she's out of pain.
Until she dies, I can't really open up and be creative," Sting finally confessed to Vic Garbarini, who had been invited to stay in Montserrat
during the sessions.

A few days later, Sting received a call from Trudie Styler in London
informing him that his mother had finally succumbed to the cancer
raging inside her. Instead of flying back to England to help his family
make preparations for the funeral, Sting remained in Montserrat to
continue recording. Garbarini reported that as Sting had predicted,
the album was completed quickly, just two weeks later. The singer
then travelled to New York to supervise the mixing process. He did
not attend his mother's funeral, asserting that he had made the decision to avoid attracting the tabloid press to his family's grief and turning the event into a "degrading circus." Yet he was not above talking
about his mother's death to lend weight to his own artistic efforts.

"I look back on this album," Sting would tell Chris Salewicz later
that year, "and I realize that the record is about my mother, although
I didn't see it at the time. It's about mothers and daughters, mistresses
and wives, sisters." This seems a little disingenuous on his part, given
that while still recording in Montserrat, Sting had told Garbarini that
he intended to call the album *In Praise of Women*—almost as if he

were quite simply attempting to redress the wrongs he had done to the women in his life.

On the album's release in November 1987, now capped with a title (... *Nothing Like the Sun*) that referenced one of Shakespeare's sonnets, it was for the most part well-received. The smooth jazz of *Dream of the Blue Turtles* had been refined into a even slicker middle-of-the-road sound. The format remained much the same as the one established for all of the Police albums from *Zenyatta Mondatta* onward: a grab bag of message songs, including "We Dance Alone," about the Chilean mothers of the "disappeared"—and those that bored through Sting's psyche. One song, "We'll Be Together," made plain his commercial ambitions; it was originally commissioned as a Japanese TV ad for Kirin beer in which Sting also appeared, performing the song. . . . *Nothing Like the Sun* would go on to sell eleven million copies and would become Sting's most commercially successful solo album. But he was not without his detractors.

In a November 1987 review of the album, titled "Bring Me the Head of Gordon Sumner," *Village Voice* writer Howard Hampton described the album as "perfumed gunk," questioned the singer's commitment to the causes he espoused, and decried what he saw as the ruthless commodification of "feelings, politics and hope" through Sting's persona as the sensitive singer-songwriter, pained by the injustice of the world.

"If Sting is the disease, then Hasil Adkins is the cure," Hampton concluded, comparing the Police front man to the legendary hillbilly rock 'n' roll icon and one-man band from Madison, West Virginia. It was a valid, if bold, comparison to make. Adkins was untutored and untamed, a wholly intuitive musician who dealt in raw emotion, rather than in manufactured empathy.

Sting apparently read the review and became so incensed by it that he fired off an extraordinary poison pen letter to the publication, a scathing attack on the critic, in which he described Hampton as a "dipshit fascist simpleton." Sting opened the letter with what was purported to be a direct quote from Oscar Wilde—"The school of criticism wherein the worst is championed as the best, and the best as the worst, is merely a form of autobiography." What Wilde in fact wrote (in his preface to *The Picture of Dorian Gray*) was the following:

> The highest, as the lowest, form of criticism is a mode of autobi-ography. Those who find ugly meanings in beautiful things are corrupt without being charming. This is a fault. Those who find beautiful meanings in beautiful things are the cultivated. For these there is hope. They are the elect to whom beautiful things mean only beauty.

If Hampton had been so inclined, he might have responded to this egregious distortion by quoting Wilde back at Sting (from his essay, "The Critic as Artist"): "I am always amused by the silly vanity of those writers and artists of our day who seem to imagine that the primary function of the critic is to chatter about their second-rate work."

Sting continued his attack on Hampton, repeatedly equating the media with Nazism, describing the critic "masturbating dryly over pic-tures of war atrocities," and railing against "the fragility of [Hampton's] self-esteem, your tenuous but essential feeling of superiority over the rest of the human race; you hate music and you hate people."

Curiously, the last point mirrored an oft-reported comment attrib-uted to Stewart Copeland about Sting himself. "Not only does he hate humanity," Copeland revealed of his former bandmate, "but every human within the species, except for his family."

By lashing out in anger during a moment of weakness, Sting revealed more about himself than he would probably ever have cared to admit. He had spent years cultivating a persona as the nice guy of rock, an intelligent and charming man; now he had laid himself bare. Yet over and over, while promoting the album, he portrayed himself as a man who had been changed by the experience of making the album. Working through his mother's death had matured him and brought him closer to his feminine side, he insisted. And as if to prove it, he had grown his hair long. "I'm a normal person," Sting insisted, "I'm not indulging in the rock-star fantasy trip any more."

But that's because he was about to indulge in another trip entirely: as a saviour of the world. Or at least a tiny part of it. A part the size of Switzerland but located in the Amazon rain forest.

Dutilleux had himself been introduced to Raoni by a man named Captain Clive Kelly. A former rock promoter from Manchester, Kelly was so moved by the spirit of the sixties that he sold up, shipped out, and went native, traveling around South America in a specially-constructed trimaran yacht called *Survival*. Kelly made his living by making and selling elaborate pieces of jewelry out of bent nails and the ivory piano keys and also opened up a string of themed pubs and clubs in Brazil. In 1973, he made a trip to a Kayapo Indian village located on the Xingu River, where he befriended Raoni and was adopted by the villagers. Kelly subsequently made it his mission to tell the outside world about the plight of the Indians, whose territory was under threat of invasion by commercial logging companies.

Raoni became the public face of the Brazilian Indians in 1978, acquiring celebrity status after Dutilleux codirected a documentary film, *Raoni: The Fight for the Amazon*, that featured him as the titular hero. Kelly, who had maintained close contacts with Raoni and the tribe since his first visit to the region in 1973, also appeared in the film, as the Englishman who had made the acquaintance of the Indians and become one with them after being initiated by Raoni through a scarification and lip-piercing ritual. The film—recut for the US excising Kelly's role and adding a narration by Marlon Brando—was launched at the Cannes Film Festival in 1977 and subsequently nominated for an Oscar for Best Documentary Feature.

Dutilleux's persistence eventually paid off, and Sting agreed to accompany him on an expedition to the Xingu River in the Mato Grosso, immediately after the completion of the Brazilian leg of a short South American tour to promote . . . *Nothing Like the Sun*. The tour began with a show at Estádio do Maracanã, an eighty-eight-thousand-capacity football stadium in Rio De Janeiro—Sting's biggest solo show to date.

But just three days before the concert, while performing warm-up dates in New York, he was hit by another heavy blow. His father died of cancer. It had not been six months since the death of his mother. Again, he opted not to attend the funeral, instead plowing ahead with the concert at Maracanã stadium, which he would describe as a huge "wake" for his father. By celebrating his own success, Sting reasoned, he was also celebrating the man who had brought him into the world. He did not stop to take stock following the death of his parents. Instead, he pushed himself harder to keep the grief and the waves of emotion welling up inside him at bay. He would maintain a punishing tour schedule through 1988, playing more than 160 shows.

Two weeks after the Rio stadium show, Sting and Styler accompanied Dutilleux and Kelly into the jungle, where they spent three days in the company of Raoni and the Kayapo Indians, touring local villages and hearing about the effects of commercial logging on the area. Sting later wrote an article about his jungle experience for *Vogue* magazine (published in June 1988). "Sting's South American tour took a detour—across Brazil, up the Amazon, visiting Indian tribes who want nothing from the 20th century," ran the strapline to the story. "For three days, Sting was one of them—then they sent him back to 'civilization' with a new look and an urgent message."

The actual article read more like a *Boy's Own* adventure rather than a plea to forestall the destruction of the rainforest, with Sting portraying himself as the conquering hero who after surviving an attack by a deadly snake had pledged his undying support for the Indians.

In 1989, Sting, Styler, and Dutilleux founded the Rainforest Foundation, a charitable organization whose stated aims were to raise awareness of the plight of the Amazonian Indians and the ecological damage caused by deforestation. Sting would immerse himself in activities connected to the foundation for the next two years, using his celebrity to promote the Indians' cause. Sting took a leaf out of Bob Geldof's book and presented his cause as one of great urgency that required immediate action. He narrated a television ad that promised dire consequences and the onset of earthquakes, hurricanes, drought, famine—an environmental apocalypse—if the deforestation was not halted.

Clive Kelly, for one, was not impressed by Sting's performance. "Sting is also an actor," said Kelly. "He makes films. When you're an actor, everything you do has to be exaggerated, that's what drama is. Drama is exaggeration. And Sting is an exaggeration of the truth. Therefore, everything he said then had to be exaggerated to make an impact."

Sting embarked on a high-profile publicity tour with Raoni and Sheriff Red Crow (aka Native American actor and singer Floyd Westerman), hitting fifteen countries, appearing on TV talk shows, and meeting world leaders and other dignitaries. The tour coincided with the publication of a book co-authored by Sting and Dutilleux titled *Jungle Stories: The Fight for the Amazon*, from which all royalties were due to go to the foundation. Shortly afterward, the goodwill toward Sting's activities began to run out.

Mark Zeller, a journalist for the French edition of *Rolling Stone* magazine, attended a fund-raising event for Dutilleux's own rainforest foundation (l'Association Pour La Foret Vierge) that took place in a fashionable Paris restaurant off the Champs-Élysées called Ledoyen. There, Zeller witnessed the invited guests supping champagne and nibbling caviar in the Napoleonic décor of the dining establishment, while Dutilleux and Styler auctioned off art prints signed by Brazilian footballer Pelé to raise money from their well-heeled patrons. Zeller wondered how a charitable organization could afford to stage such a lavish affair and still have enough change left over to effect change. He took it upon himself to write a story questioning whether the Rainforest Foundation was in fact actually meeting its stated aims.

The magazine ran the article as the cover feature of its January 1990 issue, using a picture of Sting dressed like a rakish dandy with white gloves, cane, and mustache—a promo shot taken for his role as Macheath in the Broadway production of *3 Penny Opera* that he was at that time starring in. Beside it, the headline read "Sting: Has He Raped the Virgin Forest?"

The article itself wasn't so much an investigation as accusation and allegation fueled by outrage. But the story had legs and so a television producer for the British investigative magazine show *World in Action* picked it up and ran with it, producing a thirty-minute show titled

"Sting and the Indians" that was broadcast on national TV in April 1990. (In the United States, the A&E Network produced a version of the show narrated by veteran reporter Bill Kurtis.)

Among the allegations made was that Dutilleux had kept a portion of the royalty payment from the publication of the *Jungle Stories* book for himself, a charge he categorically denied. The Rainforest Foundation was described as "a charity built on promises that has failed to deliver." Captain Clive Kelly, the man who had brought both Sting and Dutilleux to Raoni, also believed that the pair had failed to pass on the proceeds from the book which they had promised to the Kayapo Indians in order to help set up a museum.

In May 1992, Kelly attempted to vocalize his frustrations by gate-crashing the Rainforest Ball, a fundraising dinner hosted by Sting and Styler's Rainforest Foundation at the Grosvenor Hotel in London. Kelly was wearing a blue Kayapo Indian headdress as he attempted to carry an oil painting into the event of Raoni and himself (with the words "SOS Rainforest Near Extinction" across the top). He was prevented from entering the hotel by policemen and told he would be arrested.

To counteract the allegations aired in the *Rolling Stone* article and the TV documentary, Dutilleux was encouraged to fall on his sword and resign from his role as co-President of the Rainforest Foundation, thereby distancing himself and any scandal from the Foundation. Sting wrote a personal letter to Dutilleux in which he implied that he was aware that his partner had compromised the activities of the Foundation. "You can't be a trustee of the foundation and make money from related projects, no matter what you and Kelly have done in the past," Sting wrote. "The Foundation is in charge of at least $1m. We have to be ultra-conservative, absolutely straight, cleaner than clean—not only that, we must be seen to be those things."

Dutilleux would resign from the Rainforest Foundation but continued to run the France-based rainforest organizations he had set up on his own. It seemed that, like Geldof before them, Sting and Styler had waded into a complex situation and found themselves completely out of their depth. They were undoubtedly dining out on the high society soirees they organized as fund-raising events, but they also had a tendency to fudge the facts in order to shore up the importance of their organization.

The Rainforest Foundation claimed to have brought about "the recognition and demarcation of an area of more than 27,359 square kilometers" in 1993, thereby achieving its aim to help protect the Kayapo Indians' lands from advances made by commercial logging companies. In fact, most of that area had already been established as a protected area, called the Xingu National Park, back in 1961, work done not by Sting and the Rainforest Foundation but by famed Brazilian anthropologist-explorers the Villa Boas brothers (Claudio, Orlando, and Leonardo), who had criss-crossed the jungle on a seventeen-year expedition (that began in 1943). In the intervening period, incursions were made around the perimeter by logging companies and land developers, leading to the impression that the territory was under threat.

In addition, it was pointed out that by focusing all of their efforts on the Xingu National Park attention was being drawn away from injustices perpetrated against tribes in other parts of Brazil—a case in point being the Yanomamo, who occupied an area close to the border with Venezuela and, from the 1980s on, had been decimated by disease and the murderous advances of loggers who were prepared to kill in order to secure their territory.

Sting, while trying to establish his credentials as an environmental campaigner, made great mileage from having Raoni, who looked impressively native with his disk-shaped lip plug, traditional warrior face paint, and attire, stand next to him. But Raoni and the other members of his tribe were far from the naifs that unknowing foreigners might take them to be. Tribal contacts with outsiders had been established since around 1950, first by the Villa Boas brothers. When Raoni was not on official duties, he wore Levis, cotton shirts, and glasses to correct his failing eyesight.

At the close of the *Rolling Stone* article, Styler was quoted as saying, "I know this looks like a horrible mess, but our hearts are pure." Yet allegations that the Rainforest Foundation was mismanaging funds would continue to dog the organization right up to 2008. That year, a report from a charity watchdog organization, Charity Navigator, upbraided the Rainforest Foundation for "hoarding" donations. There was no indication that there was anything illegal in the way the foundation was run, but the percentage of funds allocated to charitable programs was far less than the 75 per cent standard expected of a well-managed charity. (The following year, in a quite remarkable turnaround in fortunes, the same watchdog would award the Rainforest Foundation with a four-star rating.)

Styler would become well-versed in writing self-serving puff pieces about her own charity in response to any criticism within the media, making great play on her and Sting's achievements and their connection to Raoni—despite the fact that in a 2000 interview, Raoni himself admitted he had not had any contact with Sting for ten years. During that period, Styler had become the public face of the organization, coordinating society balls every year in New York City that attracted high-profile attendants drawn from celebrity circles to raise money for the charity and an enormous amount of press attention. Meanwhile, Sting's role in the Rainforest Foundation was quietly reduced to that of figurehead and founding patron. Nevertheless, the public perception that Sting's rainforest adventures were more self-serving promotional opportunity than altruistic activity would stick. It was not helped by the information that one of the original trustees of Sting and Styler's Rainforest Foundation was Gil Friesen, the head of A&M Records—the boss of Sting's record company.

Sting continued to publicly dwell on his association with the Amazonian Indians for many years. His 2003 autobiography was framed by an account of the visions he claimed to have experienced after imbibing a psychotropic infusion of the ayahuasca vine (called the "spirit vine" by the Indians).

When the time came for Sting to promote his next album, *The Soul Cages*, he made it clear that his ecological activities had been put firmly on the back burner. "I was coopted the last three years," he said. "Coopted by various ecological groups. I used my fame and celebrity as a platform, which is fine, but it's not necessarily me. It was important for me to find myself again. I'm still committed to those things. It's just that I don't sing about them. I don't sing about ecology."

This came as a relief to Sting's manager, Miles Copeland, who did not at all approve of his client gallivanting around the world like the Lone Ranger with an Indian in tow. He wanted Sting to get back to the business of making records. But neither was he happy at Sting's open admission that *The Soul Cages* was a concept album inspired by the death of his father. "That was a big mistake," Copeland offered. "The minute you read somewhere that an album is all about death from cancer, you go . . . er . . . I don't really know if I want to hear that."

Copeland's instinct proved right. The public did not take to *The Soul Cages*. Sales stalled around the million mark, a significant drop in numbers from Sting's previous album, . . . *Nothing Like The Sun*, his most successful since the Police's *Synchronicity*. Whereas *The Soul Cages* was the first since *Zenyatta Mondatta* not to go multiplatinum. It was not as if Sting's career was in jeopardy. His finances, though, were another matter.

In October 1992, it was reported that Scotland Yard was investigating allegations that up to £6 million had "disappeared" from Sting's personal bank accounts. A fraud investigation was launched.

Since the days of the Police, Miles Copeland had built up a Byzantine network of companies to funnel the income from his various activities—including (but not limited to) management, publishing, and a record company—ploughing some profits into foreign investments in order to reduce his tax bill (as well as that of his client Sting). The man charged with masterminding this was Keith Moore, the accountant who (at Copeland's recommendation) had managed Sting's financial affairs right from the beginning of his career.

When Moore dissolved his accounting practice, Moore Sloane, in September 1992, leaving the accounts in the hands of his partner, Malcolm Patrick, an audit of Sting's accounts was commissioned that identified a shortfall of several million pounds. The police were then informed. Keith Moore was questioned without charge by police in November 1993.

A January 1994 article in the *Independent* reported that at a meeting of creditors owed money by the accountancy firm, Moore and Patrick proposed a five-year repayment plan for all uncontested debts. At that time, Sting claimed he was owed £7.7 million. But, the article continues, the meeting "degenerated into a row" when one creditor accused Sting's lawyers of trying to "bankrupt the partners" and the plan was voted down. This suggests that the singer's lawyers might have employed heavy-handed tactics in order to reject any offer of a settlement and instead force the matter to trial.

The case did not come to trial until September 1995. In court, Moore claimed in his defence that he had invested the money on behalf of the singer in a series of failed business ventures, including a chain of Indian restaurants and the conversion of Russian military aircraft into passenger planes, then embarked on a cover-up to hide the losses out of shame and embarrassment. Moore was also in financial difficulties himself and owed the tax man more than £690,000.

At the same time, Moore had been negotiating with A&M Records on Sting's behalf regarding an underpayment of royalties, which eventually resulted in a $24 million payout to the singer. Moore told Sting about the amount that was potentially due to him during a meeting at Sting's country mansion. "His response was that if that [the underpayment] is right, there was a 'big fee for your part,'" Moore told the court. "I took that opportunity . . . to tell him that I was in extreme difficulties with the Inland Revenue and asked for an advance against the fee." Shortly afterwards, Moore claimed that he acquired a signed letter of authority from Sting to draw the money he needed to settle his tax bill from the singer's account.

Sting appeared in court on the second day of the trial, dressed in a sober grey suit and, according to one report, looking "ill at ease." He denied any knowledge of authorizing either the investments or the payment to settle Moore's tax bill. But during the trial, it was also revealed that Sting had very little knowledge of his own financial affairs, leaving all of the details to Moore, who had set up no less than 108 different bank accounts to manage the singer's affairs. The prosecution alleged that Moore kept statements from one of those accounts back from the singer and used it to make transfers of money to himself that were intended to be paid out to Gramelda Investments, an investment company set up for Sting by Miles Copeland.

After a four-week trial, Moore was found guilty of making fraudulent payments to himself and sentenced to six years' imprisonment. Sting was subsequently repaid £4.8 million by his bank, Coutts & Co. But he was also cast into ridicule, as a man so rich he failed to notice when his millions went missing.

While Sting got caught up in drama after drama, the other two members of the Police had only one thing to worry about: how to carve out new careers for themselves.

Stewart Copeland was the most openly ambitious of the trio. He also had the most to prove, having been relegated to providing the backbeat in the band he had founded. When asked whether he resented the fact that Sting had become the de facto leader of the group, Copeland still doggedly insisted that the Police were "my band." Not content with scoring a Golden Globe nomination for his soundtrack to Francis Ford Coppola's film *Rumble Fish*, he took on world music, then opera and ballet.

Copeland's first big test came with a 1985 commission to score a ballet for the San Francisco Ballet—a contemporary dance version of Shakespeare's *King Lear*, no less. The drummer was hired at the recommendation of director Michael Smuin, who had choreographed the fight scenes for *Rumble Fish*. It was a prestigious commission and a considerable (but bankable) risk on the part of the company, especially considering that Copeland freely admitted to knowing little about ballet and nothing about *King Lear*.

Luckily for him, choreographer Victoria Morgan had already dispensed with much of the plot and the majority of the characters in order to boil the original play down to a twenty-minute dance performance. The story was reimagined as a sci-fi romp set in the year 2020. Lear is a rock-star CEO who decides to divide up his corporate empire, represented by a glowing sphere that he consults like a crystal ball. The beneficiaries of his largesse are to be his daughters, three punk-rocker girls costumed in "short skirts, sexy tops, and glittering tights," who dance with a "leggy menace" in their attempt to compete for their father's affections and fortune.

The timing of the commission was awkward. Copeland was about to set off for Africa to film *The Rhythmatist*, which required him to work on both projects simultaneously. "I was shooting a film— an 'extended video'—about African music while I was composing Shakespeare," he explained. "Amazingly enough, it was the perfect setting for writing ballet, on the plains of the Serengeti with the dancing wildebeest."

He included proof that he did just that in *The Rhythmatist*. In a shot that was clearly set up for the camera, he can be seen hunkered down in front of a metal trunk on a plateau that looked across a picture-postcard view of the plains. A small battery-operated Casiotone keyboard (with stickers on the keys marking the notes) is set out in front of him as he scrawls in a notebook with his left hand. Among the choices Copeland made while sitting out on the Serengeti was to score the piece as if it were "medieval." "The overall effect, I think, will be timeless," he explained. The story of King Lear was pagan, rather than medieval, in origin, but details like this got brushed aside in his unabashed enthusiasm for the project. "The idea of hearing some of my humble tunes performed by a big orchestra has a big appeal," he said. "Furthermore, to see these dancers bouncing around to it is even more appealing."

Copeland saw Lear as a "ponderous fellow with problems" and wrote musical motifs for the character that reflected this. These were sent back to Morgan, who choreographed the ballet to the music and requested changes based on her work. This process went on for nine months.

Not being familiar with music theory, Copeland relied on a rather unorthodox method of composition that involved playing all of the parts into his Fairlight synthesizer and then using the software on his Apple Mac computer to convert that into notational form. The printed sheet music was next given to Jeff Seitz, his recording engineer and former drum tech, to look over. Unlike Copeland, Seitz had graduated from music college—the drummer referred to him as "My man from Juilliard"—and was able to suggest improvements to tighten up the composition. Copeland also employed the talents of Darryl Way, his old colleague in Curved Air, as an arranger to translate his synthesized instrumentation into parts playable by a live orchestra. Even so, Copeland's lack of theoretical knowledge occasionally caused problems. He created a portion of music with duelling flute leads that sounded like a brass section and others that were not physically playable by humans. This meant that the score could be performed only by a combination of live orchestra and tape playback of the computerized sounds.

The show received an ovation on its first night but critical notice for the ballet (which opened for a week of performances midway through April 1985) and for Copeland's score, in particular, was not good. *Lear* was only one of four modern classical works that debuted that evening, but its star turn hogged all of the press. The *San Francisco Chronicle* described Copeland's music as "a fitful skein of shreds and snatches," made up of ideas that failed to be "developed beyond simple repetition." The *Examiner* dismissed it as "jejune noodling." The local *Sacramento Bee* was more polite, describing the score as "effective theatre." The response from TV media was less discerning. Copeland was interviewed for *Entertainment Tonight* and asked when he was going to begin work on his next ballet. "After I write my opera," he replied facetiously.

That interview was seen by a fifteen-year-old Police fan in Cleveland, Ohio, named Steven Bamberger, who took the comment at face value. His father, David Bamberger, happened to be the founder and director of the Cleveland Opera—the tenth-largest opera company in the United States—and so young Steven set about convincing his father to bring Copeland and his (then nonexistent) opera to Cleveland. The elder Bamberger finally relented and contacted the drummer with the intention of giving him a commission.

Copeland was as unenlightened about opera as he was about ballet, but he wasn't about to let that on to the opera director. "Stewart wasn't quite as frank about his lack of knowledge of opera as I later discovered," Bamberger recalled afterward. In fact, the thirty-three-year-old drummer had never seen an opera in his life, and his knowledge of classical music was limited to the Stravinsky records he remembered his archaeologist mother playing in the family home during his youth.

Bamberger took it upon himself to educate his new charge, but it wasn't easy. Copeland bolted like a child during the interval of the first two productions he went to see, reporting back that he found *Salome* "pounding, turgid" and Mozart "ubiquitous" with "no mystique, no angst." It sounded too much like "cartoon classical music," he said. But he claimed to have something of a revelation when he saw Jonathan Miller's controversial production of Wagner's *Tristan and Isolde* in Los Angeles. With its elaborate, day-glo modernist sets designed by David Hockney, the production looked like something out of Walt Disney's *Fantasia* and evidently appealed to the drummer's pop sensibilities. This, Copeland decided, was something he could get behind.

The drummer knew he wanted to tell a very personal story, one that was intimately connected to his childhood growing up in Beirut and Cairo. He wanted to tell a story about religion and religious intolerance. It wasn't so much history that inspired Copeland's "grand opera" but history as presented in a book titled *The Holy Blood and the Holy Grail*. A work of conspiracy masquerading as historical fact, the book purported to reveal the hidden workings of a movement dedicated to preserving the bloodline and legacy of Jesus Christ, who was said to have sired children and survived into old age (postcrucifixion). Many years later, it would become the basis of Dan Brown's novel *The Da Vinci Code*. The source of the story told in *The Holy Blood and the Holy Grail* was a series of documents found in the Bibliotheque Nationale in Paris that detailed the history of an organization called the Priory of Sion, documents that were later revealed to be a hoax perpetrated by two Frenchmen, a convicted conman named Pierre Plantard and an actor and humorist named Philippe De Cherisey.

At the time that Copeland encountered it, *Holy Blood* was at the top of the best-seller lists on both sides of the Atlantic, albeit a controversial seller due its blasphemous (if ludicrous) dismissal of the roots of Christian myth. Copeland strapped the basic premise of *Holy Blood*—with its convoluted tale of Christly bloodlines, mystical connections between the Knights Templar and the Sufi Assassins, and internecine strife between Christians and Muslims in the Holy Land—to a good old-fashioned yarn about forbidden love and then threw in some swashbuckling fight scenes for good measure. It would all take place, he decided, in Palestine. The critic for the *Wall Street Journal* later wondered whether the story had simply been lifted from Verdi's *Il Trovatore* and transplanted to the Middle East. Not being confident enough to write the story himself, Copeland enjoined a friend, English playwright Susan Shirwen, to write the libretto for him.

In all, the opera would take four years to complete. During that period, Copeland, who had by this time moved from England and set up home with his family in Los Angeles, also built a reputation of some note as a TV and film composer. He composed the theme song for the popular eighties cop show *The Equalizer* and scored two Oliver Stone movies (*Talk Radio* and *Wall Street*) and also John Hughes's irksome romantic comedy *She's Having a Baby*.

The Cleveland Opera spared no expense in bringing the finished work to realization for its run at the venerable State Theater. Bamberger brought in top-class designers and artisans to work on the production, including costumier Lewis Brown and set designer David W. Schmidt, who had worked on an acclaimed 1976 Broadway production of *The Threepenny Opera* (starring Raul Julia). The lavish sets that Schmidt designed for Copeland's *Holy Blood and Crescent Moon* looked, one observer of the finished production noted, as if they were an extension of the gaudy Italianate design of the State Theater. At its completion, the opera had a revolving cast of 120 (including a 60-member chorus) and was played by a 60-piece chamber orchestra.

As opening night bore down on the production, Copeland became so nervous that he asked whether he could join in onstage, rather than sit in the audience. Bamberger agreed. Copeland blacked-up for his role as a Muslim jihadi with a turban and scimitar, and leapt about on stage with the rest of the chorus, thoroughly perplexing reviewers who spotted his tall, lanky frame among the extras.

If nothing else, hiring Copeland was a brilliant PR move. *Holy Blood* garnered the opera house national attention. Unfortunately, it was the kind of publicity that money couldn't buy. One classical music critic described it as the "worst opera ever written." Another described Shirwen's libretto as anachronistic, pretentious, and so dramatically inept that it required "more eavesdropping here than in the contemporary CIA." The subeditors at the *Los Angeles Times* had a field day, running their (negative) review under the headline "*Holy Blood and Crescent Moon* Has No Sting." But no one at the Cleveland Opera was laughing. They had sunk a million dollars into this PR fiasco.

Bamberger had clearly been steeling himself for a barrage of bad reviews. Prior to opening night, he distributed among the board members of the Cleveland Opera a selection of the negative reactions garnered by the 1824 debut of Beethoven's Ninth Symphony. The resolve of the board had already been shaken by the resignation of one of their number (a conservative Christian) who objected to the sacrilegious theme of the opera. Commentaries from religious clergy were also printed in the programme to stave off any controversy over the play's religious message. The last thing the board wanted to do was to cause offence.

The irony of comparing Beethoven's most enduring work with Copeland's musical about the Crusades was apparently lost on Bamberger. The publicity material for the opera heralded *Holy Blood and Crescent Moon* as a "masterpiece," the first grand opera by a pop celebrity since *Porgy and Bess*. But Copeland was no Gershwin. One critic pointed out that the Police drummer was "probably the only composer to write a grand opera who has no idea what keys it's in."

Following its run in Cleveland, *Holy Blood and Crescent Moon* was scheduled to move on to Fort Worth, Texas (five months later in April 1990). It didn't open there until November, more than a year after its debut. In the intervening period, Copeland worked over the score. But the biggest change was in the staging. Director Christopher Alden decided to intercut the action between contemporary and period settings in order "to create an atmosphere of struggle through the ages." Yet this only succeeded in confounding the audience further. The production cost $200,000 to stage and lasted one weekend. "Even in this time of tight funding and lean budgets," concluded the review in the *Dallas Morning News*, "some opera companies apparently have money to waste."

The night that Copeland debuted his opera in Cleveland, Sting sent him a telegram. It read, in part: "What people forget, when they try and shoot us down, is that we have no choice. We either stick our necks out or we die."

These lines were reprinted in the *New York Times* review of *Holy Blood and Crescent Moon* as a very public show of support for his former bandmate. Sting had never been particularly sympathetic to Copeland's creative efforts. He was more likely to pour scorn on the drummer's musical contributions to the Police than offer consolation or encouragement. If the terms in which Sting chose to defend their efforts (as "death or glory") seemed overly dramatic, his defensive tone was easily explained. He was at that moment stacking up stinking reviews of his own, for his turn as Macheath in the Broadway production *3 Penny Opera*.

Sting had already spent considerable energy attempting to cultivate a screen persona. Time and again, he was drawn to the same character: the charismatic sociopath, a role he played in *Quadrophenia*, a film adaptation of Dennis Potter's play *Brimstone and Treacle*, and David Lynch's adaptation of the sci-fi novel *Dune*. But Macheath was a role for which he was clearly unsuited, possessing neither the depth of character nor the easy menace to pull it off. He had perfected the murderous glower, of course, but the charm he evinced was more lady-killer than serial killer.

Sting was not a natural screen actor, and his performances invariably came off as forced and hammy. Rock stars' winning charisma marks them as natural (if compulsive) actors in real life, but they are not often able to translate that ability to other mediums.

Sting's forays into acting had been pilloried at almost every turn. Even so, the opportunity to play Brecht's urbane criminal Macheath, one of the great literary villains, clearly held great appeal for him.

Sting had road-tested his Macheath two years earlier in a couple of performances alongside the Hamburg State Orchestra. Arranged and conducted by composer Eberhard Schoener, the event—called (with an amusing German precision) *Pop Stars Are Singing Brecht/Weill*—was recorded for broadcast on German state television. The other pop stars involved in this venture were Cream's Jack Bruce and Italian female singer-songwriter Gianni Nannini. Sting adopted a cockney accent to perform "Mack the Knife," then, in a brave but not entirely successful move, insisted on singing in stilted German, inspiring barely suppressed titters from some of the native-speaking audience.

Around the same time that he participated in the event with Schoener, Sting had also worked up enthusiasm in Hollywood producer Jerome Hellman (whose feature credits included the John Schlesinger movies *Midnight Cowboy* and *The Day of the Locust*) to stage a big-budget theatrical presentation of *3 Penny Opera*, featuring himself in the starring role. This kind of casual deal making was now a matter of course for Sting, whose social network had begun to expand greatly with Trudie Styler by his side. The couple had invested in a house in Malibu. In the nineties, Styler would utilize the contacts they had built up (and part of her partner's fortune) to help her establish a career as a film producer.

Hellman was a friend and neighbour of the couple in Malibu. Sting was clearly the main selling point of this venture. Hellman admitted that without Sting's name, he wouldn't have been "able to raise a dime" toward bringing Brecht to Broadway. The production was partly financed with Japanese money through Haruki Kadokawa, the heir to the Kadokawa Shoten publishing empire, and filmmaker Hiroshi Sugiwara.

Veteran British theatre director John Dexter was brought in to oversee the production. A new translation of the lyrics was commissioned from *Village Voice* critic Michael Feingold, who modernized and toughened up the language for a contemporary audience, with mixed results. One commentator would take Feingold to task for rhyming "happy" with "crappy" in "Mack the Knife."

The translation of performance style from concert stage to theatre stage also proved awkward for Sting. His tendency to telegraph moves for stadium audiences was not at all appropriate in the close confines of a theatre. And director Dexter, who had a reputation for being tough on his actors, was not afraid to cut the rock star down to size. "Sting-ey," he told his lead, during one rehearsal, "you're not playing to the deaf and the blind. So you don't need a gesture on every line."

Dexter took to referring to his lead as "Stingle" and "Sting-ey," accented with a kind of chummy affectation. It's just possible he was simply trying to provoke the singer. At one point during rehearsals, Sting even threatened to organize a mass walkout of the cast in protest at Dexter's harsh treatment of another actor.

Apart from the neatly trimmed moustache and a twenties-style haircut, Sting did not attempt too much of a transformation for the role. In publicity photos for the show, he looked rakishly handsome and sly as a fox. This, however, was not quite what Brecht had in mind for Macheath, who was described in the original play as "somewhat bald, like a radish, but not without dignity."

There was another, more pressing, worry. It became apparent that Sting's voice was not suited to projecting from the stage without amplification. Initial reviews of the show pointed out that his vocals were thin and had difficulty reaching the back of the theatre. For the New York run, both he and the female lead were fitted with stage mics. "But it's very subtle. They don't make your ears bleed like ours do when we play concerts," Sting joked to a reporter from the Associated Press, playing up the rock 'n' roll credentials he was bringing to Broadway.

Despite these hiccups, *3 Penny Opera*—the numeral in the title was a conscious reference to the original 1928 staging in Germany—opened on schedule midway through September 1989 at the National Theater in Washington, a venue that was often used as a testing ground for Broadway-bound productions. The opening night was heralded with great fanfare in the local press, not least because both President George H. W. Bush and First Lady Barbara were in attendance; the latter was said to be a huge fan of Sting's. "The Bushes have all of Sting's records," Kim Turner claimed to the *Washington Post* with an apparently straight face. Turner was now acting as Sting's comanager alongside Miles Copeland.

The irony of the Bush dynasty elders attending a musical that equated the bourgeoisie and the political elite with criminals and murderers was apparently lost on them. Neoconservative cultural critic Richard Grenier concluded that George Bush probably considered it "entertainment." It's just possible that his attendance was an act of rapprochement to bring about the end of the Cold War. Also in attendance that night was Soviet ambassador Yuri V. Dubinin, whose escort for the evening was an eighteen-year-old Russian beauty queen in a polka dot dress named Yulia Sahkanova. Dubinin proudly introduced Miss Sahkanova (the very first Miss USSR) to members of the American press.

Assorted senators from both sides of the aisle (including Al Gore) also turned up, hoping to press the flesh with a genuine rock star. Were he alive to see it, Brecht would no doubt have been amused to witness the spectacle of this unctuous hobnobbing by the political hoi polloi. But all things considered, it was a highly successful coming-out party for Sting's stage debut—until the reviews came out the morning after.

Lumbering, *turgid*, and *airless* were just some of the adjectives used to describe the show. It was box-office poison. Sting bore the brunt of the criticism. His acting, said the *Washington Post*, had "little resonance" and his interpretation of Macheath "doesn't extend much beyond that initial impression of arrogant superiority." Both producer and star brushed off the criticism, insisting the show was still a work in progress that was being refined every night in preparation for its move to Broadway.

After twenty preview performances, the production opened at the Lunt-Fontanne Theatre in the heart of Broadway on November 5, 1989, with $4.5 million in advance sales, breaking even on the $4 million it had cost to stage. But *3 Penny Opera*'s first night in New York received another poison-pen letter: a harsh review from *New York Times* theatre critic Frank Rich.

Rich maintained that the idea of combining Brecht's "raw aggression" with the "outlaw pose of contemporary rock" was an exciting prospect and an achievable one, citing Tom Waits's interpretation of "What Keeps Mankind Alive?" (on a 1985 anthology of Kurt Weill covers by contemporary musicians) as proof that the results could be "incendiary." Sting's renditions, he insisted, were "monotonous" and "stiff." "He seems to hope that a large cane and a smug, insistent pout will somehow convey the menace of a character who is a murderer, rapist, thief and arsonist." The show closed six weeks later on December 31, after only sixty-five performances. Sting had been contracted to play the role until June the following year.

Publicly, at least, Stewart Copeland and Sting seemed impervious to criticism, consistently chalking up any bad notices to sour grapes and pointing to the support of their peers and the cheers of the audience. "My audience is a much more voluble [*sic*] audience than Verdi's audience," said Copeland, commenting on what he brought to the classical arena, "and so I can go home after the show with more ringing in my ears than maybe for *Tosca*."

Pop music is a medium that thrives on the relationship between performer and audience. Sexual frenzy drives the market. Entertaining the crowd is crucial to the art of pop; it bears little or no function in other artistic mediums. This point the Police men singularly failed to comprehend. Sting at least gave the impression of seeming humble—even if, once one scratched the surface, this was clearly not the case. "I'm not afraid of failing. I relish failure, actually," he told National Public Radio in America the year following his Brechtian debacle, while promoting another enterprise: the narration he had lent to a new recording of Prokofiev's *Peter and the Wolf*. Yet the notion of failure becomes virtually meaningless after someone has experienced a continued and sustained success that has banked millions. At this point in his career, Sting could afford to fail and take what he considered "artistic risks."

Later in the same interview, when asked what he considered his greatest failure, he suddenly became coy. "It's a secret," he teased. "I think that's—that's how we evolve, you know? That's how art evolves, by not being interested in the purity of the original idea. I don't care about that. I'm much more interested in taking something, adapting it and making it into something new."

Unlike Sting and Copeland, Andy Summers seemed to have no desire to grandstand. He slipped into a quiet retirement from stadium rock, content to shore up his musical credentials with a series of jazz-fusion solo albums. The closest Summers came to taking on the classics was a 1999 album titled *Green Chimneys*, in which he reinterpreted the work of Thelonius Monk. But he did attempt to reinvent himself in another profession entirely: as a photographer.

Summers had started taking photographs to relieve the boredom of the long dead hours of his touring schedule with the Police. He outfitted himself with a Leica (the compact German camera used by photographers such as Henri Cartier Bresson, Robert Capa and Robert Frank) and limited himself to shooting only in black and white. It soon became an all-consuming passion, offstage and onstage. At one point, he even rigged up a switch to his guitar pedals that allowed him to take pictures of the stage and the audience remotely while playing onstage.

He reckoned to have taken more than twenty-five thousand pictures during the three or four-year period that the Police toured the world. He also took pictures that were a world away from his life in the Police. Pictures of alien city streets, sometimes deserted apart from a single figure, sometimes bustling with commuter activity, a nude woman wrapped around his guitar in a hotel room, and visual jokes set up for the camera.

British fashion photographer David Bailey, in his introduction to *Cities Like This*, a 2005 collection of Summers's street photography, placed the guitarist's work in the same lineage with Brassai and Edward Hopper. He gave no indication that he was joking. When discussing his own work, Summers, too, invoked the likes of Henri Cartier-Bresson and Robert Frank and affected a solemn air of intellectual sophistication. "I think of the composition in musical terms," he commented to one interviewer. "I've been realizing how similar a photograph is to a chord on the guitar, to the way you assemble the different notes."

The photographs themselves didn't really merit much serious consideration. They were little more than nicely-composed snapshots printed in black and white to give them a semblance of artsiness. The selections themselves were ill-defined and nebulous for the sake of generating a sense of mystery. But then Summers didn't actually edit his own photographs for exhibition. "I sent the gallery a lot of photos, and these are the ones they chose," he revealed.

The photographer seemed dissociated from his work in other ways, too: always remote and aloof from his subjects, whether it was a passer-by shot at point-blank range in the street or a self-consciously arty female nude laid out like a buffet among the bland furnishings of a hotel room. Like his guitar playing, the images were flawless in their technical execution but lacking in any emotional resonance.

No longer connected by the umbilical cord of the Police, the lives of the three men drifted apart and took radically different courses. They maintained a personal connection and met as friends, but by and large, it was with the warmth of strangers, no longer compatriots with a shared sense of mission. Discussion of whether the Police would ever reunite was strictly off the agenda.

16

RECEDE, RETIRE, RETREAD

Eventually, Sting would bow to the inevitable. The Police would reunite—but not until some twenty years had elapsed since they last played together in public as part of the Amnesty International tour. Pride and public image dictated that Sting concede in his own way. It had to sound like a gallant decision, reached spontaneously and not without a certain amount of risk on his part.

"I woke up one morning last year," Sting recalled in 2007, his words ringing like an old blues refrain, "and my classical record [*Songs from the Labyrinth*, a 2006 album of interpretations of the sixteenth-century lute music of John Dowland] had just gone into the pop charts, in both England and America. I was extremely happy, but then I thought, 'What do I do now? Do I make another record like that?' I didn't want to do that: it would be like painting myself into a corner. Did I want to make another Sting pop record? No, not really. What would surprise people? If I re-formed the Police. I thought, 'Are you out of your mind? Well then, that's what you do.'"

According to this scenario, Sting was at the peak of his powers. The numbers tell a different story. His classical lute album, although never a record that would sell in the millions, was a commercial flop, spending just five weeks on the American Billboard album chart (and only four weeks on the British album chart). It debuted with North American sales of 23,514 in the same week that Rod Stewart went straight to number one with 184,000. Sting's career peak as a solo artist came with his 1999 album, *Brand New Day*, which sold six million copies. The album that followed it, 2003's *Sacred Love*, was his second-worst-selling record, clocking up less than a million in sales.

The person directly and indirectly responsible for both developments was Miles Copeland, who continued to mastermind his client's career long after the Police had disbanded. When Sting's record sales levelled off in the 1990s, a natural occurrence for any long-standing recording artist, Copeland had pulled off one last stunt on behalf of his client that had sent Sting's career soaring once again. Then Sting abruptly decided to part ways with Copeland, ending their twenty-three-year working relationship, just as he had abruptly called a halt to the Police. Sales for Sting's next album, *Sacred Love*, went into free-fall, which at least gave Copeland the opportunity to gloat.

"I think in the end for him," Copeland offered, "one of the reasons why we separated was that when that *Brand New Day* album became so huge, he got to the point where he thought, 'Okay, I did it in the Police, with two other guys. I did it with Miles, a manager who really helped and guided me. I wonder if I can do it on my own . . . with an idiot manager.' So he went off with an idiot manager. And, unfortunately, he didn't do it on his own. The album went [Copeland points south]. And he gave up and he's gone and done the Police again."

There's a hint of sour grapes in this statement because the "idiot manager" whom Sting went off with was the singer's long-term US publicist Kathryn Schenker. She had, according to one observer, been wooing him for some time before the split. Lonn Friend, a former editor of *RIP* magazine and record industry consultant involved in the campaign for *Brand New Day*, recalled, "At that time, [Schenker] was moving in on Miles's territory, becoming all things 'manager' to Sting. She was practically lifting the board for him when he took a leak."

Friend was employed during a corporate restructuring programme in which A&M (Sting's long-term label) and Geffen Records were being merged into Interscope Records. In order to avoid disenfranchising the company's artists, Friend was employed on a six-month contract as a "sort-of ambassador and project manager" (his words) to the biggest names on the label—people like Sheryl Crow, Peter Gabriel, and Sting. Friend was to act as a sop between the musicians and the newer hard-nosed corporate management at the label.

As part of his assignment, Friend met Sting and Miles Copeland in Paris during a campaign meeting to thrash out the international marketing strategy for *Brand New Day*—the album was due for release in September 1999 and carried a message of hope for the new millennium. Later that evening, during a lavish dinner hosted at a restaurant in the Eiffel Tower, Friend felt that he had bonded with the singer during a brief discussion about the yoga techniques they both practised (Ashtanga and Kundalini). Friend was so enthused by his meeting with the singer that the next morning a vision of perfect Stingly perfection popped into his head.

"He's a prophet, a modern prophet of song and spirit," Friend explained. "The people follow him, up the mountain, to a better way. The year 2000 was six months away, and that's when we turn the clock to zero, honey, and sell the stock and spend the money, and call it up: a '*Brand New Day*.' It was so clear to me. This is the image, the message."

Friend scribbled his idea down as a makeshift video treatment that seemed to be the perfect visual accompaniment for the title track on Sting's new album, which was also planned to be the first single from the record. He resolved to give it to Sting later that day during a studio session he had been invited to attend. As the session came to a close, Friend somewhat clumsily pressed the note into Sting's hand. He later heard through another industry contact that he had "pissed someone off with that move." That person, Friend presumed, was Schenker, "whose feathers got ruffled by the gentle extension of my middle finger to the process."

The video for "Brand New Day" was delivered to the label several months later, after Friend's stint at Interscope had come to an end, and it did indeed feature Sting as a miracle-working prophet who walked on water and glowed with an incandescent godly aura as he led his flock to the promised land. But it was also intercut with half-baked skits—commercial interludes for products like "Brand New Day" washing powder—in a leaden attempt to poke fun at the singer's po-faced image. Whenever Sting sought to undermine his seriousness, he invariably fell flat on his face. Forced jollity did not suit him at all. The clip was no miracle worker, either. Sales of the album stalled at just under a million.

Plans progressed for a second single, "Desert Rose," to be released in the first few months of 2000. The song was a pet project for Miles Copeland. It featured a Middle Eastern-sounding ululating chorus that gave Copeland the idea to feature Algerian raï singer Cheb Mami on the track. In 1997, Copeland had established a new network of labels to replace the now-defunct IRS and pursue his new passion: the promotion of Arabic music in the West. Ark 21, Mondo Melodia, and Mondo Rhythmica served that purpose. A label called Pagan focused exclusively on techno and dance music. A fifth label, Pangaea, was initiated as a vanity label through which Sting would be able to release his own pet projects, but it soon became little more than a conduit for the release of film soundtracks that featured his songs. Copeland would claim that Ark 21 was the largest distributor of Arab music in the West. "Desert Rose" offered the perfect opportunity to introduce Cheb Mami, whose music was due to be released through Copeland's label, to Western audiences.

In retrospect, Mami might not have been the finest ambassador for the Arab music world. In 2006, he was arrested on suspicion of committing "voluntary violence, sequestration, and threats" on a French female photojournalist, said to be an ex-girlfriend, who was held captive in a house in Algiers while two associates of Mami's attempted to perform an abortion on her. In January 2008, Interpol formally asked Algeria to hand Mami, who refused to answer the charges and denied any wrongdoing, over to France for questioning. But back in 1999, Mami could do no wrong. He would become a huge crossover star on the back of his collaboration with Sting.

What distinguished the success of "Desert Rose" was the slickly shot promo video that was made to accompany it. It featured footage of Sting being driven on a desert road in the back of a sleek, black S-type Jaguar. His head is pressed against the tinted window, his face blank and desolate, a reflection of the landscape outside. He looks as jaded and lost as David Bowie's alien in *The Man Who Fell to Earth*. During the chorus, the scene cuts to footage of Sting and Mami performing in a nightclub. A DJ spins records, and the camera pans across scantily clad girls gyrating in slow motion, dark and sweaty.

Copeland approached car manufacturer Jaguar with the completed video and suggested that it re-edit the clip as a commercial for its new S-type model. One report suggested that Copeland had specifically shot the promo to enable him to do this. Jaguar would benefit from the association with Sting to sell its car, and "Desert Rose" would get unprecedented promotion, courtesy of Jaguar's worldwide advertising campaign, far beyond the kind of resources his record company would spend to promote a single release. "Everyone dreams of becoming a rock star, but what do rock stars dream of?" the ad asked.

The ploy worked. "Desert Rose" became a massive hit all over the world, providing Sting with his biggest seller in fifteen years and eventually tipping sales of the album over the six million mark. The trade-off was that his public image as an eco-conscious liberal took a heavy knock with the news that he was now advertising luxury vehicles. Sting was by now quite adept at making any compromise sound reasonable: "When I'm offered a Jaguar commercial, I think, 'Well, I do have a certain environmental responsibility.' And yet, if I allow them to use my song, then my song gets heard by millions of people. It's a song that I care passionately about, it's a song—you know, a duet between an Arab singer and a Western singer, and it has a political message, if you like, underneath the musical one."

The political message clearly originated with Miles Copeland, still pushing his rightist agenda through his client's career: the song posited a harmonious marriage of Western and Eastern cultures, while also indirectly promoting the interests of their two great pillars of industry—the auto industry and the oil barons on whom it depended. Sting attempted to allay any criticism by making it known that he had planted fifty thousand trees. "I'm told that balances my carbon debt for any Jaguars I might have been responsible for selling," he said.

When Schenker took over as manager, her approach to corporate sponsorship was far less subtle. She licensed a Christmas song to a compilation given away in the States through Best Buy's buyers' club and lined up computer manufacturer Compaq to sponsor Sting's tour. The singer who had once decried the use of one of his songs in a deodorant commercial (and sued his music publisher, Virgin, for allowing it to be used) was now happily shilling for corporate sponsors.

As Sting drew closer to celebrating his third decade in the entertainment industry, the shine was coming off his career. He had begun to lose his perceived vitality as a pop artist and was settling into middle-age complacency, releasing increasingly bland albums that paid fewer dividends but served as promotional opportunities for ever more lucrative live shows. He was now in the highest echelon of touring performers. Schenker cut a $50 million deal with Clear Channel Entertainment to act as the global promoter for the seventy shows on Sting's 2004 *Sacred Love* tour. Commercially, there was only one logical next move to inflate Sting's revenues further. The voice inside his head told him: "Re-form the Police. Make the call."

Sting actually instructed Schenker to make the call to the other two. She disguised the significance of what she was about to announce as part of a planned discussion with Stewart Copeland and Andy Summers to nail down the details for the release of reissues of Police albums that would mark the thirtieth anniversary of the group. When they were told that Sting wanted to re-form the band, they were delighted.

In the intervening years, Summers, now sixty-six years old, had virtually lapsed into retirement. He still performed a handful of gigs every year, sometimes with his jazz group, the Andy Summers Trio, other times as a sideman, much as he had done at the beginning of his career. He scored a few films, including Hollywood comedies *Down and Out in Beverly Hills* and *Weekend at Bernie's*. In 2006, he announced that he was composing a film soundtrack for a Danny DeVito vehicle called *One Part Sugar*. The film changed its title to *Just Add Water* before its release, but Summers's score never made the final cut.

Stewart Copeland had re-established himself in Los Angeles, earning a steady income by scoring films, TV movies, and theme music for network TV shows. In 2006, he also appeared as a judge on a 2006 reality talent show for the BBC. Called *Just the Two of Us*, the show was a cheap knockoff that combined the formats of *Pop Idol* and *Strictly Come Dancing*. Copeland realized pretty quickly that his role was to be the loud American "in charge of bullshit wisecracks," but he seemed to have no qualms about playing the fool for the cameras.

As 2006 wound to a close, both men had moved to draw a veil over their years in the Police. That year, Summers's memoir, *One Train Later*, was published and Copeland premiered a feature film at the Sundance Film Festival constructed from fifty-plus hours of Super-8 home-movie footage that he had shot during Police tours. Sting's memoir, *Broken Music,* had been published in 2003. The book was a studied retelling of his life that not only excised the more perfidious aspects of his character in an attempt to bolster his nice-guy image but left out his life with the Police almost entirely. The narrative ends just as the group is about to hit the big time. Over the years, Sting had consistently avoided any analysis or sentimentalizing of his time playing with the group. By contrast, both Summers's and Copeland's accounts almost seemed like laments for those brief, defining years of their adult lives and left the sense that both men had been deeply hurt by Sting's decision to put the Police on permanent hiatus.

Diehard Police fans had also felt cheated by Sting's unwavering commitment to the vagaries of his solo career. They had been on tenterhooks for years, working themselves up to a frenzy at every hint that the band might reunite. Momentum for a reunion had been building in earnest since the induction of the band into the Rock and Roll Hall of Fame in 2003. The Police played three songs during the ceremony: "Roxanne," "Every Breath You Take," and "Message in a Bottle." It was the first time they had performed together in public since the Amnesty International tour in 1986, and it showed. Their playing was halting and unsure. They also played a short informal set at the reception held after Sting and Trudie Styler's August 1992 wedding. Neither of these appearances blossomed into a full reunion.

In 2004, Copeland e-mailed Sting immediately after the tsunami disaster in Southeast Asia, suggesting that the Police re-form to play a benefit concert for the region, but the singer demurred. He had already been asked to play a benefit show as a solo artist at a vineyard in Perth, Australia. He had no reason to share his largesse with his former bandmates.

And then—nothing, until a single bulletin-board posting on a U2 fan site in mid-December 2006 began to snowball into rumours that a reunion was imminent. The posting reported an account of a personal conversation with U2's tour manager, Rocko Reedy, who claimed to have been approached to work on a Police tour in 2007 to commemorate the thirtieth anniversary of the group. By January, the rumour mill had gone into overdrive. The Police tour quickly became the worst-kept secret in the music industry.

The Police started to make appearances together in public that were clearly intended to stoke further speculation in the media. Fox News reported that all three members had attended Styler's fifty-second birthday party at the couple's Malibu house on January 14. Earlier that week, Summers and Copeland had also attended Sting's lute concert at the Walt Disney Concert Hall in Los Angeles, during which the singer had dedicated a lute version of "Message in a Bottle" to his bandmates. But the day before Styler's birthday, while playing a private show for the Television Critics Association in Los Angeles, Sting had played dumb regarding any reunion plans. "We started thirty years ago, so it would be nice to do something to celebrate," Sting was quoted as saying. "We don't quite know what, but we're talking about it."

Two weeks later, on January 30, the Recording Academy issued a statement confirming that the Police would reunite to play the 49th Annual Grammy Awards ceremony on February 11. The following day the Police held a press conference and played a short informal set at the Whisky A Go-Go in Los Angeles, where the band finally put the official seal on the announcement: they were to re-form and tour the world again, beginning in May 2007. "We're the Police and we're back," Sting announced when they took the stage.

Sting avowed that the Police tour was to be a one-time deal, after which he would immediately resume his own solo career. Copeland, strangely, concurred, insisting (albeit rather unconvincingly) that he had grown accustomed to life as a working stiff, which came with his position as a jobbing soundtrack composer. But Summers, who had been left in much the same position he was in before he originally joined the Police (as a freelance guitarist), talked up the possibility that the reunion might translate into a new Police album. Either way, they had all committed themselves to ten months of touring, from May 2007 until February 2008 (the tour would eventually be extended to August).

It didn't take long for the old patterns to emerge. When the band holed up in Il Palagio, Sting's six-hundred-acre Tuscany estate, to rehearse songs they hadn't played together for twenty years, spontaneous arguments started to break out over new arrangements for classic Police hits. Chris Salewicz, a British journalist favoured by the group since their heyday, sat in on some of the rehearsals. He downplayed his description of renewed hostilities by sandwiching it between demonstrative expressions of brotherly love, but the subtext was that age seemed to have exacerbated, rather than tempered, the dysfunction that had fuelled their personality conflicts: "It is glaringly apparent that Sting is the bandleader, in charge of the songs' arrangements; yet, almost as though it is a matter of principle, Copeland seems intent on ceaselessly contradicting him. Sometimes visibly reeling from the ferocity of the discourse, Summers, as ever, is cast in the role of diplomat."

Sting had already reworked some of the songs from the Police catalogue to his own taste for his 2005 *Broken Music* solo tour—which was little more than an additional promotional opportunity for his memoir—fixing music that no one (not least his bandmates) realized was broken. These new arrangements were the ones he presented to Copeland and Summers during their rehearsals for the Police tour. It was a throwback to the days when Sting would bring his home-recorded demos to the recording sessions for the later Police albums, expecting the guitarist and drummer to play over them.

"Sting's changed these tunes, but I'm insisting we're going right back to how they were," Copeland explained. The trio began to work on new arrangements as a team but soon discovered that they remained as intransigent as ever in their old age. "I'd hate not to give the people what they want to hear," Copeland insisted, while battling to come to grips with Sting's new arrangement of "Don't Stand So Close to Me"—the song that had hastened the group's demise when they attempted to remake it in 1986. But Sting was not prepared to budge. "'I'm not changing the bass line," he griped.

As had happened in the studio so often in the past, they hit an impasse where no one could agree on anything and the music remained unfinished. And so they returned again to Sting's arrangements from the *Broken Music* tour. It wasn't only the songs that were made to conform to the singer's vision; the Police were also to use Sting's current live sound engineer Mike Keating. "Perhaps I was an obvious choice to maintain some sort of coherency between [Sting's] solo stuff and the Police," Keating explained.

Any reservations that Summers and Copeland may have had that they were simply being used as adjuncts to further Sting's career were softened by the unprecedented payoff that was negotiated as payment for their labours. "We have a very equitable deal," said Copeland. "Sting could have raped us. He chose not to. We're all extremely happy." The subtext being that Sting had them over a barrel and was able to dictate all the terms and conditions of the reunion to the other two. What Copeland did not reveal was that Sting had effectively emasculated them by offering a take-it-or-leave-it split of sixty-twenty-twenty in his favour.

Nethertheless, the figures involved were still colossal. One report stated that the trio had been offered $150 million for the tour by Rolling Stones promoter Michael Cohl. As it was, Arthur Fogel at live music behemoth Live Nation got the gig, and the figure remained unconfirmed. The promoters would reap far more than that amount within ninety minutes of the tickets going on sale, selling 1,770,000 seats in a snap, at an average ticket price of a whopping $120 a seat. When the sales of merchandise were factored in on top of that, it was clear that the band was making money hand over fist, despite the vast scale of the production they were taking on the road. Their tour entourage included a physical therapist, a nutritionist, and even a "dressing room ambience coordinator," whose job it was to drape coloured fabrics around the drab stadium dressing rooms and turn them into something resembling a Moroccan bordello. Copeland boasted that "they could pay each one of these people here twenty times and I don't think the tour gross would even notice."

But as the date of the first show closed in on them, the question was, Would the Police be able to live up to their own hype and provide value for money? Copeland effectively answered that question himself in an online blog posted at his personal website on May 31, just two days after the Police played their first stadium show in Vancouver, Canada.

"Our First Disaster Gig!" read the subject line of his post. With an honesty that was so unseemly it was insensitive, Copeland proceeded to reveal how badly the Police played during their second show. "We are half a bar out of sync with each other. Andy is in Idaho," he said, later adding. "This is ubeLIEVably [*sic*] lame. We are the mighty Police and we are totally at sea."

Describing Sting's attempt at making a Pete Townshend-style rock 'n' roll leap that misfired and became more of a skip, Copeland joked that "the mighty Sting momentarily looks like a petulant pansy instead of the god of rock." The quote ricocheted around the world on a newswire the next day. Notices from the first shows had barely been posted by the press, and Copeland had already given his own band the thumbs-down. It's possible that the drummer was so anxious about how the band would be received that he attempted to preempt a critical mauling. But it was a rather bizarre gaffe to make for a man at the centre of a multimillion-dollar production. It was the last blog entry that Copeland would post on his website during the tour.

There was a tone of forced enthusiasm to even the most positive reviews of the tour. The general consensus seemed to be that much as their albums had been, the re-formed Police were a hit-and-miss affair. Their September 2007 homecoming show in London was a definite miss. The band had managed to sell out Twickenham Stadium twice over, but once inside the sound was echoey and indistinct, the atmosphere in the venue dead. The group seemed plagued by the very same synchronization problems that Copeland had identified four months earlier at the beginning of the tour. At times, they sounded as if they were all playing different sets at the same time. They seemed to be trying very hard to sound like experienced musicians who had something new to add to their canon.

Summers still clearly felt he had the most to prove, unleashing squalls of atonal guitar in the middle of what would have otherwise been quite serviceable renditions of their hits. You could almost feel the deflation that rippled through the audience every time the vast bank of video screens arrayed behind the band flashed images of the guitarist screwing up his face with what looked like excruciating agony while playing yet another ear-splitting guitar solo. Summers had not aged all that gracefully. The boyish thirty-something tyke of old had dispensed with the skin-tight jeans and now dressed in sneakers and pants that were as baggy as the skin on his face.

The other members of the band had not fared much better, either. Copeland sported a shock of white hair pushed back from his face with a sweatband and wore the kind of glasses one would expect to see on a Silicon Valley software engineer. His stage getup—consisting of a Lycra shirt and biker shorts that left little to the imagination—had not changed since the eighties but looked rather less dignified on a man in his mid-fifties. Sting, meanwhile, had gotten into the spirit of the reunion by dyeing what was left of his rapidly receding hair peroxide blond. He appeared tanned and ripped, dressed like an aging hipster lothario in a white sleeveless T-shirt with a medallion draped around his neck. Offstage, he behaved like a lothario as well, stealing the headlines from the tour when he was photographed by paparazzi leaving a brothel in Hamburg in the early hours of the morning, after a Police show in the city.

Outside the stadium itself, on the merchandise stalls, the only images of the band to be found on T-shirts (as on all promotional literature and posters advertising the tour) were of the trio in their 1980s heyday. The sole official contemporary shot of the band was taken from a photo shoot used for a *Rolling Stone* cover story published in the run-up to the tour. Other than in newspaper and magazine profiles of the group, this photograph was barely used, not even being featured on the group's official website. It was a strange state of affairs. The group had re-formed with the most extraordinary fanfare after a quarter of a decade, yet the trio seemed to be extremely self-conscious about their ages. It gave the impression that what the Police were really selling was not a re-formed version of the group at all, but a simulacrum of the old one, albeit lined and creased and rather rough around the edges from having been kept in storage for so long. What they were really selling was nostalgia.

The founding of the Rock and Roll Hall of Fame in 1983 marked the beginning of the era of nostalgia in music and signalled the death of rock 'n' roll. The Hall of Fame was a private organization wholly dedicated to the promotion of the music industry's back catalogue. From the time it was established, never again would a single defining genre of music sweep the music world, as it had done in periodic waves ever since the 1950s with the emergence of Elvis Presley. Genuine innovations in popular music still emerged from musical cultures that had grown up outside the reaches of the mainstream music industry—for example, British rave music in the late eighties, and new ever-evolving genres of electronic music and rap—but most were quickly subsumed by the industry's need to classify, contain, and consume.

If new wave smothered the potential of punk rock, then the nostalgia industry built it concrete boots and sent it to a watery grave. When the Sex Pistols were nominated for inclusion in the Rock and Roll Hall of Fame in 2006 (alongside Black Sabbath and Blondie), singer John Lydon (formerly Rotten) took extreme umbrage at the news that the Pistols were being considered for a plot in the rock 'n' roll graveyard. He described the organization as "urine in the wine," informing it, "We're not your monkeys. We're not coming." Tellingly, the Clash, the second-most-prominent band associated with the punk era, had accepted their nomination in 2003 (the same year that the Police were inducted) with nary a protest.

In a 1998 essay, Canadian academic Linda Hutcheon identified the three stages through which cultural forms traversed once the demands of commercial consumption quashed the desire for authenticity: "Irony, nostalgia and the post-modern." And this, too, seems to sum up the evolutionary curve of rock music since 1983. Irony was the response posed by the reactionary forces of new wave in response to the threat of punk, with its scorched-earth approach to altering the musical landscape. New wave allowed for an arch reinvention of rock music, one that was both postmodern and irreverent. Once irony had played itself out, nostalgia stepped in to provide a kind of commercialized authenticity that seemed to hark back to a more innocent age.

The nostalgia industry hit rewind on all of the rock idioms that had played themselves out in popular culture. Rock stars refused to bow out gracefully, existing instead in a state of suspended putrefaction, returning year in and year out like living-dead waxworks of their former selves—manicured, coiffed, nipped and tucked, performing note-perfect jukebox renditions of their greatest hits. A peculiar characteristic of the nostalgia industry is that audiences no longer went to shows to hear a "live" band; they went expecting to hear what they remembered a band sounded like. Despite the best efforts of the re-formed Police to retrofit their hits with new arrangements, the fans who came to see them were clearly only interested in hearing the Police as they remembered the band from their youth.

Lydon, weathered and leathered but no less spiky (and looking like a petrified punk rocker himself), waded into the argument as to whether a Police reunion had any relevance at all in 2007, during a radio interview to promote his own tour with the re-formed Sex Pistols. The Police, he said, were like "soggy old dead carcasses." "Listening to Stink try to squeak through 'Roxanne' one more time, that's not fun," he said. "It's like letting air out of a balloon."

Even Sting would probably admit that he was treading water. He had traded on his back catalogue with the Police for years, always making sure to slot a smattering of the classic hits into his live shows. "It's my job every night to infuse a twenty-five-year-old song with as much energy and commitment as if it had been written that afternoon. People don't want to come to a Sting show and not hear 'Roxanne,'" he said.

Miles Copeland was moved to suggest that the decision to re-form the Police was a betrayal of the original ideas that drove the band. The commercial benefits of nostalgia, he agreed, were more likely the real motivating factors behind the reunion. As of 2007, the Police had released more greatest hits albums (seven in total) than albums of original material while they were still active as a group.

"It was the thirtieth anniversary [of the release of the Police's first single] and that was a good opportunity to be reflective about it," Copeland offered. "The record company's always thinking of a hook to reinvigorate the public's awareness of the band, and the anniversary was as good a reason as any. So it's not just about the money. From an aesthetic standpoint, it's in everyone's ego to want to see your art carry on and see it be vibrant and reach a new generation."

In the period leading up to the announcement of the reunion, Miles Copeland would make several public statements that gave the impression he was party to negotiations for the tour. In August 2006, an official Police website apparently linked to Copeland's own personal website appeared online, selling Police-themed clothing. Some fans ordered T-shirts and later complained that their orders never arrived. The website was pulled shortly afterward, with a corresponding announcement by Stewart Copeland on his official website that the Police site was an unauthorized operation that had been closed down. The mystery of Miles Copeland's actual involvement was never cleared up.

Later, the Police manager would be conspicuous by his absence in all of the hoopla surrounding the band's reunion. The fourth member of the Police was nowhere to be seen. In fact, Miles Copeland had been shut out of the reunion, and he clearly wasn't happy about it. "Now it's all about money again," he said. "They had a bunch of lawyers who said, 'Let's keep Miles out, you're going to save money. We'll hook him up.' I still get my royalties and it's going to help me, too, but I thought it was undermining the essence of what the Police was all about. And, yeah, it's disappointing."

Instead, Copeland announced that he would be holding an open audition in Los Angeles to form "the new Police" on February 10, 2007, the day before the Police were to play the Grammy ceremony. Ian Copeland, who died of melanoma cancer in May 2006 and never got to see the Police re-form, had frequently posted on his official bulletin board, *Ask Uncle Ian*, of Miles Copeland's intention to form a Police tribute band and send them out on a world tour, making a documentary film of the entire process. The date came and went with no further announcement as to the fate of the "new Police." In any case, Miles Copeland already had his hands full managing the career of the Bellydance Superstars—a troupe of Western belly dancers who came off like a cross between the girls of the Coyote Ugly Saloon and the theatrical routines of *Riverdance*—which he had announced was his "new tool for world domination."

Around and around the Police tour turned for most of 2007 and 2008, traversing the world in ever-decreasing circles, hitting all the right markets and curling around the United States in circuits that allowed them the luxury of returning to play large metropolitan centres two or three times during different legs of the tour. On repeat dates in the same city, they typically played smaller venues, swapping stadiums for arenas, mopping up fans who either didn't manage to catch them the first time around or wanted to see them again. Yet those shelling out for another opportunity to see the band would find themselves caught in a rerun of the same show. The group played essentially the same set list for sixteen months. Two songs ("Synchronicity II" and "Truth Hits Everybody") were cut from the set for their 2008 jaunt; one was added ("Bring On the Night"). Otherwise, the running order remained the same. Even the ad-libs were scripted.

With a final tour gross that would be in excess of a quarter of a billion dollars, the Police claimed that they had embarked on the most successful live tour of all time, a claim tempered somewhat by news reports (in January 2008) also citing them as the touring band with the largest carbon footprint. To this, the Police responded in time-honoured fashion, bowing out with one final grandstanding PR stunt. While simultaneously announcing what was heralded as their last-ever show, at Madison Square Garden on August 9, 2008, they also agreed to donate enough money to plant a million trees in New York City. It was a peculiarly parochial gesture for a band that had flaunted its status as the world's biggest. That final show, a benefit for two public television stations in New York, was a belated acknowledgment of how much they owed the media as a band.

What legacy did the Police bequeath to the world of pop and rock? "Nothing that important," Stewart Copeland admitted in a rare moment of humility, when asked that very question while promoting his 2006 film about the Police, *Everybody Stares.* Nothing much more, he said, than introducing a reggae influence into popular music, and he wasn't even sure they could claim credit for that. The Clash, after all, had done it first and better, covering Lee Scratch Perry's "Police & Thieves." "That's exactly what we were," Copeland joked. "We were the Police and we stole their chops."

Jimi Hendrix, Eddie Van Halen, and Pete Townshend inspired new generations of kids to pick up the guitar. John Lennon and Paul McCartney inspired them to write songs. Would anyone ever aspire to be Sting? Stewart Copeland's unguarded comment does raise the question that if the legacy of the Police wasn't musical, what was it?

Perhaps the best person to answer that is ex–Police manager Miles Copeland, whose aggressive business techniques, PR-savvy, and idiosyncratic modus operandi did more than anything to establish the group's primacy in the music industry. "We were radicals," said Copeland. "People kind of liked that. We always had a sort of underdog image."

Yet there was no irony intended in the choice of name. The Police were only ever antiestablishment on the most superficial of levels. They were boys in blue, through and through—*Conservative* radicals.

They attempted to be all things to all men, climbed the heights of success, and left a flag planted in the dusty earth as proof of their dominion. Up there where the atmosphere was thin, they remained. Isolated from the world but standing tall and striding like giants— walking on the moon.

ACKNOWLEDGMENTS

To Masumi, for keeping me on the straight and narrow, day in and day out, and without whom the world simply does not exist. To my father, David, for his unceasing support. My agent Peter McGuigan, for his confidence and belief and for pushing me down a path contrary to the one I would have chosen for myself, trusting that I would find my way. To my editor, Tom Miller, for his trust, patience, and Zen-like guidance, and all the fine folks at Wiley who worked so hard to realize the book, not least Kitt Allan, Dan Crissman, Lisa Burstiner, and Patricia Waldygo. To Hannah Brown Gordon, Stéphanie Abou, and everyone at Foundry Literary + Media, for keeping everything running smoothly. To Caspar Llewellyn-Smith, for keeping me in work and for his generosity and instinct for a good story. To Sam Harrison and everyone at Aurum Press, for the incredible care and attention they lavished on this UK edition.

To all of the loyal, lifelong friends who fed and cheered and listened to me along the way. Shaun Kerr, who planted all the seeds. Naseem Allaf, for his unceasing belief and support. To Jo Bangina and Matt and Sue Harding. Haik Sahakian, who started it all. To Chris Compagno and the Zarkovic family (Boban, Sarah, and Maxim). The Sugarman family (David, Joanna, and Chloe), my second family. The Dykes family (Brian, Diana, Robert, and Nicholas) and Edward Dykes, the brother I never had. The Kobayashi family (Ryojun, Masako, Yoshiaki) for accepting me so wholeheartedly as one of their own. The Perou family (Perou, Lucy, Maximum, and Zed) for housing me when I was homeless. And Sting the pig, for bringing home the bacon.

To Lydia, whose indefatigable and independent spirit never fails to inspire me. To Peter, for his endless and selfless encouragement and moral support. To Andrew, for the Peter Berlin connection. To Matt, without whom this book would never have happened, and D.V., the ambassador of fun. To true friends Geoff Cox, Nick Abrahams, Billy Chainsaw, Sam Dunn, and Alex Godfrey. To Tibet, a guiding light. To Cameron and Gaspar, for inspiration. To B+, for keeping the spirit of music alive. Joe Ambrose, for teaching me a trick or two. Kirk Lake, a fellow writer struggling to make it all work. To Chelsea Lee, original rock chick, for her friendship. To all those who make home so special: Stu Mead, Ghazi Barakat, Becky Ofek, Philip and Liz, Miron Zownir, Nico Anfuso, Paul Carlin, Paul Bonomo, Wyndham Wallace, and Yusi. To Will De Los Santos, Gerard Damiano Jr., Adam Parfrey, and the one, the only Ramm:Ell:Zee. To Joe and Whitney, for their love. Richard Metzger, for all of his enthusiasm and inspiration. To Jessamy Calkin and Mick Brown, for their encouragement and support. To Stacey Cousino and Tamara Palmer, for their camaraderie and support early on. To Aleisher X, spirtual adviser and guerrilla marketeer, for letting me stay in his dark little flat at the end of the lane.

To all of those who shared their time and memories, not least Nigel Gray, Chris Gray, Miles Copeland, Cherry Vanilla, Jayne County, Bob Garcia, Carol Wilson, Kid Congo Powers, Jean Roussell, and Paul Morley. To David Arnoff and Akihiro Takayama for granting me permission to use their wonderful photos. To Dick O'Dell, for providing confirmation of my instincts and a final burst of energy. To Tom Vague, for listening.

To all the unsung heroes. To those who know in their heart of hearts that might is not right, that power always drains, that success is not to be measured in pounds and pennies, and that the weird will out.

This book is dedicated to the memory of Lux Interior, the last true wild man of rock 'n' roll to rape the earth.

PHOTOGRAPHER BIOGRAPHIES

This book would not have been complete without the addition of David Arnoff's and Akihiro Takayama's wonderful photographs, shot during the heyday of the Police, some of which have never been published before.

David Arnoff

Although born in Cleveland, Ohio, David Arnoff spent his teenage years in Los Angeles. He spent some time playing in garage bands (like the Collection) but in 1970 swapped his Eko bass for his father's Argus camera and took up rock photography instead. A job as a wholesale record salesman conveniently put his name on any number of guest lists, notably at the Whisky A Go-Go—which is where he shot the Police, during their second US tour in 1980. He would only shoot bands he liked, which is why he took live pictures of the Mumps but not the headline band, Van Halen. This also enabled him to become friendly with bands like the Cramps, the Damned, and Nick Cave, whom he was able to shoot offstage as well as on. His photos grace the cover of the Cramps' debut album for IRS, *Songs the Lord Taught Us,* and the cover of Stiv Bators's solo album *Disconnected.* Another appears on the back of the Fleshtones' debut album on IRS He also shot the Dream Syndicate and British band the Only Ones (during a 1980 West Coast tour with the Who). His photographs were published in publications such as *Trouser Press, New York Rocker,* and the *NME.* In 1985, he moved to England, where he continued to photograph bands (like the Scientists and Thee Hypnotics) and hosted a radio show (*The Late David Arnoff*) on fledgling indie station XfM, playing underground sixties rock. His one regret is not having a camera handy when he was reckless enough to give a lift to two girls from the Manson Family outside the Spahn Ranch, just before they killed the sixties.

David Arnoff's website is myspace.com/crucifox.

Akihiro Takayama

Ever since he began taking photographs as a child, Akihiro Takayama's two favourite subjects have been nature and music. He first used a camera obscura when he was nine years old to photograph the countryside in Nagano, the northern Japanese region where he was born. He took up photography as a profession after seeing Pink Floyd play at the resort town of Hakone. Between 1979 and 1984, he shot many foreign bands during their Japanese tours, including the Ramones, the Clash, the Stranglers, the Kinks, the Knack, Brian Eno, and Japan. He also photographed many Japanese acts, of which the best known in the West are YMO, Ryuichi Sakamoto, Sadistic Mika Band, and Sheena and the Rockets. He shot the Police in 1980 during their first trip to Japan, following the band as they kept various appointments around Tokyo. He photographed them trying out the instruments in the studio of their Japanese record company Alfa Records, playing live at the Nakano Sun Plaza, and meeting adoring female fans afterward. He was also present at a session filmed (but never used) for the *Police: Around the World* documentary, in which the band members wore traditional Japanese kimonos and Sting pretended to commit hara-kiri with a ceremonial blade. Takayama's photographs of the band were subsequently featured on the photo collage that was part of the artwork for their *Zenyatta Mondatta* album. Some of the photographs in this book were also featured in *Heibon Punch*, a Japanese pop culture magazine, to which he regularly contributed photographs. To this day, his other great passion is surfing and surf photography.

Akihiro Takayama's official website is http://akihirotakayama .hp.infoseek.co.jp.

NOTES

1 Orphans

It was Andy Summers who said that the Police found their sound during a session in the basement of a gay hairdresser's in North London that they used as an early rehearsal space. The comment was part of an anecdote related during a joint radio interview with Robert Fripp (while promoting *Bewitched*, the second of two albums they recorded as Fripp and Summers). The interview, conducted by Vic Garbarini, was released on a 1984 A&M promo LP, *Andy Summers & Robert Fripp Speak Out*.

Sting's description of "Roxanne" is contained in his memoir, *Broken Music*. Stewart Copeland's reminiscence is from a three-way interview with the group moderated by Police insider Garbarini. The exchange between the trio later in the chapter is taken from the same article. The Police frequently and vehemently disagreed with one another.

The chronology of Sting's and Summers's pre-Police years is drawn from their respective memoirs. Sting describes his flirtation with Marxist activism, including his participation in a protest outside Durham prison in support of the Price sisters (Dolores and Marian), two IRA bombers who went on a hunger strike when they were refused compassionate leave after learning about the death of their mother. (Summers's *One Train Later* was published in 2006 by Portrait.) The account of Copeland's early years comes from his older brother Ian's memoir, *Wild Thing: The Backstage, On the Road, In the Studio, Off the Charts Memoirs of Ian Copeland* (Simon & Schuster, 1995).

The description of the Newcastle Big Band, which Sting played with in his early twenties, as "twenty-five pissheads" comes from an interview with Sting and Gerry Richardson conducted by Chris Salewicz in December 2003 for Sting's official website. British journalist Salewicz and American journalist Garbarini were essentially official mouthpieces for both the Police and Sting throughout their careers and were given access to the band above and beyond that of any other writers. The trust they enjoyed ensured that their reports were far more candid than either they or the Police possibly intended.

It was Sting who referred to himself as "the Don Juan of North Shields," in Phil Sutcliffe and Hugh Fielder's 1982 book *The Police* (Proteus). This is also the source of his boast "I used to get girls pregnant all the time" and the story behind "The Bed's Too Big without You," a song that he described as "rooted in that period. It's fairly close to the A [anonymous girlfriend] episode of being a partial cause of suicide." When it came to writing his memoir, Sting decided that the song was not only rooted in that period but also written then as well—in other words, after the end to the relationship with his girlfriend but long before her death by suicide—possibly as a means to distance himself further from blame. The song was not debuted until its appearance on the second Police album, *Reggatta de Blanc*, in 1979.

The assertion that Stewart Copeland was dropped into Rupert's People by his brother Miles, their manager, was contained in an account of the group's history by *Record Collector* magazine's Nigel Lees, written for the sleeve notes of a 2007 compilation release, *The Magic World of Rupert's People*.

2 Carpetbaggers

Stewart Copeland admitted quite openly that he came up with "the Police" as a band name before he even had a band, most notably in Phil Sutcliffe and Hugh Fielder's *The Police: L'Historia Bandido*, which was the first book ever written on the Police. *Sounds* journalist Sutcliffe was a trusted confidant who had supported Copeland's and Sting's pre-Police careers. The book, which covers the band's career up until 1981, is a solid source of information. The first aborted lineup of the Police featured Copeland playing drums with an unknown London band called the Rockets, which lasted just one show.

Copeland outlined the manifesto he came up with for the Police during an interview that took place at the 2004 O'Reilly Mac OS X Conference in Santa Clara, California, and made his admission about prying Sting's phone number out of Sutcliffe's girlfriend in an interview with Police fanatic Gert Peter Bruch for French magazine *Paru Vendu* (published in June 2007). The sequence of events that led to the dissolution of Last Exit, Sting's initial jam sessions with Copeland, and his first sight of Sonja Kristina are all contained in Sting's memoir, *Broken Music*. The drug-dealing career of the Only Ones front man Peter Perrett is detailed in Nina Antonia's biography, *The One And Only: Peter Perrett—Homme Fatale*.

An insight into the London squatting culture of the seventies was gleaned from *Squatting: The Real Story*, by Nick Wates and Christian Wolmar (Bay Leaf Books, 1980), and from Vanessa Engles's 2006 film for the BBC titled *Property Is Theft*, about the radicalized occupants of the Villa Road squat in South London in 1976. Ian Copeland's *Wild Thing* provided the description of the Green Street property and the saga of its sitting tenant, Lady Georgina. Some info on Henry Padovani's arrival in London and entry into the Police also came from there, as well as from Padovani's own memoir, *Secret Police Man*, published in France (Flammarion, 2006).

Miles Copeland's comments on Stewart's nascent band and the music business also come via Sutcliffe and Fielder. His analysis of the London and New York music scenes are from an interview in German documentary filmmaker Wolfgang Büld's *Punk in London*. A lot of the material in the film is based on the bands hanging around Miles Copeland's Faulty Products office in London's West End. Other footage is from Andy Czezowski's Roxy operation. Czezowski provided additional information about the Copeland-Childers US Package of Punk tour and the genesis of the Roxy in an interview for webzine *3AM*. Czezowski also described how Gene October's sideline as a rent boy made him familiar with London club Chagueramas, the future Roxy. Cherry Vanilla and Wayne County both gave very candid and amusing interviews. Cherry Vanilla's quote about her groupie career came from a 1976 TV interview (alongside Leon Redbone) on Canadian talk show host Peter Gzowski's CBC show *90 Minutes Live*. The quote about Miles Copeland and the punk paranoia of "Big Business" and Miles Copeland comes from Vivien Goldman's article "Punk Rock," in an April 1977 edition of British music weekly *Sounds*. Various issues of Mark Perry's fanzine *Sniffin' Glue* and a May 1977 article by Tony Parsons for the *NME* on Johnny Thunders also provided valuable information.

3 Queens of New York

Cherry Vanilla and Jayne County were both very generous in sharing recollections of their tours with the Police and the Roxy shows. County's autobiography, *Man Enough to Be a Woman* (Serpent's Tail, 1995), and contemporaneous fanzine interviews with Cherry Vanilla in *Sniffin' Glue*, *Negative Reaction*, and *Zig-Zag* (the last two by Jon Romney and Kris Needs, respectively), and Q&A on Paul Marko's Punk 77 website (punk77.co.uk) were all a source of additional information and anecdotes about the tour. Cherry Vanilla spoke in her interview about Sting and Copeland hitting on girls while on tour. Johnny Thunders and the Heartbreakers' drug history is documented in detail in Nina Antonia's biography, *Johnny Thunders: In Cold Blood*. Ian Copeland's and Henry Padovani's memoirs again provided good information about both the Roxy and the early Police gigs, as did Phil Sutcliffe and Hugh Fielder's *L'Historia Bandido*. Walt Davidson wrote a good overview of the Nuit de Punk in his March 1977 review for the *NME*; Padovani's biography and Sutcliffe and Fielder filled in the behind-the-scenes stories. Miles Copeland's comment about Sting's punk-baiting antics at the Nashville Rooms is contained in Miles's book *The Police: A Visual Documentary*. His description of *Sniffin' Glue*'s Mark Perry as the "punkometer" comes via Sutcliffe and Fielder, as do Nick Jones's comments about the Police. Two members of neo-Nazi band Skrewdriver, Phil Walmsley and Grinny, provided accounts of their show with the Police at the Railway Tavern to Paul Marko. It's not entirely clear which band was the headliner, but the show has mysteriously disappeared from the Police's chronology.

4 Vive le Punk

Andy Summers took issue with the description of himself as a session guitarist during a 2000 web chat on the website guitar.com, but he was indeed employed on that basis, not only for Jon Lord but also for his work with German composer

Eberhard Schoener. An interview with Carol Wilson, who used to run Virgin Music Publishing for Richard Branson and who signed Sting to his publishing deal, provided the information that Mike Howlett's studio was in the loft of her house. Other information came from a 2008 interview with Howlett for Sting fansite LiSting. Summers's opinion of the songs Sting contributed to Howlett's project is contained in his memoir. His comment about spending too much time with "professional musos" is in Miles's *The Police: A Visual Documentary*. In a 1997 conversation with music historian Richie Unterberger, Kevin Coyne recollected seeing one of Summers's early rehearsals with the Police.

An interview with Marc Zermati provided stories of the various incidents that occurred at the Mont de Marsan festivals, including the riot instigated by the Jam's internment in the local jail. Summers's and Henry Padovani's respective memoirs provided, in excruciating detail, accounts of the fight that occurred between them over the amps.

Information about Miles Copeland's prior relationship with John Cale (through Jane Friedman) comes from Cale's autobiography (written with Victor Bockris), *What's Welsh for Zen* (Bloomsbury, 2000). Squeeze songwriters Chris Difford and Glenn Tilbrook described the unique experience they had recording with Cale around that time in *Squeeze: Song by Song* (Sanctuary Publishing, 2004). Accounts of the session with Cale, and Padovani's ejection from the Police in its aftermath, are again provided by Summers and Padovani. Sting makes no mention of this session in his memoir and glosses over Padovani's firing in one paragraph. Despite the insolence Summers expresses toward Cale in his memoir, the two men appeared on the same stage together in 1981 during a taping in London for a special edition of Spanish TV show *Musical Express*, which reunited the old Kevin Ayers band, including guitarist Ollie Halsall.

Summers also provided the account of Sting and Copeland's approaches to Cherry Vanilla's guitarist Louis Lepore and the recording sessions with Schoener. Additional information on the Munich sessions comes from Sutcliffe and Fielder.

5 Paging Doctor Rock

Nigel Gray and his brother Chris both provided enlightening accounts of the time they spent working with the Police at Surrey Sound studio. Sting gave his description of Surrey Sound in an interview with Timothy White for the July 1985 issue of *Spin* magazine. Additional information about the sessions for the album that would become *Outlandos d'Amour* is contained in Sting's and Summers's respective memoirs, as well as in Phil Sutcliffe and Hugh Fielder's and Miles's books on the band.

Sting's *Broken Music* provides an account of his modelling career and the winning manner he employed during auditions. Strangely, despite it being a widely accepted part of their origin myth, the Wrigley's Chewing Gum ad, in which the trio first appeared with the blond hair that would become their trademark, has never surfaced. Not one still from the commercial has ever been seen. If Sting's assertion (in *Broken Music*) that Tony Scott directed the ad is correct, then the footage might presumably lie in the archives of his brother Ridley's company, RSA, for which it was shot. Until it turns up, the word of the Police men is gospel. But neither is there any evidence to suggest that the ad was apocryphal, a cover story concocted to explain their radical image change.

Chris Difford and Glenn Tilbrook discuss their fifty-fifty deal with Miles Copeland in *Squeeze: Song by Song*—a business arrangement that would come back to bite the manager on the arse years later during Sting's court case against Virgin Music Publishing. Copeland was a master at rationalizing the so-called 360 deal, in which a manager cuts himself in for a slice of not only band earnings but also publishing and record company profits. Nigel Gray revealed Copeland's percentage arrangement with the Police and his own negotiations with Copeland in Sutcliffe and Fielder's *L'Historia Bandido*. Copeland himself confirmed that he was in for a cut of the publishing during an interview for this book. Information about the origins and workings of Copeland's Faulty Products empire were drawn from several interviews with Mark Perry by Tony Parsons (*NME*, 1977), Paul Stokes (*Q*, 2002), Jean Encoule (Trakmarx.com, 2001), and Jason Gross (*Perfect Sound Forever*, 2001).

Andy Summers discussed the technology that had impacted on his guitar style in a 2007 interview published in *Guitar Player* magazine. Sting made further comments about the "holes" in the Police sound in Vic Garbarini's 2000 article in *Revolver* magazine. In the same article, Stewart Copeland admitted that the BBC "ban" of "Roxanne" was a ruse to drum up publicity for the band. The quotation in which Sting expresses his outrage about said ban came from Miles's *The Police: A Visual Documentary*, as does his assessment of Stewart Copeland's songwriting. Summers expressed his own opinion of the band's snub by music critics in his memoir. The description of the Police's lack of popularity as a live band comes from a profile by Francine Illingworth for a 1979 British poster magazine, *Star Portrait*.

6 Welcome to America

The Copeland family history and biographical anecdotes are drawn from Ian Copeland's book *Wild Thing* and Phil Sutcliffe and Hugh Fielder's *L'Historia Bandido*. An interview with Miles Copeland provided the quote concerning the importance of building an "infrastructure." Ian Copeland's biography, *Wild Thing*, details his brief car-stealing career in Lebanon as a teenager.

The story of Miles Copeland's calamitous 1975 StarTruckin' tour is largely drawn from Charles Shaar Murray's August 1975 *NME* article, an uproarious firsthand account of the tour. Information about Lou Reed's noninvolvement and his various narcotic addictions came from biographies of the singer by Victor Bockris, *Transformer: The Lou Reed Story* (Simon & Schuster, 1985), and Diana Clapton, *Lou Reed & the Velvet Underground* (Bobcat, 1987). The importance of this tour (and its failings) regarding the strategy Miles Copeland later employed to break

Squeeze and the Police in America (as well as his overall business strategies) cannot be underestimated. The knock Copeland suffered to his reputation from the tour was catalogued in both a September 1979 article by Sutcliffe for *Sounds* and in comments made during Wolfgang Büld's film *Punk in London*. Geoff Richardon's quote of Copeland that Caravan should "shape up or fuck off" was included in a profile of the musician on Calyx, the Canterbury Music website (http://calyx .club.fr).

Chris Difford and Glenn Tilbrook again provided the information about the guerrilla marketing techniques Miles Copeland employed to promote Squeeze on its 1978 US tour and also used for the Police tour later that year. Other information about the mechanics of that first Police tour of the United States is drawn from Sutcliffe and Fielder's and Miles's books, interviews with Miles Copeland and Ian Copeland, and Andy Summers's memoir. Summers also provides the description of how the Police sounded at CBGB's.

The Police reunion tour in 2007 prompted numerous articles about their initial shows in the United States, which were the source of the account of their first tour there in 1979. Among these articles were John W. Barry's detailed January 2007 story about the lead-up to the Last Chance Saloon show for the *Poughkeepsie Journal* and Eric R. Danton's August 2007 article for the *Hartford Courant* about the Shaboo in Willimantic, Connecticut. WPIX DJ Jane Hamburger's recollection of meeting the Police appears on Police fan Rogier van Der Gugten's extensive Police website, as are the quotes from the November 1978 radio interview itself (www.cybercomm.nl/~gugten/s19781114.htm).

An interview with Miles Copeland provided the information about A&M's flourishing interest in the band toward the end of 1979. An interview with Bob Garcia was particularly insightful about the initial reception that the Police received within the American wing of A&M and the strategies employed by the record company to help break the group during their second tour, including the Roxanne look-alike contest held at the Agora Ballroom, Atlanta. *Boston Phoenix* music critic Kit Rachlis wrote a 1979 review that contained his impressions of the Police's live show at the Rat in Boston.

The story behind Steve Dahl's 1979 Disco Demolition Night at Comiskey Park in Chicago was laid out in Simon Steinhardt's April 2007 article for *Swindle* magazine. Additional thoughts on the background behind the battle to reaffirm the supremacy of rock over disco on the airwaves came from articles by John Rockwell and Patrick Goldman (respectively, in the *New York Times* and the *Los Angeles Times*). Goldman's article provided information on the unprecedented marketing budget assigned to break the Police in America. An interview with Miles Copeland uncovered the battle waged over the *Outlandos d'Amour* cover art.

7   Ladies and Gentlemen, the Sensational New Blow Waves

Nigel and Chris Gray again provided good information about the 1980 recording sessions for the second Police album, *Reggatta de Blanc*, and about how success had changed their relationship with the band. Sting's analysis of his own song "Message in a Bottle" is from Vic Garbarini's 2000 article for *Revolver*.

A small aside in an article by Sally Cragin for the *Boston Phoenix* (about the Police reunion tour hitting Boston) provided the tip-off about the never-to-be-heard remix of "Roxanne" by the Homosexuals. Chris Gray, who produced the band in the twilight hours at Surrey Sound after the Police had gone home to their families, provided the details of their collaboration.

Sting's memoir contains an account of his audition with director Franc Roddam for his role in *Quadrophenia*. His belief that the Police played a large part in the film's success was revealed in a comment to the *NME*'s Paul Morley for an article that was published in April 1980. And Sting made other comments about his role to Nick Kent and Chris Salewicz (both for articles in *NME*, September 1979 and February 1981, respectively).

PR guru Keith Altham's memoir *The PR Strikes Back* (Blake Publishing, 2001), which takes the form of open letters written to his ex-clients (among whom were Sting and the Police), explained the PR strategy that was employed to keep the band's name in the British tabloid newspapers. The newspaper archive at the British Library turned up a mountain of tabloid press about the band from this period. Sting's comment that he was "very aware of anything I do" came from an April 1980 article in the *Daily Mirror* written by pop columnist Pauline McLeod. Peter Berlin's quote regarding his own narcissism (which reflects back to Sting's vanity) was taken from a 2006 article in the *San Francisco Chronicle* by Neva Chonin. The excerpt of Police "slash" fiction comes from Sidewinder's extraordinary self-published book *Internal Affairs*, in which she essentially rewrites the band's entire history, arguments and all, as if they were engaged in a passionate ménage-à-trois.

The backstage footage of the Police and Miles Copeland is featured in *Outlandos to Synchronicities*, an official video history of the band.

8   The Organization

An interview with Miles Copeland included his own extremely entertaining account of how he persuaded A&M's Jerry Ross to give him a production deal for IRS Records, delivered in two voices with all the passion of someone delivering a soliloquy from Shakespeare. He also explained how it was that IRS made a splash in the eighties rock scene. Ian Copeland's *Wild Thing* and an interview with Bob Garcia provided more information about how IRS was run. Seymour Stein's comments regarding an earlier pitch by Copeland for a label deal (as well as a view of the Copeland brothers in general) were made during a panel discussion for the 2007 Musexpo in Los Angeles, a three-day annual pow-wow for worldwide music executives.

Buzzcocks bassist Steve Garvey's contention that Miles Copeland "ripped us off" (after releasing a compilation of Buzzcocks material on IRS) was made in an April 1996 interview with Margit Detweiler for *Philadelphia City Paper*.

The IRS business model and some of the acts that Copeland and Jay Boberg signed (especially the Go-Go's) received a fair amount of press from US broadsheet newspapers on both coasts, with several features appearing in the *Los Angeles Times* and one in the *Wall Street Journal*. Background information on the West Coast music scene was also gleaned from *We Got the Neutron Bomb* (Three Rivers Press, 2001) by Marc Spitz and Brendan Mullen, an entertaining oral history of the late 1970s/early 1980s LA music scene.

The material on Skafish came from a 1978 profile by Tim Holmes about the eccentric band leader Jim Skafish in the *Twin Cities Reader*. Former Cramps guitarist Kid Congo Powers gave an interview about his experience playing with the band around this time. Andy Summers made his feelings about the Cramps plain in his own book, *One Train Later*.

9   Police the World

Sting explained the ideological motivations for the Police's off-road world tour to Chris Salewicz for a 1981 *NME* feature. Miles Copeland contradicted the singer in his interview for this book, explaining that it was all strictly PR. Annie Nightingale's comment about the relentless documentation of everything connected to the Police was contained in her memoir *Chase the Fade* (Blandford Press, 1981).

Police: Around the World, the film Miles Copeland commissioned Derek and Kate Burbidge to make, is an essential behind-the-scenes documentary of the world tour, taking in footage from Tokyo, Hong Kong, Cairo, and Bombay. Some of the descriptive passages about the tour came from footage in that film.

The short passage about the band's trip to Japan was taken from the introductory paragraphs of a 1980 article in *Record Mirror* written by Mike Nicholls and is cut through with a casual racism that would almost certainly be unacceptable today. Stewart Copeland's comment about the "Nips" arrives later in the same article. The photos of Sting pretending to commit ritual suicide were shot by Watal Asanuma. But shots from the same session were also made by Akihiro Takahashi, one of which is featured in the photo section of this book.

Ian Copeland's *Wild Thing* had a very detailed account of the calamities that befell the Cairo show, as well as of the general difficulties of setting up a tour in countries that had no infrastructure to put on a show by a Western pop act. It also told the story of how the Police manager called on his father's political contacts to smooth the path. The background information on then Egyptian vice president Hassan Touhami (including his 1952 trip to Washington) was found in *The Game Player* (Aurum Press, 1971), a memoir written by the Copeland brothers' father, Miles Copeland II, about his years as an intelligence agent. Some quotes are taken from the Burbidges' film *Police: Around the World*. Miles Copeland's story about Sting's standoff with the Egyptian chief of police is drawn partly from an interview with him and partly from a quote in Miles's *The Police: A Visual Documentary*.

The story behind the Bombay show was sourced from a 2007 article about the ladies of the Time and Talents Club written for the *Hindustan Times* magazine

Brunch by ex-*Bombay* magazine editor Vir Sanghvi, as well as from Paul Morley's excellent 1981 long-form story in the *NME* that expressed all of the contradictory thoughts running through his head when he was flown out to meet the world's most famous pop star in the midst of the dirt and dust and poverty of the Indian subcontinent. Sting's comments are also drawn from that article, as is the passage about the limo and the armless beggar. In addition, Morley gave an interview for this book, providing a very perceptive overview of his experience in India, his various encounters with Sting, and critical thoughts regarding the Police at the time, all of which were woven into the narrative. Andy Summers gave his opinion of Morley in his memoir, *One Train Later*. The quote by Sting about "real poverty" is from a 1980 article by Dermot Stokes in *Hot Press*.

10   Gimme Shelter

Keith Moore's role in the Police story and the manner in which he enriched them by managing their money would only become significant many years later when he was charged with siphoning off £6 million of Sting's personal fortune. Summers's comments about his 80 per cent tax rate are from an October 1980 interview in *Record Mirror*, again by Mike Nicholls. At the beginning of 1979, the tax rate for the highest-earning Britons was 98 per cent. The Police had their first chart success in May of that year, coinciding with the formation of the Thatcher government. In June 1979, Margaret Thatcher lowered the highest rate of tax to 60 per cent. Andy Summers's comments about his life in Ireland (and other details) are drawn from both that article and *One Train Later*. His comment about the effects of the heavy workload imposed on the group was made to Chris Salewicz for a 1982 story in *Creem*. The additional quote from Sting about the pressure he personally felt came from a 1981 article in the *NME* by Lynn Hanna. The US retail sales figures for the music industry recession are official RIAA (Recording Industry Association of America) figures, as quoted in a 1992 article by Paul D. Lopes for the *American Sociological Review*.

Interviews with Nigel Gray and Chris Gray again provided stories from the *Zenyatta Mondatta* sessions at Wisseloord and details of Nigel Gray's attempts to win further remuneration for his production work. These are interspersed with Summers's take on events, which was drawn from *One Train Later*. Stewart Copeland's comment about Sting's attempt to control the sessions by arriving with fully realized songs is from Phil Sutcliffe's July 2007 cover story for *Mojo*. Copeland admitted using an old tape of Siouxsie and the Banshees as the basis for "Bomb's Away" in a 1980 interview with Chris Welch for *Musician's Only* magazine. Gray's description of the demos as sounding like "Sly and the Family Stone" is from Sutcliffe and Hugh Fielder's *L'Historia Bandido*. And Summers's contention that Sting had merely dug out and dusted off old songs he had lying around was also from Salewicz's article for *Creem*.

The account of the rained-out Rockatta de Bowl show at Milton Keynes (in July 1980) was drawn from contemporaneous reviews in *Sounds*, *Record Mirror*, and *Musicians Only*. Sting's description of the bottles raining down at him during the gig at Leixlip Castle, Dublin, was given to Dermot Stokes for his 1980 article in *Hot Press*, as was his contention (later in the text) that an album is no more than a collection of songs. Sting's reappraisal of *Zenyattá Mondatta* as "a reasonable pop album" was made to the *NME*'s Lynn Hanna. The alternate titles for the album have been widely reported. The band's explanation that *Zenyattá Mondatta* was partly drawn from the name of Kenyan dictator Jomo Kenyatta was taken at face value in Christopher Sandford's poorly researched unofficial biography of Sting, *Back on the Beat* (Carroll & Graf, 2007).

11   The New Wave Crusade

Interviews with Miles Copeland and Bob Garcia provided the meat of the material concerning the rise of IRS to the top of the new wave heap. Ian Copeland's memoir *Wild Thing* was a good source of information about this period, too, particularly the work that went into setting up the shows that would be filmed by Derek Burbidge for *Urgh! A Music War*. Jello Biafra's comments are taken from a 1980 interview conducted by Squeeze keyboard player-turned-presenter Jools Holland for *The Tube*, a television music show that Holland fronted through the eighties. This was around the time of the release of the first Dead Kennedys album, *Fresh Fruit for Rotting Vegetables*, on Copeland's IRS Records. Material was drawn from several large profile pieces in the *Los Angeles Times* between 1979 and 1983 about IRS Records and the Go-Go's (both pre and post the phenomenal success of their debut album) by writers Candace A. Wedlan, Patrick Goldstein, Robert Hilburn, Kristine McKenna, and Steve Pond.

Julien Temple's comments about UK punk and the sweeping away of the British Empire were made in an interview he gave to Chris Salewicz that was included as an extra on the DVD release of his film *The Great Rock 'n' Roll Swindle*. The comments attributed to CBS Records executive Brad Weir were from a March 1982 report, "Punks Wearing Pink," that aired on CBC radio in Canada.

Several articles from Reebee Garofalo's fascinating book *Rockin' the Boat* (South End Press, 1982) were used to piece together the rise of new wave rock in socialist dictatorships around the world. These included Tim Brace and Paul Freidlander's "Rock and Roll on the New Long March: Popular Music, Cultural Identity, and Political Opposition in the People's Republic of China" and Pablo Vila's "Rock Nacional and Dictatorship in Argentina." Also extremely insightful was a viewing of Rodrigo Garcia's 2007 film *Luca*, about Luca Prodan, a Scottish-Italian ex-pat punk rocker who became an uncompromising music star and cult figure in Argentina in the 1980s.

Although it is not cited in the text, the section on the cultural implications of new wave music was influenced by a 1986 article for the American Anthropological Association's publication *Cultural Anthropology*. In "Beyond Narcissism in American Culture of the 80s," authors Steve Barnett and JoAnn Magdoff coined the phrase "New Wave narcissism" to identify the consumerist vanity that took hold of eighties youth in America, a sociological phenomenon that they claimed was a follow-on from the "Me generation." Several other useful ideas came from two articles written by cultural studies academic Lawrence Grossberg, especially regarding the post-modernist aspects of new wave and other eighties music genres. Klaus Nomi's quote, "Some people think I'm not human" was made in a 1979 interview published in New York's *Soho News*. Bob Lewis's quote about Mark Mothersbaugh is contained in his essay "Some Thoughts on Devo: The First Postmodern Band."

Brian James of Lords of the New Church recalled the circumstances behind the recording session for "Like a Virgin" in a 1999 interview for *Damned* fanzine, "Neat Damned Noise." Miles Copeland's way of doing business meant that he fell foul of many of the bands he worked with. Stewart Copeland's comment about his brother Miles being "good on overall strategy but bad on important details" came from Phil Sutcliffe and Hugh Fielder's *L'Historia Bandido*. Nick Jones was also quoted in that book. Mark E. Smith described Miles Copeland as a "glorified con-man" in a 1986 interview with *BravEar* fanzine. The Fall's then manager Kim Carroll made her comments about Copeland in a 1978 story for the *NME*, written by Ian Penman.

An entry in Jim Skafish's personal blog provided the information that Copeland was up to his old tricks and cutting himself a slice of the publishing for his IRS acts whenever he was able to. Information about Copeland's relationship with the Cramps (and how it faltered) came from an interview with the band's former guitarist Kid Congo Powers, as well as from material in Ian Johnston's biography *The Wild Wild World of the Cramps* (Omnibus Press, 1990). Stiv Bators talked about the problems of employing one person (namely, Miles Copeland) as manager, publisher, and record company in a 1986 interview with *Rave-Up* fanzine.

12   Dystopia in Utopia

Hugh Padgham gave an extended interview for a 2004 article by Richard Buskin for *Sound on Sound* magazine. He talked about the recording setup at Air Studios and the communication problems it exacerbated within the band. In an interview done for this book, Chris Gray confirmed that Stewart Copeland was a big weed smoker. Gray noted that this was ironic considering that Stewart's brother Miles was so vehemently anti-drugs. Quotes from the band about the session were taken from both Chris Salewicz's 1982 story in *Creem* magazine and Jim Green's 1982 article in *Trouser Press*. Additional quotes from Stewart Copeland were sourced from the voiceover that the drummer recorded for his 2006 film *Everybody Stares*. Quotes from Andy Summers come from his memoir, *One Train Later*. Jean Roussel graciously found time to do an interview for this book, in which he provided an outsider's view of the frosty relations within the band and where he felt the balance of power lay (with Sting) during the short time he spent recording with them on Montserrat.

Sting explained the personal connection he had to his song "Invisible Sun" and the thinking behind his need to speak about social issues to Lynn Hanna for a 1981 *NME* article. The information that Sting's wife, Frances Tomelty, was brought in to "balance every Catholic and Protestant image" in the video that accompanied the song was included in an October 1981 article for *Melody Maker* by Paul Colbert.

Sting first mentioned his interest in Arthur Koestler in Dermot Stokes's August 1980 article for *Hot Press*. He enthused about Koestler and his book *The Ghost in the Machine* to *Penthouse* magazine journalist Timothy White in 1984 and spoke further about it to Hanna. The background on Koestler came from articles by and about David Cesarani, the author of the controversial Koestler biography *Arthur Koestler: The Homeless Mind* (Free Press, 1999).

13   Destabilize, Desynchronize

Sonja Kristina's comment about Sting and his cocaine use appears in Phil Sutcliffe's 2007 *Mojo* story about the band. The timing of Sting's affair with Trudie Styler has never been made public. It was in fact fudged to help maintain Sting's public image. But both Sting and Styler have since made comments that allude to the affair beginning a good few years before it was made public. In a 2003 appearance the couple made on the *Oprah Winfrey Show*, Sting said they had been living together for twenty-five years (although in her introduction, Winfrey chopped two years off that number), dating the start of the affair to 1978. Sting's memories of meeting Styler come from his memoir, *Broken Music*. Styler's early recollections of Sting are taken from various magazine profiles of her, most notably a 2005 article by Geordie Greig in *Tatler*. Sting talked about monogamy, sin, and the problems of maintaining a relationship to Victoria and David Scheff for a 1985 article in *Playboy*. The story of the break-in at Sting's Irish home that hastened his move back to the UK was revealed only in a 2007 article by Seamus Ross in the *Sunday Mirror* newspaper.

The story of the court case brought by Sting and Miles Copeland against Virgin Music publishing was widely reported in the British press. The extracts from Sting's diaries that were read out in court and other quotes from the case came from those newspaper reports. What wasn't reported was how the case collapsed, leading to an out-of-court settlement. This is revealed here for the first time by Carol Wilson, who signed Sting to his publishing deal with Virgin in 1976 and gave an interview for this book. All of Wilson's quotes are drawn from that interview. The battle continued after the court case ended, with Miles Copeland and Sting waging a war of words against Richard Branson in the *NME* and other tabloid newspapers.

Sting's claim that he did not know the profession of Adnan Khashoggi—the arms-dealing host of a party he was taken to by Styler during the trial—was reported by Gavin Martin in a 1991 *NME* article. Styler's past as a hostess at Xenon nightclub was revealed in a 2004 profile by Adam Higginbotham for the *Observer* newspaper. A report of the Police show at the Gateshead Arena, during which Sting shouted "Body Mist stinks!" from the stage (in reference to a deodorant commercial using one of his songs) was reported in a July 1982 *NME* review of the show by David Dorrell. Sting railed against the perception of him created by the media and the "amateur psychoanalysis" of his lyrics in a February 1993 interview with Leonard Pitts for the *Miami Herald*. Paul Bishop's book *The Dionysian Self* (Walter de Gruyter, 1995) provided a good overview of Jungian archetypes.

Sting denied that *Synchronicity* was inspired by his failing marriage and subsequent divorce in a 1985 interview with Fred Schruers for *GQ* magazine. Richard Baskin's 2004 article for *Sound on Sound* again provided information and anecdotes on the brewing tension that pervaded the *Synchronicity* sessions at Air Studios. Additional material came from Andy Summers's *One Train Later*. The impact of MTV's 1981 launch and the introduction of the compact disc on the fortunes of the music industry were explained in detail in R. Serge Denisoff and William L. Schurk's *Tarnished Gold: The Record Industry Revisited* (Transaction Publishers, 1986). The technical trickery used in the *Synchronicity* promo videos made by Godley & Creme were revealed by their cinematographer, Daniel Pearl, during three interviews he gave to Bob Fisher for the International Cinematographer's Guild magazine. Summers's recollections about the band's 1985 Shea Stadium show frame the entire narrative of his memoir.

14 Rock of Charity

The account of Sting's New York City auditions to find a new backup band was drawn from a two-part story written by Vic Garbarini for *Musician* magazine (published as "Sting's Swing Shift" and "Sting under the Gun" in the July and August 1985 issues).

The account of the lead-up to the release of Sting's *Dream of the Blue Turtles* and quotes from various people associated with him were drawn largely from Michael Apted's 1986 film *Bring On the Night*. A June 1985 cover story for *Time Out* by Chris Salewicz ("Sting: Confessions of a Complete Egomaniac," June 13, 1985) provided the information that much of the "documentary" was staged for Apted's cameras, including the press conference in Paris and the mimed performances at the Mogador Theatre.

Miles Davis's thoughts about having members of his band poached by Sting and his own forthright opinions concerning Sting's attempts to reinvent himself as a pop jazz artist are contained in his autobiography, *Miles* (Touchstone, 1989). The descriptions of Stewart Copeland's antics in Africa came from J. P. Dutilleux's 1986 film *The Rhythmatist*.

Norman Tebbit's description of Live Aid as a "triumph of international marketing" was cited in Neal Ullestad's essay "Rock and Rebellion: Subversive Effects of Live Aid and Sun City." Information about how funds raised by Live Aid fell into the hands of Ethiopian dictator Mengistu Haile Mariam came from articles by Robert D. Kaplan and David Rieff in, respectively, the *Washington Monthly* and the *Guardian*. Miles Copeland II's memoir, *The Game Player*, relates the story of the Ethiopian government official who differentiated between "horizontals" and "verticals." British journalist Robin Denselow detailed the public spat between

Police manager Miles Copeland and Paul Weller in his 1989 book about pop and politics, *When the Music's Over*. Keith Altham's claim that this almost caused Sting to split with his manager was made in his memoir, *The PR Strikes Back*.

Jack Healey's efforts to set up the Amnesty International tour were detailed in "It Was 20 Years Ago Today," an article celebrating the twentieth anniversary of the tour by Matt McGee for the U2 fan site @U2. Other facts and figures came from "Wide Awake in America," a July 1987 article about the tour by Pat Singer in the Irish music magazine *Hot Press*. The story of the behind-the-scenes machinations of the tour and the quotes associated with it (including those by Bill Graham, Jack Healey, Mary Daly, and Michael Ahearn) came largely from the chapter "Conspiracy of Hope" in *Bill Graham Presents: My Life Inside Rock and Out* (Da Capo Press, 2004), veteran rock promoter Bill Graham's blistering oral history of his career in music (cowritten with Robert Greenfield). Jack Healey was first called "Mr. Human Rights" in an article published by *US News and World Report*, then he himself adopted it as a nickname, apparently without irony.

The whole grisly story of the Police's aborted attempt to record together again was drawn from Garbarini's April 2003 article for *Guitar World* magazine, "Don't Stand So Close to Me." Additional material came from "I Think If We Came Back . . . ," Garbarini's round-table interview with all three members of the Police (published in the spring 2000 issue of *Revolver* magazine). It is one of the very rare occasions that the entire band sat down for a joint interview. It also illustrates why this situation was avoided whenever possible, the problem being the explosive chemistry between Sting and Stewart Copeland. A 1983 MTV interview with Martha Quinn, right after the band had come offstage, descended into chaos within seconds after Sting announced, "I want to have a fight," and then threw water on Copeland. Both men then raced off, leaving an exasperated Quinn to pack up.

15 Classical Gas

Vic Garbarini was again present during the recording sessions for Sting's 1987 album . . . *Nothing Like the Sun* and wrote about the experience and his candid conversations with the singer for a December 1987 article in *Spin* magazine ("Invisible Son"). Sting made additional comments to Chris Salewicz about the album's connection to the death of his mother (in an article titled "Sting: Coming Home," published in the October 28, 1987, issue of *Time Out*).

Sting's extraordinary letter to critic Howard Hampton was printed (spelling mistakes, misquotes, and all) in the November 24, 1987, issue of the *Village Voice*. Stewart Copeland's assertion about Sting—"Not only does he hate humanity"— was reprinted in a March 1993 profile of the singer in *Esquire* magazine. Sting's insistence that he was not on the "rock-star fantasy trip" was made to Tom Moon in a February 1988 article for the *Chicago Tribune*.

Sting recounted his experience of meeting Raoni in the Brazilian rain forest for a June 1988 article in *Vogue* magazine. Mark Zeller's January 1990 article for the French edition of *Rolling Stone* kick-started the inquiries into the finances of Sting, Trudie Styler, and J. P. Dutilleux's Rainforest Foundation. The title of the article ("Les Risques du Metier") shared, as the editors were probably quite aware, the title of a controversial 1967 film starring singer Jacques Brel, in which he plays a small-town teacher accused of raping a female student.

Captain Clive Kelly and his incredible life story were profiled in a 2000 article for the New York Times by Herb McCormick. Kelly himself provided further information to the author in a June 2010 interview, along with documents and information relating to the relationship between Sting and J.P. Dutilleux. Background information about the Villas Boas brothers came from a 2002 obituary of Orlando Villas Boas in the *Independent*. Raoni's activist work on behalf of the Brazilian Indians and his tour with Sting were the subject of a 1990 article by James Brooke in the *New York Times*. In a 2000 interview, Raoni told Gert Peter-Bruch that he had not had any contact with Sting for ten years. Background information on the Xingu National Park and the political implications of its formation came from an essay by Simon Garfield, "A Nationalist Environment: Indians, Nature, and the Construction of the Xingu National Park in Brazil," published in the 2004 *Luso-Brazilian Review*.

The 2008 Charity Navigator report taking the Rainforest Foundation to task for its spending on charity projects was the subject of a May 2008 article in the *New York Post*. Trudie Styler's *Huffington Post* puff piece about the Rainforest Foundation actually preceded this story, running at the end of April 2008. The quote marking Sting's step back from his ecological activist role was made to Kim Hughes for a March 1991 article in *NOW* magazine. Miles Copeland's assertion that *The Soul Cages* album was killed by its association with the death of Sting's father was made in a 1991 article by Mark Edwards for the *Sunday Times*.

The 1995 court case that put Sting's former accountant Keith Moore on trial for purloining £6 million of the singer's personal fortune was widely reported on in the British media. This account was drawn from several articles in the *Independent* and *Times* newspapers.

Stewart Copeland's score for the King Lear ballet in San Francisco was the subject of several articles in local papers. The account of its production here (and associated quotes) was based largely on an April 1985 article in the *San Francisco Chronicle*, "A Rocker Drums Up Some High-Brow Stuff." The tragicomic genesis and production of Copeland's opera *Holy Blood and Crescent Moon* for the Cleveland Opera House was described in excruciating detail in a September 1989 story by Anthony Tommasini for the *Boston Globe*. Additional information came from October 1989 articles in the *Los Angeles Times* (by Mark Swed), the *Wall Street Journal* (by opera critic Heidi Waleson), the *New York Times* (by John Rockwell), and the *Columbus Dispatch*. A report on the 1990 Dallas run of the opera appeared in the *Dallas Morning News*.

Sting's turn as Macheath in the Broadway production (transferred from a run in Washington) of *3 Penny Opera* generated almost as much ink as Copeland's opera. The account provided here draws largely from a November 1989 article by Mervyn Rothstein in the *New York Times*, as well as a letter to the editor of the same publication later that month, a November review of the Broadway opening by the paper's theatre critic Frank Rich, and another in *Time* magazine.

Stewart Copeland's comment about the audience for his classical works being more "voluble than Verdi's" was made in an article in the *Cleveland Plain Dealer*. The audience is not "voluble," of course, merely "louder." Sting's comment about "artistic risks" was made on an edition of Lynn Neary's NPR (National Public Radio) show in September 1991. Andy Summers's explanation of his photographic work appeared in a 2005 article written by Simon Hardeman for the *Independent* newspaper.

16   Recede, Retire, Retread

The narrative that led up to the 2007 reuniting of the Police was outlined through interviews that Chris Salewicz did with each member for the official tour programme. Salewicz was rewarded for his years of service to the band with an invitation to Sting's residence in Tuscany, where he watched the band struggle with rehearsals and wrote about the experience for a 2007 feature article in the UK's *Telegraph Magazine*. Quotes from Sting, Copeland, and Summers from both of those texts are used here. Information about Miles Copeland's last days as Sting's manager and his opinion of the re-formed band and how he was shut out of the reunion were all provided by Copeland himself in a 2007 interview. Lonn Friend wrote a long blog on his MySpace site in May 2008, detailing his experience working as a consultant on the *Brand New Day* album and his dealings with Kathryn Schenker, who would shortly after this become Sting's new manager.

The tumultuous life of Algerian raï singer Cheb Mami following his appearance in Sting's "Desert Rose" song and video was detailed in a May 2008 *Agence France Presse* article. As of publication, Mami's legal problems still had not been resolved. He has strenuously denied any involvement in the affair and maintains his innocence.

The Jaguar car commercial that Sting appeared in and the effect it had on his record sales received a huge amount of worldwide publicity. The contradictions in his stance toward the environment were highlighted in a 2003 article by Greg Kott for the *Chicago Tribune*, in which Sting talked about his "carbon footprint." He also discussed the ad on an edition of Robert Siegel and Michele Norris's NPR show *All Things Considered*.

The gradual lead-up to the announcement of the Police reunion also made headlines the world over. Articles from Foxnews.com and the *New York Times* (by Roger Friedman and Jeff Leeds, respectively) were used as sources to construct the narrative here. Mike Keating, Sting's sound engineer, was quoted in an August 2007 article about technical requirements for the Police tour, written by Sarah Benzuly for *The Mix* magazine.

Stewart Copeland's comment about his persona on the BBC talent show *Just the Two of Us* was made on the forum of his official website, as were his reports of the first shows on the tour. His remarks about the financial agreement between the three band members were made to Reuters journalist Dean Goodman in May 2007. And his statement that the Police had bequeathed "nothing that important" to music history was in an interview by Andre Mayer conducted for the Canadian Broadcasting Company website in June 2006.

SOURCES

Books

Altham, Keith. *The PR Strikes Back.* Blake Publishing, 2001.

Antonia, Nina. *Johnny Thunders: In Cold Blood.* Cherry Red Books, 2000.

———. *The One and Only: Peter Perrett—Homme Fatale.* SAF Publishing, 1996.

Bishop, Paul. *The Dionysian Self: C. G. Jung's Recognition of Friedrich Nietzsche.* Walter de Gruyter, 1995.

Black, Johnny. *R.E.M. Reveal the Story of R.E.M.* Backbeat Books, 2004.

Bockris, Victor. *Transformer: The Lou Reed Story.* Simon & Schuster, 1995.

Bockris, Victor, and Roberta Bayley. *Patti Smith: An Unauthorized Biography.* Simon & Schuster, 1999.

Bonomo, Joe. *Sweat: The Story of the Fleshtones, America's Garage Band.* Continuum, 2007.

Burchill, Julie, and Tony Parsons. *The Boy Looked at Johnny.* Pluto Press, 1978.

Burdon, Eric (with J. Marshall Craig). *Don't Let Me Be Misunderstood.* Thunder's Mouth Press, 2001.

Cale, John, and Victor Bockris. *What's Welsh for Zen: The Autobiography of John Cale.* Bloomsbury, 2000.

Cesarani, David. *Arthur Koestler: The Homeless Mind.* Free Press, 1999.

Clapton, Diana. *Lou Reed & the Velvet Underground.* Bobcat, 1987.

Clarkson, Wensley. *A Tale in the Sting.* Thunder's Mouth Press, 1999.

Clay, Jason W., and Bonnie K. Holcoomb. *Politics and the Ethiopian Famine, 1984–1985.* Transaction Publishers, 1986.

Cloonan, Martin. *Popular Music and the State in the UK: Culture, Trade or Industry.* Ashgate Publishing, 2007.

Copeland, Ian. *Wild Thing: The Backstage, On the Road, In the Studio, Off the Charts Memoirs of Ian Copeland.* Simon & Schuster, 1995.

Copeland, Miles. *The Game Player: Confessions of the CIA's Original Political Operative.* Aurum Press, 1989.

Costa, Salvador. *Punk: Fotografías de Salvador Costa.* Producciones Editoriales, 1977.

County, Jayne (with Rupert Smith). *Man Enough to Be a Woman*. Serpent's Tail, 1995.

Davis, Miles (with Quincy Troupe). *Miles: The Autobiography*. Touchstone, 1990.

Dellinger, Jade, and David Giffels. *Are We Not Men? We Are DEVO!* SAF Publishing, 2003.

Denisoff, R. Serge. *Tarnished Gold: The Record Industry Revisited*. Transaction Publishers, 1986.

Denselow, Robin. *When the Music's Over: The Story of Political Pop*. Faber & Faber, 1989.

Difford, Chris, and Glenn Tilbrook (with Jim Drury). *Squeeze: Song by Song*. Sanctuary Publishing, 2004.

Ford, Simon. *Hip Priest: The Story of Mark E. Smith and the Fall*. Quartet Books, 2002.

Forsythe, David P. *Human Rights and US Foreign Policy: Congress Reconsidered*. University Press of Florida, 1988.

Garofalo, Reebee (ed.). *Rockin' the Boat: Mass Music & Mass Movements*. South End Press, 1992.

Gimarc, George. *Punk Diary: The Ultimate Trainspotter's Guide to Underground Rock, 1970–1982*. Backbeat Books, 2005.

Goodman, Fred. *The Mansion on the Hill: Dylan, Young, Geffen, Springsteen, and the Head-on Collision of Rock and Commerce*. Vintage, 1998.

Graham, Bill, and Robert Greenfield. *Bill Graham Presents: My Life Inside Rock and Out*. Da Capo Press, 2004.

Holland, Jools. *Barefaced Lies and Boogie-Woogie Boasts*. Michael Joseph Ltd., 2007.

Johnston, Ian. *The Wild Wild World of the Cramps*. Omnibus Press, 1990.

Marko, Paul. *The Roxy London WC2: A Punk History*. Punk 77 Books, 2007.

Medawar, Peter. *The Strange Case of the Spotted Mice and Other Classic Essays on Science*. Oxford University Press, 1996.

Menn, Don (ed.). *Secrets from the Masters*. GPI Publications, 1992.

Miles, Barry (as Miles). *The Police*. Omnibus Press, 1981.

Montiel, Dito. *A Guide to Recognizing Your Saints*. Thunder's Mouth Press, 2003.

Nightingale, Annie. *Chase the Fade*. Blandford Press, 1981.

Padovani, Henry. *Secret Police Man*. Flammarion, 2006.

Parry, Robert. *Secrecy & Privilege: Rise of the Bush Dynasty from Watergate to Iraq*. The Media Consortium, 2004.

Perry, Mark. *Sniffin' Glue: The Essential Punk Accessory*. Sanctuary Publishing, 2000.

Porter, Dick. *The Cramps: A Short History of Rock 'n' Roll Psychosis*. Plexus Publishing, 2007.

Rimmer, Dave. *Like Punk Never Happened: Culture Club and the New Pop*. Faber and Faber, 1985.

Sandford, Christopher. *Sting: Back on the Beat*. Carroll & Graf, 1998, 2007.

Savage, Jon. *England's Dreaming: Anarchy, Sex Pistols, Punk Rock and Beyond.* St. Martin's Griffin, 2001.

Shattuck, B. H. *Jocko-Homo Heavenbound.* Self-published, 1924.

Sidewinder. *Internal Affairs.* Rockfic Press LLC, 2006.

Spitz, Marc, and Brendon Mullen. *We Got the Neutron Bomb: The Untold Story of L.A. Punk.* Three Rivers Press, 2001.

Sting. *Broken Music: A Memoir.* Dial Press, 2003.

———. *Lyrics.* Dial Press, 2007.

Summers, Andy. *One Train Later: A Memoir.* Portrait, 2006.

Sullivan, Denise. *R.E.M. Talk about the Passion: An Oral History.* Da Capo Press, 1998.

Sutcliffe, Phil, and Hugh Fielder. *The Police: L'Historia Bandido.* Proteus Books, 1981.

Thompson, Dave. *Alternative Rock: Third Ear—The Essential Listening Companion.* Miller Freeman Books, 2000.

Wates, Nick, and Christian Wolmar. *Squatting: The Real Story.* Bay Leaf Books, 1980.

Weibel, Peter (ed.). *Beyond Art: A Third Culture: A Comparative Study in Cultures, Art and Science in 20th Century Austria and Hungary.* Springer, 2005.

The Police Released. Big O Publishing Ltd., 1980.

Articles

Austin, Hal. "Cocaine Made Me a Monster, Says Sting." *Daily Mail,* September 30, 1993.

Baker, Mark (ed.). "The Official Police Files," nos. 1–21. Diamond Publishing Group, 1980–1982.

Barnett, Steve, and JoAnn Magdoff. "Beyond Narcissism in American Culture of the 1980s." *Cultural Anthropology* 1, no. 4 (November 1986).

Barry, John W. "Police Show at Last Chance Remains Stuff of Legends." *Poughkeepsie Journal,* January 30, 2007.

Bell, John (letter to ed.). "'Threepenny Opera': Brecht Did Too Want to Entertain." *New York Times,* November 19, 1989.

Bell, Max. "Safely Successful." *Times,* December 30, 1983.

Benzuly, Sarah. "Tour Profile: The Police." *Mix,* August 1, 2007.

Blair, Iain. "Sting: The Chief of Police." *Playgirl,* October 1982.

Blake, John, and Lisa Robinson. "Kids by Sting." *Mirror,* December 19, 1985.

Blake, John. "Why Police Have Broken Up." *Daily Mirror,* March 28, 1985.

Bradbury, David, and Christian Gysin. "You Ain't Seen Nothing Yet." *Daily Mirror,* March 31, 1984.

Braid, Mary. "Sting's Adviser Tells of Shame over Pounds 6m Losses." *Independent,* October 11, 1995.

Breskin, David. "Bob Geldof: The Rolling Stone Interview." *Spin,* Aug, 1986.

Bright, Terry. "Soviet Crusade against Pop." *Popular Music* 5 (1985).

Brooke, James. "Kapoto Journal: Rain Forest Indians Holding off Threat of Change." *New York Times,* December 3, 1990.

Bruch, Gert Peter. "A La Une: Stewart Copeland." *Paru Vendu* June 7–14, 2007.

———. "Raoni: L'interview." *Gertonline.free.fr,* May 2000.

Buchan, Alasdair, and Bryan Rimmer. "The Mod Squad." *Daily Mirror,* August 24, 1979.

Burchill, Julie. "Review: *Zenyatta Mondatta.*" *NME,* November 1, 1980.

Buskin, Richard. "Recording the Police's 'Every Breath You Take.'" *Sound on Sound,* March 2004.

Cateforis, Theo. "Performing the Avant-Garde Groove: Devo and the Whiteness of the New Wave." *American Music,* vol. 22, no. 4 (Winter, 2004).

Chonin, Neva. "Peter Berlin Made a Work of Art out of His Sex Life." *San Francisco Chronicle,* February 13, 2006.

Chrimes, Penny. "Baby for Sting." *Daily Mirror,* September 12, 1981.

Christgau, Robert. "Rock 'n' Roller Coaster: The Music Biz on a Joyride." *Village Voice,* February 7, 1984.

Colbert, Paul. "High Spirits in the Material World." *Melody Maker,* October 17, 1981.

Connew, Paul. "Sting Hates Rock!" *Daily Mirror,* January 6, 1984.

———. "Sting Plastered!" *Daily Mirror* October 7, 1983.

———. "Sting Takes Wing." *Daily Mirror,* September 28, 1983.

———. "Police Hit Banned by the Beeb." *Daily Mirror,* September 23, 1981.

Copeland, Stewart. "Judge Hard Place & the BBC." Stewartcopeland.net, September 28, 2006.

Cragin, Sally. "Police Force." *Boston Phoenix,* July 25, 2007.

Danton, Eric R. "Memorable Nights at the Shaboo." *Hartford Courant,* August 12, 2007.

Davidson, Walt. "Nuit de Punk Review." *NME,* March 28, 1977.

Dorrell, David. "A Sour Spirit's Bitter Venom . . . ." *NME,* July 1982.

Douglas, Pete. "Review: Rockatta De Bowl." *Musician's Only,* August 1980.

Dyer, Richard. "'Holy Blood': Million-Dollar Disappointment." *Boston Globe,* October 17, 1989.

Edwards, Mark. "Policeman on a New Beat." *Sunday Times,* March 1993.

Eggar, Robin, "The Stinger." *Daily Mirror,* November 24, 1983.

———. "What a Row." *Daily Mirror,* August 7, 1982.

———. "What It Took to Soothe Sting." *Daily Mirror,* August 3, 1982.

———. "Who Switches on the Stars?" *Daily Mirror,* June 7, 1983.

Eggar, Robin, and Sharon Feinstein. "My Police." *Daily Mirror,* December 21, 1983.

Encoule, Jean. "Mark Perry: Smash the Computers." *Trakmarx.com,* January 2001.

Ferrari, Simon. "Sting: My Dark Past." *Mirror,* November 19, 1985.

Fisher, Bob. "A Conversation with Daniel Pearl." *International Cinematographer's Guild* magazine, 1999.

———. "The Last Word: Daniel Pearl." *International Cinematographer's Guild* magazine, 1997.

————. "Pearl Looks Forward to Future, 25 Years after *Texas Chainsaw Massacre*." *International Cinematographer's Guild* magazine, 1999.

Fricke, David. "Review: *Zenyatta Mondatta*." *Rolling Stone,* December 1980.

Friedman, Roger. "Sting May Be Reuniting with the Police." *Foxnews.com,* January 5, 2007.

Friend, Lonn. "Freedom, Beauty, Truth and Love." *MySpace blog,* May 30, 2008.

Garbarini, Vic. "Don't Stand So Close to Me." *Guitar World,* April 2003.

————. "Invisible Son." *Spin,* December 1987.

————. "Police Reunion!" *Revolver,* April 2000.

————. "Sting's Swing Shift." *Musician,* July 1985.

————. "Sting under the Gun." *Musician,* August 1985.

Garfield, Seth. "A Nationalist Environment: Indians, Nature, and the Construction of the Xingu National Park in Brazil." *Luso-Brazilian Review* (University of Wisconsin), 2004.

Geldof, Bob. "Response to *Spin*'s Live Aid article," *Spin,* Aug 1986.

Getweiler, Margit. "Steve Garvey of the Buzzcocks." *Philadelphia City Paper,* April 18–25, 1996.

Goldman, Vivien. "Punk Rock." *Sounds,* April 2, 1977.

Goldstein, Patrick. "Marketing the Police . . . ." *Los Angeles Times,* April 1979.

————. "Pop Music, Police Set for Jailhouse Rock." *Los Angeles Times,* November 18, 1979.

Goodman, Dean. "Interview with Stewart Copeland (the Police)." Deangoodman.com, May 25, 2007.

Green, Jim. "Police Have More Fun . . . ." *Trouser Press,* May 1982.

Greig, Geordie. "Trudie, Madly, Deeply." *Tatler,* September 2005.

Gross, Jason. "Alternative TV: Mark Perry interview." *Perfect Sound Forever* (furious.com), February 2001.

Grossberg, lawrence. "The Politics of Youth Culture: Some Observations on Rock and Roll in American Culture." *Social Text* (Duke University Press), no. 8 (Winter 1983–1984).

————"Rockin' with Reagan, or the Mainstreaming of Postmodernity." *Cultural Critique* (University of Minnesota Press), no. 10 (Autumn, 1988).

Gysin, Christian. "In a Class of His Own." *Mirror,* May 17, 1985.

————. "Sting: Milkman's Son to Millionaire Pop Superstar." *Mirror,* May 16, 1985.

Hanna, Lynn. "The Thinking Man of Pop." *NME,* September 26, 1981.

Hardeman, Simon. "Camera Noir." *Independent,* March 29, 2005.

Harding, Colin. "Obituary: Orlando Villas Boas." *Independent,* December 14, 2002.

Henk, James. "Policing the World." *Rolling Stone,* February 1981.

Henry III, William A. "Warmed Over and Not So Hot." *Time,* November 27, 1989.

Higginbotham, Adam. "Truly Trudie." *Observer Magazine,* August 4, 2002.

Hilburn, Robert. "A&M Whistles for the Police." *Los Angeles Times,* March 3, 1979.

————. "Amnesty Tour: Keeping the Doors Open." *Los Angeles Times,* June 22, 1986.

————. "Go-Go's." *Los Angeles Times,* March 7, 1982.

Holden, Stephen. "The Pop Life: Sting's New Label." *New York Times*, June 29, 1988.

Holmes, Tim. "Skafish: Not Mere Swishiness." *Twin Cities Reader*, 1978.

Hughes, Kim. "Sting's Commercial Success . . ." *NOW*, March 1991.

Hutcheon, Linda. "Irony, Nostalgia, and the Postmodern." *Studies in Comparative Literature*, March 2000.

Illingworth, Francie. "The Group with a Sting." *Star Portrait*, no. 17, publisher unknown, 1979.

Iozzia, Dave. "Interview with Lonn Friend." Rockislife.com, Winter 2006.

Irwin, Ken. "Why the Police Don't Want Sting to Be a Sex Symbol." *Daily Mirror*, December 15, 1981.

Jackman, Brian. "Sting on the Warpath." *Australian*, October 1988.

Johnstone, Iain. "Star with Remote Control—Bring On the Night." *Sunday Times*, June 26, 1986.

Joseph, Joe. "Sting Gives Court Command Performance." *Times*, September 22, 1995.

Kaplan, Robert D. "The African Killing Fields." *Washington Monthly*, September 1988.

Keating, Robert. "Live Aid, the Terible Truth," *Spin*, Jul 1986.

———. "Sympathy for the Devil." *Spin*, Sep 1986.

Kent, Nick. "The Long Yarn of the Lore." *NME*, September 1, 1979.

Kingsley, Hilary. "Sting's Set to Be a TV Angel." *Daily Mirror*, January 24, 1981.

Knight, Kathryn. "Bank Repaid £4.8M Taken from Sting's 47 Accounts." *Times*, September 22, 1995.

———. "Six Years for Accountant Who Stole Sting's £6M." *Times*, October 18, 1995.

———. "Sting Used to Work at the Inland Revenue." *Times*, September 23, 1995.

Kott, Greg. "Sting Rides Again: Sports Car Ad Puts the Musician Back in Winner's Circle." *Chicago Tribune*, October 3, 2003.

Lang, Michael. "The Fall—Mark E. Smith Interview." *BravEar* 3, no. 5, 1986.

Leeds, Jeff. "The Police Will Kick Off the Grammys." *New York Times*, January 30, 2007.

Lees, Nigel. Sleeve notes for *The Magic World of Rupert's People*. CD, *Circle Records*, 2007.

Leff, Laurel. "How the Weird Can Get Started In Recording." *Wall Street Journal*, April 23, 1981.

Lewis, Bob. "Some Thoughts on Devo: The First Postmodern Band." Johnlydon.com, 2006.

LiSting. Mike Howlett Interview. Listing.free.fr, June 2008.

Lopes, Paul D. "Innovation and Diversity in the Popular Music Industry, 1969 to 1990." *American Sociological Review* 57, no. 1 (February 1992).

Lydon, John. "Never Trust a Laptop Hippie." Johnlydon.com, July 2, 2007.

McCall, Cheryl, "Ethiopia's Ruthless Regime Uses Famine as a Weapon," *Life*, May 1985.

McCormick, Herb. "The Boating Report: An Amazon Chief Paves Captain's Way." *New York Times,* November 19, 2000.

McGee, Matt. "It Was 20 Years Ago Today: Remembering the Conspiracy of Hope Tour." *@U2 fan-site (*atu2.com*),* June 4, 2006.

McKay, Peter. "Bowie Drops Out of the Treacle." *Daily Mirror,* September 17, 1981.

McKenna, Kristine. "Pop Beat: New Deal for New Wave Acts." *Los Angeles Times,* November 17, 1979.

McLaughlin, Maureen, and John Beal. "An Interview with Klaus Nomi." *Soho News,* 1979.

McLeod, Pauline. "Fair Cops." *Daily Mirror,* January 8, 1980.

———. "In This Business Everything Is for Sale. The Looks Are Just a Part of It." *Daily Mirror,* April 25, 1980.

———. "Jogging Away from It All." *Daily Mirror,* October 13, 1980.

———. "My Green Heaven!" *Daily Mirror,* October 15, 1980.

———."The Police Cop a Hit." *Daily Mirror,* June 18, 1979.

———. "Someday I'm Bound to Get Killed." *Daily Mirror,* October 14, 1980.

McShane, John. "Rock Star in Love Child Claim." *Daily Mirror,* February 14, 1985.

Maitland, Alexander. "Review: Ring of Fire by Lawrence Blair; Lorne Blair." *Geographical Journal* 155, no. 2 (July 1989).

Marko, Paul. "Better Off Crazy: An Interview with Grinny from Skrewdriver." Punk77.co.uk, October 2003.

———. "Cherry Vanilla Interview." Punk77.co.uk, February 2007.

———. "Phil Walmsley Sets the Record Straight—Skrewdriver 1976–78." Punk77 .co.uk, April 2004.

Marshall, William. "Princes of the City." *Daily Mirror,* January 25, 1982.

Martin, Gavin. "Help the Caged!" *NME,* April 1991.

Mayer, Andre. "Candid Camera." Canadian Broadcasting Company, June 15, 2006.

Miles. "Review, Kevin Coyne: New Theatre, London." *NME,* May 1, 1976.

Mitchell,Tony, Betty Page, and Robbi Millar."Mudflatta de Bowl." *Sounds,* August 2, 1980.

Molenda, Michael. "Police Man Back on the Beat." *Guitar Player,* April 2007.

Moon, Tom. "The Pop Singer Proves That Rock Isn't Kid Stuff." *Chicago Tribune,* February 21, 1988.

Morley, Paul. "A Passage to India." *NME,* April 12, 1980.

Moyes, Jojo. "Sting 'Failed to Notice £6M Was Missing.'" *Independent,* September 22, 1995.

Murray, Charles Shaar. "Ike and Tina Turner, Caravan, John McLaughlin et al.: Startruckin' 75." *NME,* August 23, 1975.

Needs, Kris. "Cherry Vanilla." *Zig-Zag,* no. 2, April 1977.

Nicholls, Mike. "Police in Japan." *Record Mirror,* March 1980.

———. "An Upraised Arm Strikes the Balmy Irish Air." *Record Mirror,* October 4, 1980.

Ostrov, Devorah. "Stiv Bators Interview." *Rave-Up* fanzine, no. 12, 1986.

Parsons, Tony. "Get Your Chinese Rocks Off . . . and End Up Like Johnny Thunders." *NME,* May 1977.

——. "*Glue* Scribe Speaks Out." *NME,* February 12, 1977.

Peacock, John. "Sting's Single!" *Daily Mirror,* March 10, 1984.

Pener, Degen. "Egos & Ids: Rocking for the Rain Forest." *New York Times,* March 7, 1993.

Penman, Ian. "Between Innocence and Forbidden Knowledge . . . Comes the Fall." *NME,* August 19, 1978.

Pitts, Leonard. "Iceman Cometh in Concert." *Miami Herald,* February 1993.

Pond, Steve. "Pop Music: IRS Records Gets up for the Go-Go's." *Los Angeles Times,* July 26, 1981.

Pringle, Gill. "I Won't Wed." *Mirror,* May 13, 1985.

——. "Police: All Set to Get Together." *Mirror,* May 28, 1985.

Poulsen, Henrik Bech. Brian James Interview, "Neat Damned Noise." *Damned* fanzine no. 12, 1999.

Rachlis, Kit. "Police Take Notice." *Boston Phoenix,* April 17, 1979.

Rich, Frank. "Review/Theater; 'Threepenny Opera,' with Sting." *New York Times,* November 6, 1989.

Rieff, David. "Dangerous Pity." *Prospect,* June 23, 2005.

Robertson, Sandy. "A Transsexual in Transit—the Wayne County Interview." *Sounds,* August 26, 1978.

Rockwell, John. "Pop View: Rock vs. Disco: Who Won the War?" *New York Times,* September 16, 1990.

——. "Reviews/Music: 'Holy Blood,' Opera Written by a Rock Drummer." *New York Times,* October 12, 1989.

Rolston, Bill. "'This Is Not a Rebel Song': The Irish Conflict and Popular Music." *Race & Class,* Institute of Race Relations, 2001.

Romney, Jon. "Cherry Vanilla." *Negative Reaction,* no. 3, August–September 1977.

Ross, Seamus. "Don't Live So Close to Me." *Sunday Mirror,* April 29, 2007.

Rothstein, Mervyn. "A Macheath for the 90s?" *New York Times,* November 5, 1989.

Salewicz, Chris. "Back on the Beat." *Telegraph,* July 2007.

——. "Demolition Men in the Machine: Everything the Police Do Is Magic." *Creem,* April 1982.

——. "How to Enjoy Life in a Police State." *NME,* February 7, 1981.

——. "The Police: 2007 Tour Programme." 2007.

——. "Sting & Gerry Richardson: So, How Did You Two Meet Each Other . . . ?" Sting.com, December 2003.

——. "Sting: Coming Home." *Time Out,* issue no. 897, October 28–November 4, 1987.

——. "Sting: Confessions of a Complete Egomaniac." *Time Out,* issue no. 775, June 13–19, 1985.

Sanghvi, Vir. "Oh! Bombay." *Brunch,* 2007.

Scheff, David, and Victoria Scheff. "Sting." *Playboy,* November 1985.

Schruers, Fred. "Sting Cops Out." *GQ,* June 1985.

Sethia, Narendra. "The Captain—Robin Hood of the Amazon." *Caribbean Compass,* September 2000.

Shaw, Dan. "The Night: Right as the Rain Forest." *New York Times,* April 17, 1994.

Shearlaw, John. "Review: Rockatta de Bowl." *Record Mirror,* August 1980.

Shernoff, Andy. "Review: *Zenyatta Mondatta.*" *Creem,* November 1980.

Siegle, Robert, and Michele Norris. "Artist Sting Talks about His Career, His Music and His Life." NPR, *All Things Considered,* October 1, 2003.

Sinclair, David. "Jazz-Rock." *Times,* May 27, 1985.

Singer, Pat. "Wide Awake in America." *Hot Press,* July 17, 1986.

Stanton, Doug. "Yoga with Sting at the Ritz." *Esquire,* vol. 119, no. 3. March, 1993.

Stein, Seymour (participant). "Panel: Music's Window on the World" transcript. *Musexpo Los Angeles,* May 10, 2007.

Steinhardt, Simon. "Disco Demolition Night." *Swindle,* no. 9, April 2007.

Stevens, Andrew. "Turning Rebellion into Money: Andrew Stevens Interviews Andy Czezowski and Susan Carrington." *3AM,* 2003.

Sting. Letter to the Editor. *Village Voice,* December 1, 1987.

———. "Primal Sting." *Vogue,* June 1988.

Stokes, Dermot. "*Sniffin' Glue* fanzine: We Love UHU." *Q Special Editions,* April 2002.

———. "Sussed!" *Hot Press,* August 1980.

Styler, Trudie. "Why Sting and I Set Up the Rainforest Foundation Fund." *Huffington Post,* April 23, 2008.

Summers, Andy. Web chat, guitar.com, May 21, 2000.

Sutcliffe, Phil. "Making It." *Sounds,* January 8, 1977.

———. "Three Man Army." *Mojo,* July 2007.

Swed, Mark. "'Holy Blood and Crescent Moon' Has No Sting." *Los Angeles Times,* October 12, 1989.

Swedenburg, Ted. "Arab 'World Music' in the US." *Middle East Report,* no. 219 (Summer 2001).

Tommasini, Anthony. "Roll Over, Wagner." *Boston Globe,* September 24, 1989.

Turner, Steve. "Sex Pistols: The Anarchic Rock of the Young and Doleful." *Guardian,* December 3, 1976.

Ullestad, Neal. "Rock and Rebellion: Subversive Effects of Live Aid and Sun City." *Popular Music,* vol. 6, No. 1, (Jan., 1987).

Unterberger, Richie. "Kevin Coyne Interview." richieunterberger.com, 1997.

Vincent, Isabel. "It's a Charity Pall." *New York Post,* May 4, 2008.

Waleson, Heidi. "Ex-Rocker Tries His Hand at Serious Opera." *Wall Street Journal,* October 12, 1989.

———. "Stewart Copeland Has Written One Opera." *Wall Street Journal,* October 3, 1981.

Wartzman, Rick. "Pop Musicians Start to Rock the Boat for Activist Causes." *Wall Street Journal,* September 12, 1985.

Watts, Michael. "Police Plough Profits Back to the People." *Times,* December 11–17, 1981.

Wedlan, Candace A. "Small Record Firms Ride Crest of New Wave." *Los Angeles Times*, February 8, 1983.

Welch, Chris. "There's Nobody between Us and the Beatles Now!" *Musicians Only*, October 1980.

White, Timothy. "King of Pain." *Penthouse*, January 1984.

———. "Sting II." *Spin*, July 1985.

Williams, Richard. "The Police, Wembley Arena." *Times*, December 16, 1981.

Wilson, Edwin. "Broadway: Brecht with Sting but Little Bite." *Wall Street Journal*, November 8, 1980.

Wright, Steve. "Losing the Sting?" *Mirror*, February 15, 1986.

Zeller, Mark. "Les Risques du Metier." *Rolling Stone* (French edition), January, 1990.

Unattributed Articles

"Copeland Casting Aside Rock to Make Noises in Opera World." *The Columbus Dispatch*, October 8, 1989.

"The Despair of Sting When He Was on the Dole." *Daily Mirror*, July 14, 1982.

"Futuristic 'Lear' Is Tragedy-in-Brief but Stylish Approach, Powerful Score Make Intriguing Ballet." *Sacramento Bee*, April 18, 1985.

"I Know What I'm Worth." *Times*, October 18, 1995.

"My Trust in a Woman Cost Me Millions." *Daily Mirror*, July 15, 1982.

"Opera Has Miles to Go: Stewart Copeland's Revamped Show Is Paper Thin." *Dallas Morning News*, November 19, 1990.

"Police Creator Lives Classical Dilemma." *The Plain Dealer*, October 29, 1993.

"Pop Beat for the Duchess." *Daily Mirror*, June 28, 1980.

"A Rocker Drums up Some High-Brow Stuff." *San Francisco Chronicle*, April 14, 1985.

"Rock Star's Financial Adviser Charged." *Times*, October 4, 1994.

"S.F. Ballet Stumbles with New 'Lear.'" *San Francisco Chronicle*, April 18, 1985.

"Singer Sting Faces Divorce." *Daily Mirror*, March 15, 1983.

"So Lonely . . . Sting Strands Accountants." *The Independent*, January 16, 1994.

"Sting Accountant Charged." *Independent*, October 4, 1994.

"Sting and Wife Get a Break." *Daily Mirror*, July 17, 1982.

"Sting Claims £6M Fraud." *The Independent*, October 24, 1992.

"Sting on a Wing." *Daily Mirror*, December 28, 1981.

"Sting on Drugs at Twelve." *Daily Mirror*, October 25, 1983.

"Sting Settles Out of Court." *Times*, July 28, 1982.

"Sting—Sex King." *Daily Mirror*, June 9, 1981.

"War of the Words." *New Musical Express*, August 7, 1982.

Interviews

Miles Copeland, interviewed by the author on August 1, 2007.

Jayne County, interviewed by the author on September 24, 2007.

Bob Garcia, interviewed by the author on April 1, 2008.

Chris Gray, interviewed by the author on March 27, 2008.

Nigel Gray, interviewed by the author on October 10, 2007.
Clive Kelly, interviewed by the author on June 07, 2010
Paul Morley, interviewed by the author on September 26, 2007.
Kid Congo Powers, interviewed by the author on March 5, 2008.
Cherry Vanilla, interviewed by the author on September 7, 2007.
Carol Wilson, interviewed by the author on March 20, 2008.
Marc Zermati, interviewed by the author, October 2007.

Film/DVD

Bring On the Night. Michael Apted (dir.), A&M Films, 1985.
Everyone Stares: The Police Inside Out. Stewart Copeland (dir.), Universal, 2006.
The Filth and the Fury. Julien Temple (dir.), FilmFour, 2000.
The Great Rock 'n' Roll Swindle. Julien Temple (dir.), Virgin Films, 1980.
Luca. Rodrigo Espina (dir.), Baraka Cine, 2008.
Police: Around the World. Derek Burbidge (dir.), A&M, 1982.
The Police: Every Breath You Take—the Videos. Derek Burbidge, Lol Creme, and Kevin Godley (dir.), Polygram Video, 1987.
The Police: Outlandos to Synchronicities. Polygram Video, 1995.
Property Is Theft. Vanessa Engle (dir.), BBC, 2006.
Punk in London. Wolfgang Büld (dir.), Hochschule für Fernsehen und Film München, 1977.
Quadrophenia. Franc Roddam (dir.), The Who Films, 1979.
The Rhythmatist. Jean-Pierre Dutilleux (dir.), CCCP/A&M Films, 1985.
That Boy. Peter Berlin (dir.), Hand in Hand Films, 1974.
That Man: Peter Berlin. Jim Tushinski (dir.), Gorilla Factory Productions, 2005.
Urgh! A Music War. Derek Burbidge (dir.), Lorimar Productions, 1981.

Television

MTV. Martha Quinn interviews the Police backstage after a concert in Chicago, July 23, 1983.
90 Minutes Live. Peter Gzowski (host) and Cherry Vanilla and Leon Redbone (guests), CBC, 1976.
Oprah Winfrey Show. Oprah Winfrey interviews Sting and Trudie Styler. CBS, October 28, 2003.
The Tube. Jools Holland interviews Jello Biafra. Channel Four, 1980.

Audio

John Lydon, interviewed on the *Christian O'Connell Breakfast Show*, Virgin Radio, September 20, 2007.
The Police, interviewed on WPIX-FM New York by Jane Hamburger, November 1978.

"Punks Wearing Pink." *Ideas*, CBC Radio, March 25, 1982.

"The Secrets of Stewart Copeland, the Think Different Drummer." Interview and podcast. O'Reilly Mac OS X Conference, Santa Clara, California, 2004.

"Sting Goes Solo to Narrate 'Peter & the Wolf.'" Lynn Neary, NPR, September 29, 1991

Andy Summers & Robert Fripp Speak Out. A&M promo LP, 1984.

INDEX

A&M Records, 48, 60, 63, 64, 65 74, 82, 83, 86, 87, 114, 134, 136, 142–4, 147, 164, 238, 256
  Bob Garcia and, 78, 103–104, 112, 114, 164
  Bring On the Night and, 204, 206
  IRS and, 102–109, 150, 167
  Jerry Moss and, 78, 91, 101–108, 147
  Marketing the Police and, 82–3
  Miles Copeland III's dealings with, 48, 56–57, 60, 73–4, 78, 81, 101–109
  new wave and, 91, 158
  roster, 104
Ahearn, Michael, 223
Air Studios, 165–172, 194, 230
Alberto y Lost Trios Paranoias, 86, 110
Alternative Tentacles, 148
Alternative TV, 54, 108
Altham, Keith, 95–96, 219
Amnesty International, 220, 222, 223, 254, 261
Animals, the, 7, 8, 9, 46
Apted, Michael, 204–208, 209
Atwood, Colleen, 207
Ayers, Kevin, 7, 8, 42, 43

Bailey, David, 252–3
Bamberger, David, 243–246
Bangles, the, 164
Bators, Stiv, 160, 162, 164, 274
BBC, 63–64, 114–115, 117, 168, 175, 214–215, 260
Beatles, the, 6, 55, 62, 199–200
"Bed's Too Big without You, The" (the Police), 12
Bellydance Superstars, 269

Belushi, John, 181
Berber, Anita, 159
Berlin, Peter, 98–9
Biafra, Jello, 148–148
Blondie, 47, 80, 104, 148, 176, 267
Boberg, Jay, 103, 148, 164
Body Mist (deodorant), 184, 190
"Bombs Away" (the Police), 135
Boomtown Rats, 85, 176, 212
Boorman, John, 131
Booz Allen Hamilton, 119
Bowie, David, 26, 146, 248
Brand New Day (Sting), 255–257
Branson, Richard, 14, 188–190
Bride, The, 226
Bright, Terry, 152
Brimstone and Treacle, 247
Bring On the Night, 204–11
"Bring On the Night" (the Police), 270
British Talent Managers, 13, 70, 189
BTM Records, 13, 38, 160
Burbidge, Derek and Kate, 91–92, 115–116, 120, 146, 175, 198
Burchill, Julie, 143
Burdon, Eric, 8, 9
Bush, George H. W., 249–250
Bush, George W., 107
Buzzcocks, 105–106, 107–109

Cale, John, 105, 108
  as producer of the Police, 47–49
Campbell, Lady Georgina, 20–21
"Can't Stand Losing You" (the Police), 66–67, 92, 97
Caravan, 55, 70–71, 73, 189
Casale, Gerard, 158

Cateforis, Theo, 158
CBGB, 28, 76, 77, 146
"charity rock," 212–215, 220–224
Chelsea, 31–32, 102, 160
Childers, Leee Black, 25–27, 28
Childs, Harold, 80–1
Christgau, Robert, 156
CIA (Central Intelligence Agency), 13, 69, 102, 118–119, 149, 151, 162, 218, 246
Clash, the, 21, 26, 33, 45, 126, 205, 267, 270
Cleveland Opera, 243–246
Climax Blues Band, 70, 71, 73, 102, 105
Collins, Phil, 167
Columbia Records, 8, 54, 153–154, 164
Copeland, Ian, 13, 20–1, 120
    Ask Uncle Ian (Web site), 269
    biographical information and character of, 68–70
    contributions to the Police, 22
    Frontier Booking International (F.B.I.) and, 47, 107, 146
    IRS Records, contributions to, 150
    Paragon agency, work for, 105
    strategies used to book the Police, 73, 75–6, 120
    Urgh! A Music War, contributions to, 145–147
Copeland, Miles II, 12, 20, 68–9, 120–121
    Game Player, The, 151, 217–218
Copeland, Miles III (manager), 13–14, 23, 46, 58–59, 65, 88, 98, 152
    Ark 21 and associated labels, 257
    biographical information, 68–70, 121
    character of, 69–70, 102, 144, 222
    image of the Police and, 95, 117, 119, 125–126
    management style of, 70–73, 109–110, 115, 160–164
    neo–conservative political views of, 92, 147–148, 151, 162, 217–218, 259
    new wave and, 145–165
    Nigel Gray and, 132, 133–135, 142
    office at Dryden Chambers, 25, 28, 72
    plans to form "the new Police," 269
    political ambitions of, 150–152
    reaction to "Roxanne," 55–56

Squeeze and, 47–48, 57, 59, 73–74, 102, 184, 189
    Startruckin' 75 tour, 70–72
    Sting's solo career and, 210, 213, 219, 220–224, 239, 255–259
    Sting vs. Virgin Records, legal case and, 187–189
    US Package of Punk, 27, 30, 47 See also International Record Syndicate (IRS); Police, the
Copeland, Stewart, 2, 58
    biographical information, 2, 12–14
    character of, 2, 3, 34, 70, 263
    "Don't Care" (Klark Kent), 65–66
    drug use by, 35–36, 170
    Everybody Stares, 86, 270
    formation of the Police and, 16–17
    The Holy Blood and the Holy Grail (opera), 244–248
    homes of, 20–21, 88, 242
    illegitimate child of (Patrick), 181, 182
    infidelities, 35, 36, 183–4
    Just the Two of Us, appearance on, 260
    King Lear ballet by, 241–242
    as Klark Kent, 65–65, 130–131
    "Miss Gradenko," 196
    relationship with Miles Copeland III, 142, 162
    relationship with Sonja Kristina, 14, 17, 20, 21, 180–181
    The Rhythmatist, 211–212, 233, 242
    Rumble Fish (soundtrack), 241
    solo career of, 241–247, 251–252, 259
    worldview of, 117, 122, 129, 137, 196, 203–204, 211 See also Police, the; individual names of albums and songs
Coppola, Francis Ford, 131, 241
County, Jayne (née Wayne), 26–27, 28, 36–38, 51
    on Miles Copeland, 28
    on the Police, 33–34
Coyne, Kevin, 7, 42, 43, 44, 171
Cramps, the, 150, 159, 160, 161, 162–163
    Andy Summers's view of, 111
    Miles Copeland III and, 160–161, 162164
    problems with IRS Records, 163–164
    UK tour with the Police, 111–113

Culture Club, 21, 155, 156

Curved Air, 24, 25, 29, 47, 65, 73, 243
   final shows, 15, 17, 22
   Stewart Copeland's joining of, 14–15

Czezowski, Andy, 27, 149
   role in founding the Roxy club, 30, 31–2

Dahl, Steve, 79–80

Daly, Mary, 222–224

Damned, the, 26, 32, 45

Davis, Miles, 208, 209–211
   on Sting, 209

"Dead End Job" (the Police), 33

Dead Kennedys, 147–148

"De Do Do Do, De Da Da Da" (the
   Police), 136, 143, 226, 228

"Demolition Man" (the Police), 168, 177,
   182
   writing and interpretation of, 182–183

Denver, John, 142

Deptford Fun City, 48, 73

"Desert Rose" (Sting), 257–258

Devo, 146
   new wave music and, 157–158

Dickies, the, 104, 154–155

Difford, Chris, 49, 74

Disco Demolition Night, 79–80

Dix, Otto, 159

"Don't Stand So Close to Me" (the Police),
   136, 141
   attempts at re–recording, 225, 227, 263
   Body Mist commercial and, 184, 193

Dream of the Blue Turtles (Sting), 205–6,
   231
   meaning of album title, 205
   players on, 206–207
   recordings of, 206–207

"Driven to Tears" (the Police), 135

Dune, 247

Duran Duran, 99, 155, 198

Dutilleux, J. P., 211
   involvement with Rainforest
   Foundation, 233, 234–235

Electric Chairs, the, 36–37, 38, 51

Electric Eels, the, 157–158

Ellis, Terry, 18–19

EMI, 54

Esquibel, Zecca, 27, 35, 36

Ethiopia, famine, 212–218

"Every Breath You Take" (the Police), 195,
   198–199, 261
   interpretation of, 191–192

"Every Little Thing She Does Is Magic"
   (the Police), 172, 195
   Strontium 90's version of, 42–43
   troubled recording of, 160–70

Fall, the, 29, 160–161

"Fall Out" (the Police), 24, 64–65

Faulty Products, 29, 54, 55, 65, 73, 101,
   106, 147, 160, 164
   Dead Kennedys and, 147, 148

Feingold, Michael, 248–249

"Fortress around Your Heart" (Sting),
   203, 207

Freidman, Jane, 47, 105

Friend, Lonn, 255–256

Friesen, Gil, 103, 145, 206, 238

Frontier Booking International (F.B.I.),
   105, 150

Gang of Four, 155, 175–176

Garbarini, Vic, 202–203, 206, 209, 225,
   226, 227

Garcia, Bob, 78, 83, 103–104, 108, 109,
   114, 164

Garvey, Steve, 105

Geffen Records, 162, 256

Geldof, Bob, 212–216 *See also* Boomtown
   Rats; Live Aid, Mengistu, Haile
   Mariam

Ghost in the Machine (the Police)
   critical reception of, 178–179
   naming of, 173–174
   recording of, 166–173, 184

Glitterbest, 25

Godley & Creme, 133, 141–142, 198–199

Go–Go's, the, 106, 107, 148–149, 150,
   163–164

Gormley, Mike, 81, 161, 162

Graham, Bill, 220–225

Gravelle, Peter, 66

Gray, Chris, 53, 55, 61, 62, 87, 89–90, 135,
   142

Gray, Nigel, 62, 166–167

A&M Records, dealings with, 60, 88, 132, 134, 140–142
Miles Copeland III, dealings with, 55, 60, 137–138
production style of, 53, 54, 62, 87–88, 132, 142–143
as "Rock Doc," 90, 133, 142
Surrey Sound studio and, 53–56, 60, 65, 88–92, 90, 133
Greenfield, Robert, 221
Grossberg, Lawrence, 155–156, 159
Guinness, Marina, 180–181
Gurdjieff, G. I., 176

Hakim, Omar, 203, 208
Hamburger, Jane, 76, 77
Hammersmith Odeon, 100, 146
Hampton, Howard, 231–232
Healey, Jack, 220–225
Hellman, Jerome, 248
Henry Cow, 42
Hilburn, Robert, 149
"Hole in My Life" (the Police), 62
Holland, Jools, 54, 147, 168
Homosexuals, the, 88–89
Howlett, Mike, 42, 44, 169
Human League, the, 155–156
Hutcheon, Linda, 267

"If You Love Somebody Set Them Free" (Sting), 203
Illegal Records, 47, 73
Impey, Lawrence, 23–24, 189
Interior, Lux, 110
International Record Syndicate (IRS), 257
conflicts with artists, 162–166
creation of, 102–109
Go-Go's and, 151–152, 163–164
new wave and, 162–167
street teams, 103
Urgh! A Music War and, 146, 147
Interscope Records, 256, 257
"Invisible Son" (the Police), 175, 190
as political protest song, 178–180

Jaguar, 258
Jam, the, 37, 38, 45, 218

James, Brian, 159–160
Johnstone, Iain, 211
Jones, Darryl, 203, 208, 210–211
Jones, Grace, 168
Jung, Carl Gustav, 177, 193, 194, 196, 198

Kajagoogoo, 156
Kaye, Lenny, 37
Kelly, Captain Clive, 233, 234, 236
Khashoggi, Adnan, 186
"King of Pain" (the Police), 191
Kirkland, Kenny, 202–2–3, 209
Koestler, Arthur, 174, 177–179, 182, 193
Kristina, Sonja, 14, 17, 20, 21, 180–181

Last Exit, 11, 17, 203
demise of, 17–18, 22–23
musical style of, 11, 134
publishing deal, 14
Sting vs. Virgin Records, 187–189
Lefever, Ernest W., 218
Leixlip Castle, 136, 137, 181
Lepore, Louis, 27, 35, 50
"Like a Virgin" (Madonna), 160
Live Aid, 212–215, 219, 220 *See also* Geldof, Bob; Mengistu, Haile Mariam
Live Nation, 264
Lords of the New Church, 159–160, 162
Los Angeles Personal Direction (L.A.P.D.), 162. *See also* Copeland, Miles III; Gormley, Mike
Lydon, John, (Johnny Rotten), 25, 127, 267, 268. *See also* Sex Pistols

Mami, Cheb, 257–8
Markham, Pippa, 18, 57, 93
Marley, Bob (and the Wailers), 2, 171
Marsalis, Branford, 202–203, 208, 210
Marsalis, Wynton, 202–2–3, 208
Martin, George, 165, 166, 230
"Masoko Tanga" (the Police), 62
Max's Kansas City, 26, 29, 33, 159
McLaren, Malcolm, 25, 84–85
McLeod, Pauline, 99
Mengistu, Haile Mariam, 215–216

"Message in a Bottle" (the Police), 87–88, 94, 97–98, 175, 194
Mills McCartney, Heather, 186
Mishima, Yukio, 117
mods, 93–95
Money, George "Zoot" (and Big Roll Band), 7, 51, 171
Mont de Marsan festival, 45–47
Moore, Keith, 129, 131
   trial for fraud, 239–241
Morgan, Victoria, 241
Morley, Paul, 67, 176
   in India with the Police, 121–127
Moss, Jerry, 78, 91, 147, 162
   IRS Records and, 102–109
MTV, 5, 91–92, 114, 156, 221
   the Police on, 197–199, 204
Mulligan, Paul, 21, 24, 40
Murray, Charles Shaar, 71–72
music industry, 5
   advent of music videos, 91–92, 197–198
   compassion politics and, 213
   impact of MTV on, 198–200
   introduction of CDs and, 197
   promotion of nostalgia, 266–268
   reaction to disco, 79–80, 154
   recession in, 6, 131–132, 197
   threat of music piracy and, 197

Napier–Bell, Simon, 21
Nariz, Wazmo, 106, 109
Nasser, Gamal, 1118–119
new wave, 4, 26, 34, 45, 51, 93, 97–99, 267
   advent of in US, 79, 106, 157
   artificiality of, 161
   as cultural meme, 152–153
   as depoliticized punk rock, 150, 154–155, 157, 267
   impact in Soviet Union, 152
   IRS Records and, 104–107, 152, 161
   Miles Copeland III and, 149, 153, 163–164
   as performance art, 157–159
   the Police as vanguard of, 95
   variations of in authoritarian regimes, 153

New York Dolls, 29
Nightingale, Annie, 114–115
Nomi, Klaus, 146, 158–159
"Nothing Achieving" (the Police), 24
. . . Nothing Like the Sun (Sting), 213, 231–233
   criticism of, 232–234
Nugent, Ted, 122
"Nuit de Punk," 37–38

October, Gene, 31–2, 102, 160
Oingo Boingo, 108, 162
O'Toole, Peter, 182–183
Outlandos d'Amour (the Police), 68
   album cover, 84–85
   on Billboard chart, 78, 80
   critical reception to, 67–68, 123
   naming of, 67
   recording of, 53–55, 60–62

Padgham, Hugh, 166–7, 170, 194, 195
Padovani, Henry, 32, 33, 35, 37
   ejection from the Police, 43–51
   joining the Police, 21–25
Patrick, Malcolm, 239–240
Pearson, Ronnie, 18–19, 187
Perrett, Peter (the Only Ones), 23
Perry, André, 168–169
Perry, Lee "Scratch," 270
Perry, Mark, 28–29, 54
   influence on the London punk scene, 38–39
Playgirl, 98, 186
Police, the
   association with IRS Records, 103–113
   blond hairdos of, 4, 58–59, 78, 81, 97
   concert performances by, 38, 44–46, 61, 76–78, 83, 139–140, 202–204, 264
   dissolution of, 204–206, 209, 229
   greatest hits albums, 224–227, 267
   image of, 22, 58–9, 82, 84, 97–98, 116, 121, 180, 200, 263–264
   legacy of, 270–271
   musical ability of, 33, 38, 61–62
   origin of band name, 16–17
   playing as Strontium 90 (aka the Elevators), 42–43

Police: Around the World, The, 115–118
  (*See also* Burbidge, Derek and Kate)
reunions of, 221–225, 255–256, 260–1,
  262, 268–270
rivalry among members, 89–90, 93,
  130–131, 134, 137–139, 172–178,
  173–177, 200–201
royalty arrangements, 59–60, 133,
  189
Shea Stadium concert by, 199–200
slash fiction personas of, 99–100
sound of, 55–57, 137, 175
tax status of, 129–132, 239–241
as teen idols, 5, 97–98, 119
on US Package of Punk tour, 27–31,
  33–37
Wrigley's Chewing Gum commercial,
  appearance in, 58–59 *See also*
  Copeland, Miles III; Copeland,
  Stewart; Sting; Summers, Andy;
  individual names of albums and songs
Powers, Kid Congo, 109–110, 163–164
Prokofiev, Sergei, 204, 251–252
punk, 4, 16–17, 21, 22, 33, 58–59,
  153–167, 264
  demise of, 85–96, 266
  dress code of, 31, 39, 86
  as motivational force, 154
  press reaction to, 16–17, 25–26
  proto–punk groups, 157–158
  as reaction to vestiges of British empire,
    150
  rivalry with teddy boys, 39–40
  sociocultural roots of, 19–20, 154, 158
  US music industry view of, 157–158

Quadrophenia (the Who), 95–97, 131,
  226, 246
Quatrochi, Danny, 120, 167

Rachlis, Kit, 82
Rafferty, Gerry, 62
Rainforest Foundation, 234
  controversy surrounding, 234–238
Raoni, 233–236
Red Wedge, 218–219 *See also* Weller, Paul
Reed, Lou, 47, 70, 71
reggae, 2, 4, 61–62, 80, 82, 91, 213, 269

Reggatta de Blanc (the Police), 97
  recording of, 88–89, 103
"Rehumanize Yourself" (the Police), 177
R.E.M., 150, 159
Renaissance, 13, 71, 73, 102, 150, 189
Richard, Cliff, 113
Richardson, Gerry, 11–12, 18, 22–23, 51
Ridgway, Stan, 161
Rimmer, Dave, 155
Rock and Roll Hall of Fame, 261, 266–267
Roddam, Franc, 93–4, 131, 226
Rolling Stone, 126, 143, 235–238, 266
Rolling Stones, 8, 67, 96, 113, 158, 208
Rolston, Bill, 174–175
Rook, Jean, 125
Root Boy Slim, 106–107
Rorschach, Ivy (aka Poison Ivy), 109, 100
Roussel, Jean–Alain, 169–172
"Roxanne" (the Police), 1–2, 5, 58–59, 60,
  66, 92, 96–97, 261, 268
  "banning" of, 63–64
  the Homosexuals and, 89–90
  interpretation of, 63, 136, 193
  look–alike contest, 83–84
  marketing of, 62–63, 85
  promotional video for, 92–93
  recording of, 54–57
  role in breaking the Police in the US,
    79–83
Roxy, the (London), 28, 33, 34, 149
"Russians" (Sting), 203–204

Sacred Love (Sting), 255, 259
Sanghvi, Vir, 121
Schenker, Kathryn, 255–257, 259
Schmidt, David W., 245
Schoener, Eberhard, 51–52, 105, 247
Scott, Tony, 58
"Secret Journey" (Police), 176–177
Seitz, Jeff, 167, 242–3
Sensational New Blow Waves, 84–85
Sex Pistols, 25
  appearance on Bill Grundy show, 25
  Great Rock 'n' Roll Swindle, The, 85–86,
    150
  press reaction to, 16, 25
  US music industry opinion of, 154

"Shadows in the Rain" (the Police), 138, 203
Shakin' Stevens, 39
Sioux, Siouxsie (and the Banshees), 25, 133, 135
Sire Records, 102, 104, 148
Skafish, Jim, 106, 137, 162
Skrewdriver, 39, 40
slash fiction, 99–100
Smith, Mark E., 161–162
Smith, Patti, 34, 37, 47
Sniffin' Glue, 28–29, 33–34, 38–39, 83
Soft Machine, the, 8–9, 42, 50, 71–72
"So Lonely" (the Police), 115, 117
Songs from the Labyrinth (Sting), 254
Soul Cages, The (Sting), 238–239
"Spirits in the Material World" (the Police), 176, 181
squatting, 19–20
Squeeze, 54, 78, 107, 108, 139, 157–158
John Cale and, 48, 49
Miles Copeland and, 23, 57, 59, 75, 77, 104, 188, 192
Startruckin' 75 tour, 70–72, 146
Stein, Seymour, 102
Step Forward Records, 29, 74, 164–165
Stiff Records, 62, 106
Sting, 5, 258–259
acting career, 86–87, 95–97, 134, 207–214, 226, 236, 246–251
Amnesty International and, 220–225
attempts to interpret Brecht, 211, 246–251
Bring On the Night, 204–211
Broken Music (autobiography), 18, 20, 53, 187, 188, 193, 239, 260, 262–263
Broken Music (tour), 262–263
character of, 32, 38, 58, 90, 93, 123, 128–129, 183, 195, 197–198, 209–210, 233
childhood of, 2–3, 8–12
children of (Fuschia, Jake, Joe), 19, 173, 186–187, 188, 194, 211
court appearances by, 186–193, 239–241
death of parents and, 231–235
divorce of, 185–191, 196–197, 207, 209 (*See also* Tomelty, Frances)

drug use by, 35–36, 185
environmental activism of, 234–239
homes of, 5, 133–134, 189, 262
image of, 59, 100–103, 126–131, 195–196
infidelities, 35, 37 (*See also* Styler, Trudie)
Jungian analysis and, 205
Jungle Stories, 235–238
Koestler's influence on, 178, 181, 184, 196
narcissism of, 11, 97, 126–128, 197
nickname origin, 11
parents of (Ernie, Audrey), 9, 57, 197
political views of, 4, 94, 133, 156, 178–180, 220
relationship with Miles Copeland III, 188, 192, 220, 223, 255
sexual activities of, 4, 11, 266
sexual persona of, 100–102
solo career of, 4, 202–211, 230–241
tabloid interest in, 99, 100–101, 125, 188, 193, 194–195, 214, 231
views on women, 11, 64, 100, 197–198, 231–232
work as male model, 57–58
work in commercials of, 57–59, 188, 232, 258–259 *See also* Last Exit; Police, the; *individual names of albums and songs*
Stuart, Ian, 40. *See also* Skrewdriver
Styler, Trudie, 4, 211, 212, 214, 231, 247, 261
affair with Sting, 185–187, 189–190, 194–196
character of, 185, 238
hostess career of, 190
Rainforest Foundation and, 235–238
Summers, Andy, 5
"Behind My Camel," 142–143
"Be My Girl," 196
character of, 3, 61, 114, 130–131, 185
childhood, 7
cocaine use of, 145, 185
daughter of (Layla), 77, 130
early career of, 8–9, 14, 41–42
homes of, 43, 132–133
image of, 58–59, 97

later career of, 252–253, 259–260
marriage of, 8, 43, 79, 135, 177
"Mother," 196
One Train Later, 7, 42, 43, 47, 49–50, 65, 114, 116, 129, 176, 184, 203–204, 260
parents of (Maurice, Jean), 7
photography of, 252–253
sensitivity to criticism, 41, 64–65, 114, 125 *See also* Police, the; *individual names of albums and songs*
Summers, Kate, 8, 43, 79, 133, 176
Sumner, Gordon Matthew Thomas. *See* Sting
Sutcliffe, Peter (Yorkshire Ripper), 63
Sutcliffe, Phil, 15–16, 18, 68
Synchronicity (the Police), 5, 181
album cover of, 200
commercial success of, 201, 203
music videos for, 201–203
recording of, 198–200
"Synchronicity II" (the Police), 196–197, 203

Tebbit, Norman, 214
Television (band), 47, 107
Temple, Julien, 85, 154
Thatcher, Margaret, 92–93, 132, 156, 178, 218
3 Penny Opera, 235, 244, 246–250
Thunders, Johnny (and the Heartbreakers), 24–26, 29–30, 32, 36, 44
Time and Talents Club, 121
Tomelty, Frances, 18, 19, 35, 57, 88, 95, 172, 178–179
as manager of Last Exit, 12
separation and divorce from Sting, 185–191, 194–196, 209
songs about, 195, 197, 207
Touhami, Hassan, 118–120
Turner, Ike and Tina, 71–72
Turner, Kim, 66, 77, 171, 210, 249

U2, 193, 261

Amnesty International tour and, 222–225
Urgh! A Music War, 145–147

Vanilla, Cherry, 26–30, 50, 147
on the Roxy, 32–33
touring with the Police, 34–35
Velvet Underground, 47
Vicious, Sid, 85
Virgin Music, 14, 42, 187–194, 223, 259
Virgin Records, 14, 42
"Visions of the Night" (the Police), 42, 49

"Walking on the Moon" (the Police), 90–92
Way, Darryl, 243
"We Dance Alone" (Sting), 231
"We'll Be Together" (Sting), 231
Weller, Paul, 218, 219 *See also* Jam, the; Red Wedge
Westerman, Floyd (Sheriff Red Crow), 235
"We Work the Black Seam" (Sting), 203, 219–220
Whisky A Go–Go, 93, 150, 261
White, Michael, 145
Who, the, 46, 94, 96, 99, 200
Wilde, Oscar, 231–232
Wilson, Carol, 14, 18, 42
role in Sting vs. Virgin trial, 188–189, 191–192
Wishbone Ash, 13, 71–73, 75, 77, 193
Wisseloord studio, 135–136, 142, 144
"Wrapped Around Your Finger" (the Police), 192, 199

Zeller, Mark, 235–236
Zenyatta Mondatta (Police), 169
album cover of, 148
critical reception to, 146–147
naming of, 147
recording of, 134–139, 141–146
Zermati, Marc, 44–45, 46